THE REVOLUTION OF THE DONS

*Cambridge and Society
in Victorian England*

Fr Bob -

Rebirth! (and without
introspection?) *

Fondly,

Sheldon

* or: some weed killers
don't work.

The Revolution of the Dons

CAMBRIDGE AND SOCIETY
IN VICTORIAN ENGLAND

SHELDON ROTHBLATT

CAMBRIDGE UNIVERSITY PRESS

Cambridge

London   New York   New Rochelle

Melbourne   Sydney

Published by the Press Syndicate of the University of Cambridge
The Pitt Building, Trumpington Street, Cambridge CB2 1RP
32 East 57th Street, New York, NY 10022, USA
296 Beaconsfield Parade, Middle Park, Melbourne 3206, Australia

First published by Faber & Faber and Basic Books 1968
First published by the Cambridge University Press 1981

Printed in Great Britain at the
University Press, Cambridge

British Library Cataloguing in Publication Data

Rothblatt, Sheldon
The revolution of the dons.
1. University of Cambridge – History
2. Cambridge (Cambridgeshire)
– Intellectual life
I. Title
378.426'59 LF118 80–41865

ISBN 0 521 23958 3 hard covers
ISBN 0 521 28370 1 paperback

FOR MY PARENTS

PREFACE TO THE
CAMBRIDGE UNIVERSITY PRESS
EDITION

'How many assertions owe their
strength to the lucky circumstances
that as suggestions they were not
understood?'

André Gide

The Revolution of the Dons was born in the optimism of
Cambridge (and in the exhilaration of the Plateglass
University era) and completed a few years later in the gathering
pessimism of Berkeley and the crisis of American power and
morality. Doubtless it reflects this transatlantic mix, as related
to other polarities. I notice in it a belief in the regenerative
capacity of universities or their ambidextrous ability to maintain continuity and provide for innovation, and forebodings
about their real ability to survive changes of great cultural
magnitude. In a later work[1] the problematic aspects of educational change in relation to culture have dominated my
thinking; but as I look back upon *The Revolution of the Dons* it
seems as if there was still hope. The marks of its birth lay heavily
upon it, and indeed this seems right. Not all forceps deliveries
issue in the wild consequences of *Tristram Shandy*. Victorian
England mediated the effects of one of the greatest social and
economic transformations in all of recorded history by an over-
riding historical presence of mind, by moving forward while
looking backward, by preserving and changing at exactly the
same time. But this is now well understood, although the details of it can always be reviewed and added to, and the measure
of it, the retrospective personal appraisal that inevitably inter-
penetrates historical scholarship, will produce contradictory
assessments as long as scholars quite rightly view the past as
relevant to the human experience and understanding.

[1] *Tradition and Change in English Liberal Education, An Essay in History and
Culture* (London, 1976).

I

PREFACE

The pattern of change described in this book – a backward-looking habit of mind, a 'centre' and 'periphery' institutional outlook incorporating an étatist inheritance, European but not Continental, thus allowing for a high degree of self-government, and the transformation of English society into a system of occupational status groups with professions near the top – resulted in the renewal of Cambridge academic life in the special ways discussed here. I would like to mention that by Cambridge I meant from the outset to suggest Oxford as well. There are differences between them of degree and kind. The relative strength of the colleges, the methods of financing, the different traditions of scholarship have to be acknowledged when drawing comparisons, and in addition there are the party games of more than a century that contrast cool, rational, sober, scientific Cambridge to aesthetic, literary, playful and dreaming Oxford.[1] To the off-shore observer, however, the two senior universities of England have always been institutions of the same type and complexion. Historically their cultural and institutional reticulation has been similar. Thus they possessed the same 'centre' mentality, the same connexion with the developing professional sector, the same system of instruction, the same ties to the network of Victorian schools and the same clientele. The 'revolution' that occurred in Cambridge happened at Oxford as well, with the same consequences and significance.

The materials available for the study of university history remain as daunting as ever. New studies and collections in the history of higher education, on its national, comparative and sociological dimensions continue to appear; but I am as yet not persuaded that our understanding of how universities change in relation to other institutions has been very precisely advanced. There remains the tendency immediately or directly to correlate internal with external changes even though it is appreciated that short-term connexions are exceedingly difficult to prove and long-term ones frequently truisms. To take only one instance, most historians of higher education still see the university in a supply and demand relationship to modern industrial society, with demand generating supply; whereas close and

[1] Or attempt other fundamental distinctions, such as 'Oxford is – Oxford: not a mere receptacle for youth, like Cambridge.' E. M. Forster, *Howards End*.

PREFACE

detailed study of matriculations or of such major changes as the establishment of research laboratories, the introduction of new subjects and the elaboration of the machinery of academic professionalism shows that supply has very often led demand. Innovations have taken forms inexplicable in the simpler assumptions of a demand model. The inner circuitry of university life still deserves mapping. The materials of this are to hand, but their scale and variety require considerable scholarly cooperation.

Since first publication of *The Revolution of the Dons* in 1968 new information has surfaced that would lead me to correct a point or two, adjust an observation here and there, alter an emphasis or elaborate with additional fact what were originally suggestions.[1] No one can be more aware than an author

[1] Charles Kingsley's part in Seeley's selection as Regius Professor has been explained by Owen Chadwick, 'Charles Kingsley at Cambridge', in *The Historical Journal*, XVIII (June 1975) 303–26, and by Deborah Wormell, *Sir John Seeley and the Uses of History* (Cambridge, 1980). Seeley was not Gladstone's first choice. Michael Sanderson has successfully developed the connexions between business and universities in a series of important articles and an indispensable book, *The Universities and British Industry 1850–1970* (London, 1972). Valuable or useful information and materials also appear in *The University in Society*, ed. Lawrence Stone, I (Princeton, 1974), A. H. Halsey and Martin Trow, *The British Academics* (London, 1971), J. P. T. Bury, *Romilly's Cambridge Diary, 1832–42* (Cambridge, 1967), T. J. N. Hilken, *Engineering at Cambridge University, 1783–1965* (Cambridge, 1967), Edwin Welch, *The Peripatetic University: Cambridge Local Lectures, 1873–1973* (Cambridge, 1973), E. E. Rich, ed., *St Catharine's College, Cambridge, 1473–1973* (Leeds, n.d. but 1973), Peter Allen, *The Cambridge Apostles, The Early Years* (Cambridge, 1978), John Roach, *Public Examinations, 1850–1900* (Cambridge, 1971), David Newsome, *On the Edge of Paradise, A. C. Benson: The Diarist* (Chicago, 1980). For a start on women in universities some recent writings are Rita McWilliams-Tullberg, *Women at Cambridge, A Men's University – Though of a Mixed Type* (London, 1975), Margaret Bryant, *The Unexpected Revolution* (London, 1979), and Joyce Pederson, 'The Reform of Women's Secondary and Higher Education in 19th Century England: A Study in Elite Groups' (Unpublished doctoral dissertation, University of California, Berkeley, 1974). For Oxford, besides the materials in Stone, there are E. G. W. Bill, *University Reform in Nineteenth-Century Oxford, A Study of Henry Halford Vaughan, 1811–1885* (Oxford, 1973), E. G. W. Bill and J. F. A. Mason, *Christ Church and Reform, 1850–1867* (Oxford, 1970), J. L. Heilbron, *H. G. J. Moseley, The Life and Letters of an English Physicist, 1887–1915* (Berkeley and Los Angeles, 1974). For a rare comparative view, Fritz K. Ringer, *Education and Society in Modern Europe* (Bloomington and London, 1979). Articles, biographies, memoirs and

3

of the inherently flawed nature of all views, opinions and judgments and of the easy slide into error that time makes manifest. But the economics of publishing today render any substantial revision inconceivable; and perhaps this is only just. Once decided upon the form of a book is uncooperative: it teasingly moves aside with each gesture of the hand. Yet in general I would not withdraw any of the basic conclusions or arguments of the book, and I would maintain that the relationships between Cambridge and society as first discussed are essentially correct. As for the mistakes, I hold with George Malcolm Young who held with Edward Gibbon that where error is irreparable, repentance is useless.

These are some of the afterthoughts that authors commonly attach to the reissue of a book out of print. I would like to take an additional liberty and briefly mention another aspect of *The Revolution of the Dons*. From the outset I had in mind a book that would not only study the transformation in higher education that accompanied urbanism and industrialism, but would also be a piece of bookmaking, perhaps of the type my teachers called for when they discussed the historian's craft with me. I wanted to write a book that would address itself to the perennial distinction between what a particular historian thinks about the past and the actual historical experience itself, between the patterns that the past seems to offer the trained historical mind, which brings to its inquiries assumptions about human behaviour and social change and treats events as a series of academic 'problems' – in other words, all the professional machinery by which the past is remembered – and the past as it might have appeared to those who were its principal actors in a dramatic action to be related. Each of these ways of knowing carries with it important philosophical implications (or sociological prescriptions). Analogy is frequently the result of the first; irony and paradox the outcome of the second.

---

histories appear frequently, so this list can hardly aspire to completeness. For bibliography E. H. Cordeaux and D. H. Merry, *A Bibliography of Printed Works Relating to the University of Oxford* (Oxford, 1968) is superb, and there is no Cambridge equivalent. For research in higher education generally there are *Work in Progress and Publications on the History of European Universities*, ed. John M. Fletcher, and Harold Silver and S. John Teague, *The History of British Universities, 1800–1969* (London, 1971).

PREFACE

The kind of knowing or meaning that analogy produces, what can less charitably be called the retrospective fallacy, is not completely absent from *The Revolution of the Dons*, as I can recognize. But it is continually being fought in favour of the other outlook, as old as analogy but profoundly separate from it. Historical irony and paradox produce no theory of behavioural modification or social engineering, and so perhaps they incline to the tragic view of human conduct and ambition. But for purposes of historical explanation perhaps it is better to regard them as optimistic or pessimistic only in relation to what the observer hopes or expects from the past. I have already noted at the beginning of this preface that my own outlook on the ability of universities to influence twentieth-century culture was hopeful, at least when I first began to write. And by 'hopeful' I meant essentially that the more determined view of change that many other historians of higher education noticed, the somewhat lock-step relationship between university reform and reform generally, appeared to me oversimplified. The complexity of institutional change was being ignored. Its unpredictable character and chaotic progress, the paradoxes attendant on its transformation were what needed emphasizing. Historical irony seemed a valuable way to correct the temptation of scholars to make the past directly serviceable to the present, which, as so many have warned, really amounts to using the present to gerrymander the past into convenient and compliant units. But historical irony could also capture the atmosphere of uncertainty, the bewildering options with unpredictable consequences that not only accompanied but actually coaxed Cambridge University into its present form. I thought it was ungracious of historians to describe a logic of change unknown to those who had undergone the experience.

My task, therefore, became similar to the one confronting the author of *The Eighteenth Brumaire of Louis Bonaparte* who tried to locate within the developing structure of a narrative (and analysis is a form of narrative) an explanation for the outcome of events that adjusts a preformulated view to an emerging, unexpected pattern of change realizing itself over a period of time. The original main themes are not abandoned: they are reconsidered and reworked in the light of new evidence and an ironic perspective.

5

PREFACE

I wanted to construct the book so that its themes, intentions and even 'lessons' were conveyed as much by form and organization as by the actual words of the argument. Only in this way could the necessary emphasis be conveyed to the reader, the necessary identification or recognition between reader and actor be created, the necessary tension be derived from catching on the edge of its spring the emotive release of the human experience, the transforming anxiety of men in particular historical situations. I took seriously Jacob Burckhardt's words that 'the form in which events, even the greatest, are told to the living and to posterity is anything but a matter of indifference'.[1]

The 'formal' characteristics of the early chapters of the book require no particular gloss. They set out much of the sociometrical evidence on the social composition of Cambridge and its feeder schools available when the book was written. The middle chapters, however, cannot be read exactly as they appear. Seemingly biographical or essays in the history of ideas, they are strictly speaking neither. What is attempted there is an examination of psychological strain in an institutional context. The chapters set out the boundaries of the discussion, the range of options, available to Victorian educational reformers. They recreate anxiety over role and career. They explicate the interpenetration of personal and 'objective' considerations which create what some sociologists call a 'generalized disturbance' so that the solution to one set of problems is inextricably tied to another. The Victorians understood this phenomenon. 'A man has many biographies, moving in parallel lines,' wrote one of them.[2] The chapters are meant to be read as if they were vertical or stacked, rather than sequential or linear as is the customary way. The purpose of adopting this form was to emphasize that anxiety, thinking and action occur simultaneously in life. It is these entangled processes that make human decisions confusing, and their outcomes uncertain. My object throughout was to achieve some degree of verisimilitude, to recover the many levels of thinking and behaviour which existed in a set of given circumstances, to use the form of presentation to insist on the contradiction and surprise that characterized Victorian Cambridge as it underwent the trans-

[1] *The Civilization of the Renaissance in Italy* (New York, 1954), p. 114.
[2] Herbert Morrah, *The Oxford Union* (London, 1923), p. 78.

formation that has taken it successfully to the present. Only some special arrangement of the literary text, some dislocation in the reader's customary way of noticing events, akin to what experimental novelists of the earliest twentieth century sought, could in my opinion convey the meaning of what had occurred. Clifford Geertz, amongst others, calls this procedure 'art', and he defines it memorably as crossing the conceptual wires of the observer.[1] Put in another way, such formal considerations remove 'The patina of the obvious that encrusts human actions: this is the first and last enemy of the historian.'[2]

The Victorians themselves had a cultural varnish which stripped their understanding of the obvious. They called it 'paradox'. It was a characteristic product of mid-nineteenth-century ratiocination and the mental mechanism by which they coped with change. Therefore it was entirely appropriate for me to resolve 'the revolution of the dons' into a set of para-doxical conclusions which at once reviewed the events of the past and asked historians to be careful. It was paradoxical, for example, that utilitarianism which had once been proposed as the mainspring of social reconstruction should have become suspect even by leading utilitarians. It was paradoxical that the collegiate structure of education which had been responsible for some of the most unsuccessful parts of the Georgian university should have provided the basis for the reform of the Victorian one. It was paradoxical that so much university teaching should have adopted the pedagogical assumptions of the colleges, despite the looming presence of the German example. It was paradoxical that a new student subculture of vigour and originality should have provided the inspiration for a series of innovations that cut away at its independence.[3] It was paradoxical that a strong interventionist outlook should have emerged in a society commonly depicted as liberal and

[1] Clifford Geertz, *The Interpretation of Cultures* (New York, 1973), p. 447.

[2] Peter Brown, *Religion and Society in the Age of Saint Augustine* (New York, 1972), p. 19. See also the startling, unforgettable essay by Robert Brentano, 'Bishops and Saints', in *The Historian's Workshop*, ed. L. P. Curtis, Jr. (New York, 1970), pp. 23–46. The exemplum might well be that closeness in time breeds a deceptive familiarity.

[3] For a follow-up essay see Sheldon Rothblatt, 'The Student Sub-culture and the Examination System in Early 19th-Century Oxbridge,' in Stone (ed.) *The University in Society*, I.

laissez-faire, and paradoxical, therefore, that the solution to the crisis of 1850–60, the ideal of a teaching university that prepared students for leadership roles by providing them with a professional ethic, should have ultimately put the university at the service of the State when it was intended to be a gesture of autonomy. It was paradoxical that an industrial society should have allowed one of its most prestigious institutions to reform itself in such a way that it actually became a source of values antagonistic to business. And finally it was paradoxical that the Victorian university revival was not predicated on a significant shift in the class structure of England, was not an accommodating response to a wholly middle-class culture, but was based on a section of its traditional clientele, now with different cultural expectations, and on its own traditions of learning and education.

To illuminate these paradoxes I was inevitably drawn directly into the lives of the dons, into the ironies of their thinking, into their private and public anxieties, the texture of their daily world. Occasionally I echoed their words or baited their own logical traps or entered into their conversations, which became as important to me as to them. To be sure, I wished to preserve historical hindsight, to keep *a posteriori* control of the overall pattern of change and to let nothing in human affairs pass for mystery. But at the same time, in order to emphasize the ironical and the paradoxical which gave (and give) meaning to change, I deliberately kept from the reader the several hints needed in advance to identify the exact nature of the revolution of the dons – to apprehend the special purpose of the book's title, that if dons could make a revolution, it would naturally be a donnish one. To demonstrate the manner in which human problems are sometimes historically resolved, it was necessary to make the reader share with the dons their own progressive discoveries, and like them, ultimately back into the solutions.

Berkeley, 1980

ACKNOWLEDGEMENTS

I wish to thank for their exceptional kindness and help and permission to use materials in their keeping, the Master and Fellows of Sidney Sussex College, Cambridge, especially Dr. R. C. Smail, Fellow, and Dr. M. C. Spencer, Fellow and Librarian; the Master and Fellows of Christ's College, Cambridge; the Master and Fellows of Pembroke College, Cambridge, and Professor Matthew Hodgart of the University of Sussex, former Fellow and Librarian; the Master and Fellows of Trinity College, Cambridge, and particularly Dr. R. Robson, Tutor for Advanced Students; the Provost and Fellows of King's College, Cambridge, especially Dr. A. N. L. Munby, Fellow and Librarian; Miss Heather E. Peek, Keeper of the Archives, Cambridge University; the Librarian of Cambridge University Library and the staff of the Anderson Room of the Cambridge University Library. Miss Philothea Thompson has very generously allowed me to use materials pertaining to Sir John Robert Seeley. To Professor John Roach of Sheffield University, former Fellow of Corpus Christi College, Cambridge, for his advice on sources and assistance in general, my gratitude; his work on the history of Cambridge has made it easier for others. Very special thanks go to my wife Barbara for her immense help, to my brother Ben for his inspiration and to my friends – John Ziman, Thomas Barnes, Robert Brentano, Fred Weinstein, George W. Stocking, Jr. and Irwin Scheiner – for their stimulating conversation and sensitive criticism. They prove how much scholarship is a mutual effort. I am especially indebted to my two teachers: George H. Guttridge, Sather Professor of History, Emeritus, University of California at Berkeley;

9

ACKNOWLEDGEMENTS

and Lord Annan, Provost of University College, London. To them I am very grateful.

London
New Year's Day, 1967

Sheldon Rothblatt

CONTENTS

ABBREVIATIONS

DNB	Dictionary of National Biography
B.M.	British Museum
C.U.L.	Cambridge University Library
T.C.L.	Trinity College Library
K.C.L.	King's College Library
PSYB	*Public Schools Year Book*
UC	D. A. Winstanley, *Unreformed Cambridge* (Cambridge, 1935)
EVC	D. A. Winstanley, *Early Victorian Cambridge* (Cambridge, 1940)
LVC	D. A. Winstanley, *Later Victorian Cambridge* (Cambridge, 1947)
H.C. Deb.	House of Commons Debates
H.L. Deb.	House of Lords Debates

INTRODUCTION

Today, on both sides of the Atlantic, the university in the modern world is a subject of continual discussion. Never before – hyperbole may for a moment be permitted – have the hopes and fears of civilization depended so completely on institutions of higher learning. The faith which the nineteenth century placed in the evolution of parliamentary government has now shifted to universities. Where the nineteenth century believed the historical aspirations of mankind would be fulfilled by the progressive development of representative institutions, the twentieth century looks to universities to confront the profound implications of technology and population growth. The public is almost daily assured, and the academic community flattered, that without the large, modern, research-oriented university, contemporary society could hardly meet the obligations before it.

The modern university is like Proteus, many things at once, and the colour or form it assumes depends on how it is viewed or grasped. The functions it must perform for industrial society are almost beyond imagination. It must provide both immediate and long-term advice to business and to governments, local and national. It must supply professions new and old with standards and leaders, devise solutions for urban congestion and environmental polution, and outline procedures for securing the high degree of labour mobility essential to a computer world. The modern university is often an important component of economic progress in a direct way. It can be a major employer of labour and a major consumer and therefore essential to the prosperity of contiguous communities. The modern university must provide for the culture of the inner man as well as the comfort and security of the outer. In the United States it must frequently make up the cultural deficiencies of urban, suburban or rural areas in which it may be situated, providing art, music and architecture that the surrounding community has neglected and may be in danger of forfeiting. In both the United States and Britain, as computer technology alters the work ethic which has done so much service to industrialization, the university faces its greatest challenge in education for leisure. The older ideals of a liberal education and self-cultivation, as some have prophesied, may well prove even more important a function of the university than staffing the technocracy.

In view of these multiple functions, it is not surprising that the university has attracted so much attention from scholars, critics and administrators. But it is surprising that so little writing of an historical nature has appeared. The immense volume of university literature is mainly fugitive, descriptive, sociological, programmatic, polemical and educationalist; it is only infrequently historical. None of the English universities, not even the famous older institutions, have been subjected to historical analysis in categories which are familiar to the present. Virtually all the topics of current discussion have yet to be given an historical context. Comparatively little is known of the social structure of the university, the relationship between social class and curricula, the history of academic freedom, the definition of a liberal education, the structure of teaching, the relations of students and teachers, the formation of an academic community, the growth of research as a university activity, the response of the university to change and the place of the Church of England in higher education. The source material for such studies is rich, varied and relatively untouched. College and university bursaries, muniment rooms, libraries and archives await the historian's visit. Private and official correspondence, financial records, admissions books and matriculation lists, scholarship records, biographies, magazines and newspapers, examination records, flysheets, the minutes of clubs and societies, committee reports, scholarly books and scientific treatises, architectural plans and even accounts of academic dress and dining habits are available and can be made into university history.

INTRODUCTION

The relative paucity of systematic inquiries into the history of the university is all the more curious in light of its great antiquity. It is an institution which has survived and flourished through centuries. It has undergone periodic change and adapted itself to new social and cultural conditions, but at the same time remaining a repository of past experience and insisting on the importance of continuity. If there is to be any understanding of how the university will meet the challenge of the twentieth century, then surely its past must be consulted – not, it should be said, for the sake of analogy – for analogy is limiting – but for the sake of recognition.

2.

Some of the more suggestive and innovative writings on English university history have not been studies of the university *per se* but accounts of individual dons or chapters in the lives of famous men. These usually comment on select university problems and contain themes that could well be elaborated into university history. Institutional histories proper vary considerably in purpose, scope and content. Some are relatively straightforward, impressively detailed and pioneering narrative studies or descriptions of university growth in terms of faculties, facilities, curricula and numbers of students, with additional miscellaneous information. Other accounts, especially those of Oxford or Cambridge, paraphrase or adopt the models and assumptions of nineteenth century constitutional, political or administrative history; improvement or growth and change remain their general themes. These may be classified as whig history and include the many notable volumes D. A. Winstanley produced on Cambridge. The whig interpretation proceeds on the assumption that university history may be fruitfully discussed in political terms. Professors, masters and fellows are as much politicians as they are teachers, scholars and scientists, and as politicians they must be considered an important addition to the late Georgian world of place-hunting. The whig interpretation states that in the early nineteenth century, before the great reforms of the mid-Victorian period, the ancient universities were useful instruments of an established Church, an oligarchic government and a hierarchical society, more rural or provincial in its setting than urban. After a series of famous franchise and municipal reforms, England's aristocracy was obliged to share its authority with an influential industrial and commercial bourgeoisie; but Oxford and Cambridge were slow to shift their loyalty and allegiance, remaining faithful in tone, values and structure to older arrangements. Because the ancient universities could not be persuaded to join in the general reform of English institutions, or because the university reforms that were carried out were too gradual and limited, Oxford and Cambridge did not progress; they fell behind the times and became increasingly parochial, archaic and anachronistic. Especially was this apparent when the two senior universities were compared to the growing German universities with their elaborate network of professorships and fundamental advances in science, psychology and comparative history, or even when they were measured against English secondary schools where important changes were occurring. Dons remaining in the ancient endowed colleges–having failed to raise university teaching to professional status–became almost functionless when electoral reforms effected outside the university virtually cancelled their former political usefulness. They became isolated and consequently eccentric, peevish and narrow-minded, distinctly quaint, amusing survivals like the institutions which housed them, vulnerable subjects for condescending anecdote.

By their refusal to meet the social and educational challenge of industrialism, the whig interpretation concludes, Oxford and Cambridge exhausted the patience of the nation and compromised their autonomy. By their internecine collegiate quarrels they showed themselves incapable of necessary self-reform, and finally their statutes and constitutions were altered for them by a succession of royal commissions, one of the great bureaucratic inventions of the nineteenth century. No longer were the ancient universities to be allowed the luxuries of comparative indolence and privilege or the privacy and repose of a rector's drawing room. They were to be transformed into national institutions providing for national needs and in the service of the entire nation; no longer were they to be useful merely to clergy, gentry and aristocracy.

The whig or constitutional interpretation of university history may incorporate certain assumptions that have received publicity through the writings of Sir Lewis Namier. Although in general Namier's theories about society and history are antithetical to whiggism, notably in the definition of progress and in the subliminal importance attributed to political activity, particular influences are discernible. High educational ideals or ideological statements about the relationship between ethics and education are regarded with suspicion. Dons and professors are no more idealistic or high-minded than politicians and bureaucrats. They too act in their own self-interest and any praise of their wisdom or inspiration is likely to be misleading. In order to see dons as they really are, historians ought to disregard the prophetic and self-effacing pronouncements of the Victorians and concentrate on their less lofty performances in college, convocation or committee. At this point the conclusions of Namier about human nature join the older whig interpretation: the Victorian dons were politicians, their universities were a mirror-image of the political nation. The best means for studying the history of Victorian Oxford or Cambridge is to observe the traffic between court, parliament, government and masters' lodges and to articulate the network of university offices and clerical livings that made the ancient universities so essential a part of the aristocratic spoils system.[1]

The whig interpretation shows the marks of its origins in the nineteenth century. Whig writers stressed the need for society and its institutions to be in agreement in order to reduce the areas of social friction. Hence, too, their emphasis on political rather than social change, on the progressive extension of the franchise and the establishment of representative government. Late nineteenth-century liberal political theory frequently emphasized the need of politics to be above class interest so that workers, when they entered parliament, would legislate in the interests of all. The whig insistence on the primacy of constitutional change was intended to soften unfortunate labour struggles, working-class millenarianism and demands for the end to social injustice which might result in revolution and wide-scale disturbance.

Another interpretation of the history of Oxford and Cambridge, which may be called the class conflict or class interest

---

[1] For a recent example of the modified whig approach see W. R. Ward, *Victorian Oxford* (London, 1965).

theory, has not yet been translated into full-length university history but may be derived from strands of labour history or from a general theory of social change in industrial society. The conflict theory sees university and institutional change as primarily a reflection of the struggle for power and influence among competing classes. In several respects the conflict or class interest theory resembles the whig, except that the university is a mirror-image of the socio-economic structure of England rather than its political structure. The function of the university is to serve whichever social class is in power. The allegiance of the university is easily transfered from social class to social class; Cambridge or Oxford would, if historical circumstances required, as willingly provide social status for the middle classes as it would job for the aristocracy. In the class conflict theory, educational change always parallels and reflects the struggle for influence and control that takes place among rival classes.

The class conflict theory reverses the judgment of the whig interpretation. Whereas in general whig historians regard educational change with favour and approve the reforms of the nineteenth century as in the best national interest, the conflict theory emphasizes class interest and exploitation. At one point in their history, at the time the colleges were founded, Oxford and Cambridge were meant to serve the entire nation–nation is defined socially rather than politically. Their amenities and educational facilities were meant to be enjoyed by all members of the population intellectually capable of benefitting from a university education. Indeed, so anxious was the university to guarantee merit its due that special scholarships and other emoluments were set aside specifically for the poor but able who might otherwise never reach the university. This practice, although perhaps not always followed, was essentially maintained until the great reforms of the third quarter of the nineteenth century. Under pressure, the aristocracy agreed to share political power with the economically more important middle classes who subsequently nationalized the university and the major secondary schools in their own interest. The special scholarships which wise and benevolent patrons had bequeathed to the poor were pocketed by the wealthier classes. Whereas Winstanley looked upon the great reforms with favour, the conflict interpretation finds them regressive and punitive. Their most important effect was to render the university inaccessible to the poorer classes. Far from being national, Oxford and Cambridge became more socially exclusive than ever before, a step in the climb of the parvenu bourgeoisie to status and influence.

A chief difficulty of the whig or constitutional theory of historical change is that while it admirably sets out the unique relationship between the university, the Church and the structure of political life in England in the first part of the nineteenth century, it places too much confidence in the unaided long-term effects of franchise reform and therefore neglects elements of class exclusion or bias in English education. Today a democratic franchise is not by itself thought to be the answer to public distress and social reconstruction. As an explanation of the possible social consequences of educational reform the conflict theory fares better, even though its roots also lie in the nineteenth century, and it is of special interest because many of the key, current problems of English education derive from arrangements decided upon in the mid-Victorian period. Commentators continually remark on the appeal expensive and therefore relatively exclusive private or endowed schools still have. Communications media repeatedly draw attention to the class basis of so much of English education, its aristocratic, élitist tradition, gentlemanly pretensions and outright snobbery.

Schools of the Headmasters' Conference, an important percentage of which are direct government grant, still complain about the attacks made upon them in the name of egalitarianism. In defence they cite the need for an élite in modern democracies and point to the higher proportion of 'A' and 'O' level passes received by their students than by grammar school boys.[1] Nevertheless, they remain open to criticism that their enrolments are still weighted against wage-earning families and their élite therefore not recruited from all available sources of talent. The problem of social privilege is the essential issue in all discussions of the eleven-plus, of the comprehensive secondary school and of the environmental and cultural factors which produce early

[1] See Graham Kalton, *The Public Schools—A Factual Survey* (London, 1966). In 1965–6 however, Oxford found that male candidates from maintained schools achieved a higher standard at 'A' level than those from independent schools. University of Oxford, Report of Commission of Inquiry–Franks Report (Oxford, 1966), I, p. 74.

success in examinations. And the problem of class and education is still very much alive in current discussions about the place of Oxford and Cambridge in a national scheme of higher education and the relation of both institutions to socially-exclusive secondary schools.

The problem of class in Oxford and Cambridge ultimately originates in the schools which feed into the university, but it is also related to the admissions system. Historically, the individual colleges of Oxford and Cambridge have had almost sole responsibility for deciding undergraduate admissions. Recently, and belatedly, the ancient universities joined the Universities Central Council for Admissions, an admissions clearing house composed of all universities in the kingdom. The absence of a satisfactory admissions system, however, makes it unlikely that the colleges will readily relinquish their prerogative. It is admitted that the collegiate method of selection presents special problems for students from working-class backgrounds, most of whom are educated in schools maintained by local authorities. The working-class student from a maintained school finds collegiate admission procedures strange and complicated. He may vaguely suspect a class bias in selection, he may find the interview an unfamiliar experience or he may discover that his sixth-form preparation for collegiate entrance examinations was not as extensive as that provided in the 'express streams' or longer sixth-form periods of the older, direct-grant grammar schools and independent public schools. The result is that in 1961, approximately 40 per cent of the undergraduates at Oxford came from maintained schools as against approximately 70 per cent of the undergraduates at modern and Victorian universities. The exact percentage of working-class students from maintained schools is difficult to determine in the absence of any recent data. In the mid-fifties it was possible to say that only about 9 per cent of Cambridge undergraduates and 13 per cent of Oxford undergraduates came from families of manual workers; the corresponding figure at Manchester, Leeds and Birmingham Universities was one-third.[1]

The degree to which Oxford and Cambridge have absorbed the sons of low-income families is a traditional social problem, but the question of social stratification finds expression in a

[1] Franks Report, I, pp. 77, 63–96.

newer form as well. It has been argued that the modern universities, to include Victorian foundations, are by tradition and structure more responsive to technological requirements, more adaptable to contemporary needs and more apt to play a critical role in the life of industrial society than the older collegiate establishments. The newer universities, it is said, are less bound to the past, less encumbered with beautiful and expensive grounds and buildings, more readily able to shift the direction of research as may be required by modern society.[1] Although it is easy to refute this optimism by pointing to the intellectual inventiveness of Oxford and Cambridge today, the very ease with which modern universities respond to technological demands may actually lead to a new kind of social stratification. Technological subjects appear to attract proportionately more students of working-class origin than do other disciplines. Since there is a strong possibility that the main technological burden of the future will be assigned to the modern universities, a new set of social distinctions may arise, by no means unknown in the past but now intensified as Oxford and Cambridge continue pre-eminent in the traditional humanistic culture so attractive to professional families.[2]

The problem of the relationship between education and social status is also involved in discussions of the recent governmental decision to establish a 'binary system' of higher education. For many years scientists and technologists educated in superior Colleges of Advanced Technology have complained of relative status deprivation because their institutions were not accorded university rank. This grievance has been partially remedied in the binary system. Colleges of Advanced Technology have been brought into closer association with the universities; several, at one time informally referred to as Special Institutions for Scientific and Technological Education and Research ('SISTERS'), have been given the high status and attention they deserve as establishments similar in character to the École Polytechnique or the Massachusetts Institute of

---

[1] 'The Popularity of Oxford and Cambridge', *Universities Quarterly*, XV (1960–1), pp. 327–41.
[2] See A. H. Halsey, 'British Universities and Intellectual Life', in A. H. Halsey, Jean Floud, and C. Arnold Anderson, *Education, Economy and Society* (New York, 1961), p. 511.

Technology. Colleges of education, however, and regional, area or local technical schools, may be in danger of losing whatever informal and unofficial associations with universities they may have previously enjoyed. They are to comprise an educational sector of their own, one possible result of which would be to prevent the majority of elementary and secondary school teachers from obtaining the higher professional recognition university affiliation brings. The binary system remains controversial, especially since Lord Robbins himself, chairman of the famous inquiry into higher education conducted in the period 1961 to 1963, has warned that in the binary system 'we are now confronted with the prospects of an educational caste system more rigid and hierarchical than before.'[1]

Because no proposals for educational reform in Britain today can be made without considering their possible effect on the class structure, the conflict or class interest theory of change appears more relevant than its whig alternative. Actually, however, the two theories are not necessarily mutually exclusive. In one respect in fact they complement each other; it only remains to insert in the whig interpretation a factor implicit in its own fundamental assumptions. If indeed historical progress depended on the orderly development of representative institutions and the gradual movement towards political democracy, then class factors in education can not possibly be ignored, for the health of a democracy depends upon the intelligence and literacy of its entire population. It is precisely this problem which consumed so much of the thinking of nineteenth-century intellectuals and made them acutely anxious about culture and the mass society. If political democracy were to succeed, then each major extension of the franchise had to be preceded or accompanied by a corresponding extension of education to neglected groups. The reforms of 1832 took place in the midst of the establishment of the proprietary school and the beginnings of the Arnoldian revolution; those of 1867 during the momentous reorganization of the public and the grammar schools; those of 1884 just after the establishment of a state-supported elementary school system. The correlation between educational expansion and franchise reform was never sufficiently exact or far-reaching to satisfy the Victorian intellectual aristocracy.

[1] Lord Robbins, *The University in the Modern World* (London, 1966), p. 151.

INTRODUCTION

Some predicted ochlocracy, others called for the immediate introduction of the culture utopia and still others expressed relief that a politics of deference would avert the calamity expected from educational disparities in times of political reform.

By its topicality the conflict theory has special appeal, but it is not without its dangers. Like most causal theories, it claims too much for itself; it is too quick to find expressions of simple class interest in complicated cultural and psychological responses to social change. Class conflict and rivalry is a factor in social change, but the conflict may have to be defined differently. Not all social problems of rivalry and competition begin or end in the thought of exploitation or absolute domination of one class by another. The motives of men are far more complex than they themselves suspect. The same criticism may be made of the Namier elements in the whig interpretation of university history. Dons may be politicians acting in their own self-interest, and we are right to suspect hidden or unconscious motives; but dons are also clergymen, or professional men, or snobs, idealists, romantics, neurotics and high-minded reformers. The statements and actions that one suspects may be politically motivated may in fact be generated by other considerations. The unconscious does not disclose its secrets in any straightforward manner. The historical context, always fluctuating, must decide which factors are of primary and which of secondary importance.

Both the whig and conflict theories have done a notable service to the history of education by showing how impossible it is to discuss educational change outside a larger historical context composed of social, political, intellectual, religious or economic ingredients. But there is one important area in which both theories are incomplete. Both presume too exact a correlation, too close an agreement between the principal direction of social or political change and specific educational reforms. Their emphasis is on normative values, on how a school or university is made to conform to particular socio-economic or political changes, how education is always bent to the service of society in exactly the way society wishes. Society is depicted as distant and omnipotent, an abstraction whose will cannot be denied. Disagreement between society and its institutions is regarded, implicitly or explicitly, as a situation which society

25

cannot possibly tolerate. Inherent in both theories is a dislike of plural elements, of strains and counter-strains, of the curious rivalries and unresolved tensions so common to history that make absolute social unity difficult. In a plural society, however, or one in the process of pluralization, it is entirely possible that the university and society will be in subtle and complex states of disagreement as well as agreement with one another, that the direction of university change may not be completely obvious, that surprises will occur. It is entirely possible that disagreement and agreement together constitute the peculiar quality of the modern university. A traditional institution like Cambridge, under public but not authoritarian pressure, may draw upon its own history, heritage and ideals to interpret the demands upon it in a unique and unexpected way. A university which is being asked to reform, but is still allowed a high degree of internal freedom, may restructure itself to acquire an identity and function which few expected. When Peer Gynt, searching for his true self, left the kingdom of trolls, he found the vague, formless and invisible Boyg blocking his path and was advised by a voice from the blackness to continue his quest by going 'round about'. It is the 'round about', so little emphasized in current discussions of education and so frequently neglected in histories of universities, which needs special attention.

PART ONE

A PROBLEM OF SOCIAL CHANGE

Chapter 1

CLOSED SCHOLARSHIPS, THE GRAMMAR SCHOOLS AND SOCIAL MOBILITY

In England discussions of the relationship between education and social mobility during the industrial revolution have centred on the failure of the nineteenth century to promote the moral and material welfare of the working classes commensurate with some of the more democratic claims of laissez-faire theory. Indeed it has been argued in one variant of the immiseration thesis that such educational opportunities that workers did enjoy were carefully and systematically taken from them in the great reforms in secondary education in the 1860's. Specifically it is stated that the industrial bourgeoisie – or those social groups that may be described as new in wealth and influence – took from the poor and humble privileges formerly reserved for them alone. Special closed scholarships (called 'close') and restricted financial awards which were the principal means by which boys from working-class backgrounds moved from the old grammar schools to the ancient universities and from the ancient universities to respectable and responsible positions within society were expropriated by the parvenu middle class. The poor were no longer to be suffered.

There can be little doubt that educational institutions may impede as well as encourage social mobility, nor can it be denied that in general the educational position of industrial workers and agrarian labourers did not advance as quickly as that of other groups and classes; but whether their position deteriorated – or what is more to the point, whether important changes in the structure of Victorian higher education can be traced to the desire of the rich and powerful to advance themselves at the expense of workers–is a matter for discussion. Especially does the fate of closed scholarships bear critical examination.

Unfortunately the state of current research does not allow altogether satisfactory generalizations regarding the connexion between the ancient grammar schools and the process of social mobility. Too little is known of the exact social composition of the schools before the nineteenth century, and reliable statistics on periodic changes are scarcely available. Nevertheless, it may be stated that in the argument for decreasing social mobility is a residual arcadianism which obscures rather than clarifies the course of social change in the late eighteenth and nineteenth centuries.[1] Georgian integrity does not hold up better than Victorian snobbery. If the grammar schools had ever been a genuine channel to the universities for boys of poor and humble social background, they had certainly ceased to be so long before the famous educational decisions of the 1860's.

The present view of the fate of the closed scholarships derives from complaints of the 1860's that poor boys would be denied their ancient right to a grammar school and university education if special preferences and privileges were abolished in order to promote open competition. The evidence for this view, however, depends mainly on statements made by Albert Mansbridge, the founder of the Workers' Educational Association, in

---

[1] See for example the curious statement in Nicholas Hans, *New Trends in Education in the Eighteenth Century* (London, 1951), p. 210: 'The gulf between the wealthy employers of labour and the proletarian factory hands and miners of the Victorian era was deeper than the ha-ha ditch which separated the squire from the farmer and wider than the distance between the merchant and the craftsman of the eighteenth century.' There were miners in the eighteenth century as well as in the nineteenth century, and a more apt comparison than farmer and squire, at least consistent with manufacturer and proletarian, is landowner and agrarian labourer. On the same page Hans writes that 'The closely knit rural community of the first half of the century gave ample chance for a bright boy of the labouring class.' But his own statistical table on pages 26 and 27 does not bear out this conclusion, and certainly not as far as the university is concerned. Only twenty-two identifiable 'craftsmen and retailers' attended Cambridge out of a total number of six hundred and twenty-five members of Hans' selected élite educated at Cambridge. A similar sentimental bias appears in W. G. Hoskins, *The Midland Peasant, the Economic and Social History of a Leicestershire Village* (London, 1957), p. 276.

a book which he published in 1923. It was he who gave the greatest publicity to the opinion that the elimination of closed scholarships was disastrous. Although willing to admit there were occasional instances of humanity, Mansbridge was of the opinion that 'the most difficult time for the poor scholar to get to Oxford or Cambridge was from 1854–1904.'[1] His conclusion, as summarized in his book, follows:

'In so far as the poor men lost in this way [open competition] to the Universities were of inferior parts, only able to lumber into a pulpit or a schoolroom on the strength of a degree, not much harm was done; but with such disappeared many men of real ability, who, because of inferior tuition, as compared with that provided in the great Public Schools, found the open classical scholarships entirely out of their reach. They had a better chance in the scholarships at Cambridge, because on the whole mathematical ability could be developed to a higher standard than classical in local grammar schools. Even so, a Whewell of 1860 would probably have been, not Master of Trinity, but a carpenter such as we should have liked to employ, unless he had become a trade union leader. Yet Trinity never actually turned its back on the poor scholar, and Cambridge retained its Sizars when Oxford jettisoned its Servitors. . . . Anyhow, the fact remains that from 1850 to 1900 the poor boy of parts had no chance of getting either to Oxford or to Cambridge unless he happened to be in a place towards which the Colleges recognized a special duty or where the schools had been strong enough to hold to their time-honoured privileges.'[2]

The observation on mathematics can be instantly dismissed. Only a few of the local grammar schools taught mathematics at a level suited to Cambridge standards and especially as those standards improved. Private tuition, both before and after university matriculation, was the more common means of instruction; and private tuition was expensive, unless a recent Cambridge graduate or the local parson offered his services free.

Mansbridge's conclusion was in part contradicted by the Royal Commission on Oxford and Cambridge of which he was a member. In its report of 1922 the Commission raised the

[1] Albert Mansbridge, *The Older Universities of England* (London, 1923), p. 109.
[2] Mansbridge, pp. 166–7.

possibility that there may have been a short term, transitional reduction in the amount of assistance available for poor boys from smaller grammar schools, but its general conclusion was that 'The number of poor men in residence at both Universities increased materially during the last half of the nineteenth century.'[1] Neither the Royal Commission nor Mansbridge offered decisive evidence for their conclusions, but Mansbridge nevertheless has remained unusually persuasive, his statements reappearing in a number of quite distinct studies or commentaries on Victorian Oxford and Cambridge. 'The career carved out for himself by William Whewell,' writes the author of a recent, valuable account of Cambridge, 'who was the son of a Lancaster master-carpenter and had gone up to Cambridge with an exhibition from Heversham Grammar School, would have been far more difficult to achieve in the last quarter of the nineteenth century than it had been in the first. The days of state aid and of an efficient system of secondary schools were yet to come, while the old local preferences, which had often helped poor men, had disappeared.'[2]

Mansbridge made one concession: he stated that the university commissioners of 1850 desired to open the universities to talent irrespective of class.[3] But Brian Simon, *Studies in the History of Education, 1780–1870*, disagrees. 'The colleges founded at both universities from the fourteenth to the sixteenth century,' he begins, 'were intended to provide places for the scholar unable to pay for his own board and tuition; after the Reformation there had been an influx of sons of the nobility and gentry but subsequently additional scholarships and exhibitions for the poor student had been established, particularly in the seventeenth century, often attached to local grammar schools. Many of these reserved places were now swept away; only where vested interests were powerful, as in the case of Winchester and Eton, were they maintained. The poverty clauses governing the award of scholarships and exhibitions were abolished, as well as those confined to particular districts and families. Instead, awards were thrown open to competition on the basis of "merit"

---

[1] Royal Commission on Oxford and Cambridge Universities, 1922 (Cmd. 1588), x, Report, p. 132.

[2] J. P. C. Roach, 'Victorian Universities and the National Intelligentsia', *Victorian Studies*, III (December, 1959), p. 145.

[3] Mansbridge, p. 166.

−a step which naturally favoured the wealthier schools and pupils. This was done on grounds of efficiency, and certainly with some justification. . . . the idea that a working-class child should get to Oxford or Cambridge never crossed the minds of those introducing reforms. Their avowed concern was to sweep away clerical privileges and restrictions and to create truly national universities. . . . So far as the working class were concerned, for one exclusive monopoly was substituted another, even harder to break.'[1]

Despite the use of such qualifying phrases as 'many of these reserved places were now swept away,' 'only where vested interests were powerful,' and 'with some justification,' Simon's desire is to prepare a general indictment of the Victorians; but like others who essentially follow Mansbridge, he brings no convincing evidence in support of the hypothesis. Closed scholarships with poverty clauses are automatically assumed to be the possession of poor boys, defined in the Mansbridge tradition as boys from artisan and working-class backgrounds. Open competition, by contrast, must bring higher standards, better schools and richer boys, that is, boys who are middle class. Overlooked is the possibility that poverty clauses may in practice have been disregarded, that obtaining a closed scholarship may have involved years of financial sacrifice scarcely possible for someone living at or just above the subsistence level or that the best of founders' intentions were frequently upset by economic, social and political developments of a local or regional nature.

The difficulties arising from too close an adherence to Mansbridge's interpretation can be illustrated by the grammar school career of the great William Whewell, the most frequently cited success story. The meagre facts of Whewell's early life are contained in Mrs. Stair Douglas' conventional biography. Whewell's father was a Lancaster carpenter who possessed some house property in town. William was rescued from a joiner's life by his parish priest, the headmaster of Lancaster Grammar

---

[1] Brian Simon, *Studies in the History of Education, 1780–1870* (London, 1960), p. 299. Mansbridge's conclusion is also repeated by C. Arnold Anderson and Miriam Schnaper, *School and Society in England: Social Backgrounds of Oxford and Cambridge Students* (Washington, 1952), p. 5 et seq. This sampling brings nothing fresh to the problem. G. Kitson Clark, *The Making of Victorian England* (London, 1962), p. 258, is in general more guarded in judgment but still echoes Mansbridge's original statement.

School, who managed to convince the senior Whewell that his son's education would be free. After some instruction at Lancaster, Whewell was sent north to Heversham Grammar School in Westmoreland, a distance of about twelve miles, to qualify for an exhibition to Trinity College, Cambridge; the exhibition was in the gift of the local squire, a descendant of the founder of Heversham Grammar.[1] He remained at the school for two years. He had almost certainly to pay for tuition, since he was not a native of Heversham, and he had also to pay for private coaching in mathematics, which he received from a well-known scholar resident in Kendal, five miles north of Heversham. Board and room may have cost him as much as 25 guineas per annum.[2] None of these expenditures guaranteed him the Trinity exhibition, since qualified Heversham parishioners automatically received first consideration. Even the exhibition was not valuable enough to enable a boy of limited means to attend Cambridge: Whewell had to supplement his award with the money raised in a public subscription.[3]

It is difficult to see how the Whewell experience can be made to support the arcadian dream. The condition of the grammar schools and the socio-economic position of the labouring classes, urban and rural, militated against the possibility that a grammar school education could be made accessible to all.[4] The special exhibitions available to boys from artisan families were

---

[1] Neither Mrs. Stair Douglas, *Life of William Whewell* (London, 1881), pp. 1–6, nor W. G. Clark, 'William Whewell, In Memoriam', *Macmillan's Magazine*, XIII (April, 1866), pp. 545–52, say positively that Whewell boarded in town or at the grammar school, but this is a fair assumption; and Clark does use the word 'removed'.

[2] This was true of Heversham in 1818, six years after Whewell left. Town boarding may have been cheaper. Nicholas Carlisle, *A Concise Description of the Endowed Grammar Schools in England and Wales* (London, 1818), II, pp. 707–10. In general the pound sterling increased in value in the course of the nineteenth century. There were inflationary periods in the first half of the nineteenth century, but secular trends after 1850 are decidedly deflationary. See the Gayer-Rostow-Schwartz, Rousseaux, Sauerbeck-Statist and Board of Trade Wholesale Price Indices in Brian R. Mitchell and Phyllis Deane, *Abstract of British Historical Statistics* (Cambridge, 1962).

[3] Athol Laverick Murray, *Royal Grammar School, Lancaster* (Cambridge, n.d.), p. 91.

[4] Even Hans admits that 'On the whole the Grammar Schools may be described as schools of the middle class' (pp. 29 and 30).

geographically maldistributed. They were neither plentiful nor cheap. A bright and ambitious boy might find himself called upon to pay for tuition, transportation and board in his search for an appropriate pre-university education. Possibly he could rely on some private or community support; but the amount of such assistance available at any one time was never capable of sustaining more than a very small number of poor boys. The final irony was that a closed award could be so restricted that the poor boy who had undergone elaborate and relatively expensive preparation might fail to qualify after all.

Merely because Whewell received an exhibition to Trinity does not mean that closed awards with poverty clauses were available to the poorest members of eighteenth-century provincial society. As the son of a master carpenter who owned a small amount of town property and very likely employed a journeyman or two, Whewell cannot be said to have occupied the lowest rung in the social ladder.[1] And surely it is pointless to repeat that Whewell, the eldest son of a master carpenter, rose to become Master of Trinity in 1841 unless equal publicity is given to Charles Smith, the fourth son of a Huntingdon cobbler, who became Master of Sidney Sussex in 1890.

In 1818 Nicholas Carlisle described four hundred and seventy-five endowed schools, and half a century later a royal commission investigated about eight hundred secondary schools. It is impossible to summarize the condition of each of these schools at any one time or over a long period of time. But there is evidence, nevertheless, to show that unfortunately the boy of limited means rarely occupied a special position in the grammar schools. In one opinion, 'The scholars, usually described in the school statutes as "children" or "youth" for whom the Grammar Schools were intended, were of no one class in particular. The school was to be for such as required an education in grammar, and among them there would be boys of all classes, but many more of those above the labouring class than of those in that class. The "poor" are frequently named in the school

---

[1] The Webbs report that sometimes artisans drew status distinctions between themselves. Certain of the hand woolcombers of Nottingham and Leicester, for example, insisted on being called 'gentlemen woolcombers' and would not drink with other men at the ale house. Sidney and Beatrice Webb, *The History of Trade Unionism* (London, 1894), p. 38.

statutes, but rather in a way indicating a desire to keep the school available for them, than in expectation that they would in fact form the majority of the scholars.'[1]

The grammar schools were intended to serve the inhabitants of the town and neighbouring countryside. The social structure of the schools depended on the nature of the curricula, the prosperity of the school, the state of local commerce and employment, migration, the introduction of industrial techniques and the size and composition of the community. Seamen, pilots, shipowners and shipbuilders, merchants engaged in export and import, builders, suppliers, and small producers of naval and marine stores were among the principal inhabitants of seaport towns. In agricultural areas farmers and agrarian labourers comprised a sizable proportion of the local population. The new textile barons and large wholesalers, retailers, and distributors could be found in the emerging industrial communities. Everywhere was the usual core of tradesmen and shopkeepers (butchers, bakers, grocers, tailors, publicans, booksellers, printers, auctioneers and valuers, ironmongers, drapers); skilled workers and artisans in traditional trades and services and in newer occupations concerned with the design and construction of machinery; county and borough officials, excisemen, lesser professionals (solicitors, pharmacists, engineers, surveyors, architects, draftsmen, accountants); town and estate bailiffs, clerks, clergymen, physicians and surgeons, dissenting ministers, widows, and retired naval and military officers; commission and land agents and brokers, and perhaps a number of rentiers describing themselves as gentlemen. There were also large numbers of labourers, indigent or unemployed.

Throughout the eighteenth century the demand for a traditional grammar school education was sporadic and uneven. Few boys stayed on past the ages of twelve or fourteen to complete their secondary education and qualify for university entrance. At best many of the grammar schools were providing elementary or higher elementary education and failed completely to supply the universities with suitably trained scholars.

---

[1] Board of Education, Report of the Consultative Committee on Secondary Education, with special reference to Grammar Schools and Technical High Schools (H.M.S.O., 1938, reprinted 1959), p. 6. Mansbridge was also a member of this committee.

Explanations are not hard to find. Nonconformists looked with a jaundiced eye on institutions run by Anglican clergymen. They and other representatives of business established an extensive system of academies and private schools which often featured a commercial and vocational education more suited to the needs of urban commerce and manufacturing. Some grammar schools followed suit, abandoned their classical curricula or supplemented it with instruction in English grammar, writing, accounting, mensuration, arithmetic, mechanical drawing, some history and geography, and foreign languages such as French or German. The town of Hull introduced Italian into the local grammar school to further the citrus trade recently established with Sicily and the Adriatic.[1] The introduction of non-classical subjects strained the resources of those grammar schools which attempted to stretch limited endowments and one or two teachers over a wide variety of subjects. Sometimes, in defiance of the wishes of benefactors, foundation money was diverted to the support of teaching in non-classical subjects; but the usual solution was to charge small fees, a guinea or two per subject per annum, to augment the foundation and provide the salary of a poorly-trained part-time writing master or language teacher. Salaries were frequently so low—even for headmasters—that able men went elsewhere, began private schools of their own or devoted themselves to a variety of jobs in order to accumulate a respectable income; in the meantime, the forms of a school were left without guidance or instruction. It was an age of legitimate and illegitimate pluralism.

Peculation and embezzlement of funds were common. At Nottingham, the town corporation which controlled the local grammar school was guilty of misusing endowments. The municipal corporations commissioners of the 1830's discovered that school property had been sold, the money diverted to noncharitable purposes. School surpluses were misapplied, endowments were squandered on feasts, and the nomination of students to the school's foundation was frequently determined by nepotism and political affiliation.[2] Even where the integrity

[1] John Lawson, *A Town Grammar School through Six Centuries* (London, 1963), p. 185, *et passim*.
[2] Adam Waugh Thomas, *A History of Nottingham High School* (Nottingham, 1957), p. 132 et seq.

of the masters was beyond reproach and endowments were theoretically adequate, the money required to improve the existing educational facilities or to maintain scholars was not necessarily available. At Leicester, long troubled by declining income, exhibitioners could not depend on regular payments.[1] At Manchester, where the ethical standard was usually higher than at Nottingham, poor business practice accounted for the decline in profits from the grammar school's monopoly in grinding malt.[2] Graft, waste, inefficiency and incompetency in the grammar schools throughout the eighteenth and early nineteenth centuries were reason enough to justify inquiry by county J.P.'s in their capacity as charity commissioners.

The grammar schools were free in only a limited sense. Sometimes, as at the Free Grammar School of Leicester or at the grammar school in Nottingham, foundation statutes limited free instruction in the classics to sons of freemen.[3] The qualifications for freeman status varied radically under the unreformed franchise, but few, it can be maintained, enjoyed corporate privileges and were entitled to be called freeman – less than 2 per cent of the inhabitants of Ipswich, for example, and an even smaller fraction of the inhabitants of Plymouth.[4] In some areas the grammar school was only free to parishioners, non-parishioners being expected to pay tuition fees ranging from 2 to 8 guineas per annum. Commercial subjects, modern languages, mathematics, even occasionally Greek,[5] were extras wholly or partly supported by fees. In addition all students could expect entrance fees and trifling assessments for fuel, potation and

[1] M. Claire Cross, *The Free Grammar School of Leicester* (Leicester, 1953), p. 45.

[2] A. A. Mumford, *The Manchester Grammar School, 1515–1915* (London, 1919), p. 256.

[3] A. Temple Patterson, *Radical Leicester* (Leicester, 1954), p. 17. Thomas, p. 106.

[4] Frederic William Maitland, *The Constitutional History of England* (Cambridge, 1961), p. 359. In the seventeenth century wage labourers were not considered free because they held no property even in their own labour. Even the Levellers excluded them from the franchise. 'Work and Leisure in Pre-Industrial Society: Conference Paper and Report', *Past and Present*, Number 29 (December, 1964), p. 63.

[5] The grammar school was sometimes called the Latin School, since this was the subject traditionally emphasized. Report of the Consultative Committee on Secondary Education, p. 5.

sometimes books. Even in prosperous times the poorest members of the locality found the payment of fees a heavy burden – this was still a period when the kitchen garden was necessary to the maintenance of subsistence levels – but the effect in times of short harvest or depressed trade was disastrous. Headmasters could never count on regular attendance, and some, like the headmaster of Batley, an impoverished grammar school in Yorkshire, used the excuse of irregular attendance to obtain the dismissal of textile operatives' children altogether.[1]

In order to restore both their own incomes and the reputation of their schools, headmasters began to provide boarding accommodations at high costs for boys who lived outside the town. At Heversham in 1818 boarding fees totalled a stiff 25 guineas per annum, but they were 50–60 guineas at Hull at the turn of the century, and an incredible 60–140 guineas at Manchester in the first third of the nineteenth century.[2] The income from boarding relieved a number of long-standing problems. It provided a substantial salary for a headmaster in search of gentility hitherto dependent on a meagre cure and the chaplaincy of the town jail. It was likely to be steady, for boys from a distance were not as subject to trade fluctuations as boys with parents in local employ and could be counted upon to keep the enrolment more stable. It could be used to employ additional masters and part-time instructors in old and new subjects, or it simply allowed a classical foundation to function in the face of more utilitarian demands, at the same time preserving the school from embarrassing compromises with nonconformists. The boarding side provided the classics master with a unique opportunity to teach the subject he knew best, to impart Augustan ideals to a group of students without the restraining pressures of parents and municipal corporations and, at the same time, to establish a reputation outside the immediate area. There was the added satisfaction of associating with a wealthier set and even an occasional fashionable boy. It was certainly obvious that only the wealthier boy could be counted upon to remain

[1] Derek Noel Reed Lester, *The History of Batley Grammar School* (Batley, 1963), pp. 83–4. The headmaster defended his action by saying 'that the only conditions for admission that he had required were cleanliness and willingness to learn' (p. 104).

[2] Lawson, p. 192; Mumford, p. 260 et seq.

at the school long enough to qualify for university admission, and it could be predicted that he would receive preferential treatment.

At Leicester in 1797, the decision to establish a boarding side at the Free Grammar School provided a short term solution to a thirty-year old fiscal problem. The school had become practically defunct, partly because its classical education had no value for the growing nonconformist community; and there were hardly any foundation scholars at all. The corporation hired a new headmaster who brought with him forty boarders from a private school he had been conducting. At the same time the corporation closed the lower school, claiming that it had been giving a non-classical education to a few students contrary to statute; but a number of freemen thought otherwise and several years later protested that the lower school had been closed, and their children turned out, because the corporation was admitting boarders.[1]

At Hull, a succession of headmasters, hard-pressed by the competition of a rival academy, had advertised for boarders, 'gentlemen of the neighbourhood'. By 1814 there were about ten boarders and by 1817 sixty day boys, half of whom were technically on the foundation but actually paying more than £2 per annum, depending on the number of subjects they studied.[2]

Manchester, a grammar school favoured by substantial endowments, had been accommodating boarding students in sizable numbers from at least the middle of the eighteenth century. To some extent boarders were first attracted to Manchester by its school-leaving exhibitions derived from the tax on corn and malt.[3] In the period 1740–65, eighty-four out of one hundred and ninety-six boarding students passed on to the universities, the number of day boys being only sixteen out of four hundred and seventy-seven.[4] Of the one hundred and eighty-three students from Manchester attending Oxford or Cambridge in the period 1749 to 1784, approximately 84 per

---

[1] Patterson, pp. 17–18, 240–1.　　[2] Lawson, ibid.　　[3] Mumford, p. 198.
[4] Ibid., p. 171. Mumford's distinction between the boarder and the day student is based on the distance a boy resided from school. The Manchester Grammar School registers make no such distinction so Mumford's figures are not infallible.

cent had been boarders, the remainder being sons of local clergy or others seeking professional careers.[1] In the period 1807 to 1837, when Jeremiah Smith revived the fortunes of the school after a late-century decline, the number of boarders increased again at the expense of day boys. By 1836 boarders comprised a quarter of the school.[2] They received special instruction, virtually monopolized the school exhibitions[3] and were obviously in an ideal position to receive the closed scholarships that Manchester Grammar enjoyed at Brasenose College, Oxford, and St. John's, Cambridge. Among the boarders could be found substantial tradesmen like Joah Bates, the son of a Halifax innkeeper who went from Manchester to King's College, Cambridge, or the sons of prosperous farmers residing at a distance; but on the whole Mumford's judgment is justifiably harsh: 'Although theoretically the benefits of the School were available for able boys of restricted means, as an actual fact this had largely ceased to be the case in the eighteenth century.'[4]

The introduction of a boarding side did not guarantee that a school's fortunes would be revived or that its ties to the

---

[1] Ibid., p. 193.   [2] Ibid., p. 270.   [3] Ibid., p. 262.

[4] Mumford, pp. 194, 217. See also p. 273: 'If a scholar of humble origin but of unusual ability turned up at the old Grammar School, he could only obtain advancement by the personal interest and efforts of some particular patron, and as such might conceivably even be awarded a University Exhibition. Such a case did actually once occur, but the unctuousness with which it was announced on prize day showed how unexpected and rare a circumstance it was.' Carlisle writes of King Edward the Sixth, Birmingham: 'The young Gentlemen who come as Boarders to this School, have equal privileges with the boys upon The Foundation, – And, it frequently happens, that the "*Strangers*" have been appointed to the Exhibitions [ten of £35 p.a., tenable for seven years at any college in Oxford or Cambridge].' Carlisle, II, p. 637, also p. 335. At Blundell's School, Tiverton, Devon, an Elizabethan foundation with close scholarships at Sidney Sussex College, Cambridge, tuition in 1818 amounted to 4–5 guineas per annum, £30 for board (Carlisle, I, p. 356). It has been calculated that in June 1845 there were eighty students at the school, forty-four of whom were boarders. According to one source, of the first two thousand three hundred and forty-five entries in the Register (to August 1840) only three hundred and forty-three boys were born or brought up in Tiverton and of these only seventy-eight remained in school to age sixteen, a situation which of course favoured boarders. Of the seventy-eight, only nineteen of twenty-six candidates had been elected to school scholarships and exhibitions. Arthur Fisher, *The Register of Blundell's School, Part I, 1770–1882* (Exeter, 1904), p. 2.

university would be re-established. At Hull most boys still left school between the ages of twelve and fourteen, and the curriculum was remodelled to meet their more practical needs. This meant that the education required to place a boy in the university was not available. John Scott, a wrangler from Magdalene College, Cambridge, and headmaster of Hull from 1801–24, sent only two boys to Cambridge. The first, the son of a master mariner, went up to Queens' College; the second, the son of a bankrupt alderman, ran up a deficit of £150 at St. Catharine's, which the Hull corporation paid. Both received school leaving exhibitions but neither qualified for the Metcalfe Scholarship at Clare College, a closed award for Hull students.[1]

From 1796 to 1872 Hull virtually ceased to supply suitable candidates for the Metcalfe Scholarship.[2] The Metcalfe Scholar in 1796 was the son of a Hull vicar. The next award was not given until 1816, when it went to the son of a victualler who was followed in 1822 by the son of a timber merchant and shipowner who had spent a year at Glasgow and Edinburgh.[3] Nine years later the son of another Hull clergyman became Metcalfe Scholar, and there was one scholar in each of the next two decades.[4] In the seventy-one years from 1725, when John Blythe, the orphan son of a Hull grocer received the first Metcalfe, until 1796 the award was given fourteen times.[5] In the fifty-seven years from 1872 to 1929 it was given sixteen times. By comparison the intervening period was certainly bleak.

Hull had simply few qualified applicants to offer Clare. The Metcalfe demanded a certain level of classical education which Hull no longer maintained. Inevitably the college was led to

---

[1] Lawson, pp. 189–90. The tenure of the Metcalfe is not indicated.

[2] William John Harrison, *Notes on the Masters, Fellows, Scholars and Exhibitioners of Clare College, Cambridge* (Cambridge, 1953), pp. 83–4.

[3] Lawson, p. 193.

[4] Lawson writes that from 1838 to 1868 only one Hull Grammar boy successfully applied for the Metcalfe, Septimus Green Wood, who went up to Clare in 1845 (p. 218). Harrison, however, lists a John Ward who held the scholarship in 1855. Venn, *Alumni Cantabrigienses*, provides no information on either boy, except to note that Wood took holy orders.

[5] Of the fourteen Metcalfes, two were sons of clergymen, one the son of a grocer, one probably the son of the Chamberlain of Hull. Ten of the fourteen students took holy orders, five are identified as sizars, a category reserved for the poorer undergraduates of Cambridge. No other information is available from Venn.

reject many of the potential candidates. The justice of this policy was tacitly recognized in 1862 when one poorly-prepared rejection, the son of a tailor and outfitter, was successfully coached into St. John's by his parish priest, a recent Cambridge graduate.[1] Not until 1897 was Clare allowed to broaden the selection basis of the Metcalfe by liberalizing the statutes to include candidates from any Hull school if no suitable applicant from the Grammar School appeared.[2] Until then the Metcalfe frequently went unclaimed.[3] Historians who criticize the concept of the open scholarship fail to consider that unused awards benefit no social class, even those regarded as lowest.

The Perse School, Cambridge, is an example of an endowed foundation which was also entitled to close university awards. Stephen Perse, a physician and senior fellow of Gonville and Caius, provided six scholarships at his college to which Perse students were to be given preference. From 1623 to 1678 there were at least seventy boys at Caius from the Perse, but from the end of the seventeenth century until 1833 only two or three boys are recorded. 'It would be interesting to account for this extraordinary falling off.'[4]

The closed scholarships attached to the old grammar schools of England and Wales had long ceased to be an effective way of placing the genuinely poor boy in the university. The academic future of the prospective scholar was too dependent on the fate of the grammar school, which in turn was determined by local policy and conditions. It was a prize to be won by opposing political factions, an institution to be neglected or exploited for personal profit, a business concern run badly and gone to seed, an innocent outpost assailed by the impersonal forces of social and economic change, or a helpless, weakly-endowed memorial to past piety.

---

[1] Lawson, p. 223.   [2] Harrison, p. 83.

[3] Besides the Metcalfe, former pupils of Hull Grammar School could compete for school leaving exhibitions worth £75 per annum in the late 1820's. After 1836, however, these awards were entirely dissociated from the school and were made available without examination to the inhabitants of the town of Hull. In 1840 a scholarship was established by public subscription, and the grammar school was not asked to supply candidates. By 1840, therefore, the ability of the grammar school to support poor students in their search for a university education was further reduced. Lawson, p. 218.

[4] John Venn, *The Perse School, Cambridge* (Cambridge, 1890), p. 15.

The boy who aspired to a closed scholarship in the hope of financing a university career could expect his chances to fluctuate with the social composition, selection policies and administrative efficiency of the body or bodies which controlled his school. The old borough council of Nottingham, for example, venal and dishonest in its day, had been composed of artisans and tradesmen, and most of the boys nominated to the grammar school had come from these classes.[1] But here, as in Manchester and Batley–other rapidly expanding industrial centres–the selection of students was in part simplified by the fact that men of new fortune, for reasons already described, abandoned the grammar schools and sent their sons away to board. After 1835 there was a shift in the control of Nottingham Grammar School. Control of the reformed and reorganized town council passed into the hands of manufacturers of lace and stockings, empowered by the new constitution to nominate the charity trustees who would in future supervise the grammar school. In 1836 the trustees were represented by eight manufacturers, four merchants, one physician, a banker and a gentleman, and as trustees died or retired they were usually replaced, if at all, by others of the same occupation.[2]

This change however, was not accompanied by any improvement in the quality of the education provided. The prosperity of the school was arrested in a three-cornered dispute between the charity commissioners, the charity trustees and the reconstituted town council. Until 1869 no boy entered the grammar school unless sponsored by a trustee or, afterwards, by a £50 donor whose nomination took precedence over that of a trustee.[3] The system of donatees and the policy of systematically charging fees had been introduced in 1859. By the time the schools inquiry commissioners reported in 1868, all the boys at the grammar school, now Nottingham High School, were fee-payers, although the trustees reserved the right to remit fees in part or whole. Boarders were introduced, a handful of scholarships established,

---

[1] Thomas, pp. 132 et. seq. Hull was equally guilty of nepotism in the selection of exhibitioners. Lawson, p. 201.

[2] Thomas, pp. 204 et seq.

[3] Thomas, p. 206. Thirty-nine donors accounted for one hundred and three students at any one time, but the author claims this privilege was not generally abused.

a number of school-leaving exhibitions obtained from wealthy benefactors.[1] The reorganization of the school was not complete until 1882 and by far the greater number of boys still left by age fifteen to take up clerical and commercial positions.[2] But the foundation had been laid for the revival of the school; its best boys could again attend the university. In this recovery it may be supposed that Nicholas Carlisle's lament – 'The School may now . . . be regarded as a useful Seminary for teaching boys English Grammar, reading, writing, and arithmetic, – But its former celebrity in CLASSICAL LEARNING *is at an end*'[3] – was at long last set aside.

The themes of financial insolvency, neglect and jurisdictional dispute in the thirty or forty years following the reform of the English boroughs are repeated in the history of Hull. In practice control of the grammar school was awkwardly divided between an elected town council, a grammar school committee and a body of nineteen trustees, none of which had sufficient authority to augment its endowment. No more than an elementary school supplying rudimentary education to town tradesmen and a few minor professionals, Hull was saved from outright extinction in 1865 when the charity trustees opposed the scheme of a local shipowner – backed by at least six of the seven members of the grammar school committee – to merge the endowment of the grammar school in a new, privately supported proprietary college. The Metcalfe Scholarship, its only university tie, continued to gather dust in Clare.[4]

When the schools inquiry commission appointed to investigate the endowed schools of England reported in 1868, they found that five hundred and fifty institutions classified as grammar schools sent no boys to the university, and only forty of the remaining eighty or ninety sent as many as three boys every year.[5] This was the inevitable result of the haphazard development and cumulative circumstances which produced the decay of the old grammar schools. A century of instability had made them an ineffective and unreliable means for the recruitment of poor boys into the universities. Endowed mainly for

[1] Thomas, pp. 187–8.　　[2] Thomas, p. 209.　　[3] Carlisle, II, p. 278.
[4] Lawson, p. 228, *et passim*.
[5] R. L. Archer, *Secondary Education in the Nineteenth Century* (Cambridge, 1921), p. 167.

Latin, crippled by the effects of falling incomes produced by declining enrolments, mismanaged funds or a sharp fall in the value of money, grammar schools turned to the boarding side as an antidote. Headmasters accused of favouring richer boys could always reply that these were the only boys who completed the sixth forms, the only students the school could recommend to the tutors of Cambridge colleges.

The working classes did not have to be 'edged out of grammar schools where a free education had hitherto been available'[1] by the Universities Acts of 1854 and 1856, by the Public Schools Act of 1868 and by the Endowed Schools Act of 1869. The millions of urban and agrarian labourers who populate the history of England had rarely attended the grammar schools; and the greater majority of the sons of artisans and shopkeepers in attendance at grammar schools hardly remained long enough to qualify for a closed scholarship. The eighteenth and the first half of the nineteenth centuries were still periods in which the labour of children appeared essential to the maintenance of subsistence levels of income for domestic and factory workers. Relatively few were willing or able to send their children to school regularly, and in many industrial areas satisfactory schools were not even available. Relatively few employers were willing to sacrifice a labour source which was cheap and docile and well-suited to special tasks like winding the remnants of silk or cotton thread from bobbins in lace factories. It remained for future generations to overcome parental suspicions that education was wasteful and to convince employers that children should be in school rather than in factories. In the long run only a combination of factory legislation properly enforced, technological innovation and rising productivity – reflected in the increased capitalization of industry and higher working-class incomes – could effect the economic, cultural and family changes which would allow children a chance to obtain higher levels of education.

The old grammar schools were a poor substitute for a State-supported system of compulsory secondary education. They were not idyllic places of the romantic imagination, eager to welcome and guide towards closed scholarships potential senior wranglers from artisan families. From the late eighteenth cen-

[1] Simon, p. 335.

tury to the decade of the schools inquiry commission, there were continuous protests that the intentions of founders had been disregarded.[1] It can be said that the first genuine attempt to systematically provide a secondary education for the truly poor boy of working-class origin belongs to the twentieth century. No real precedent existed, not even in the holy intentions of charitable men of the past.

[1] Patterson, pp. 240–1; Simon, p. 108; Lester, pp. 83–4, 104; Thomas, pp. 152–3, 137 n.

CHAPTER 2

EDUCATIONAL COSTS
AND SOCIAL MOBILITY

1. The Public Schools

Like the grammar schools public schools have been severely criticized for their social exclusiveness by both liberal and marxian historians. While it is agreed that the Georgian aristocracy was initially responsible for the deplorable snobbery of the schools, the Victorian middle classes come in for the harshest reprimand. They are accused of impudence and self-seeking and condemned for the haste with which they sought to expand the system of public school education. As in the grammar schools their foremost crime was closing the public schools and consequently the universities to the poorer classes. The medium of dispossession was again the closed scholarship. By eliminating this source of time-honoured assistance the middle classes removed the only access to public schools less fortunate classes possessed, and at the same time they so improved the teaching in the public schools that admission to the ancient universities became virtually unthinkable without an expensive sixth-form preparation. Exclusive as were the public schools before 1860, they were even more so after 1860; and proof of their influence and success can be seen in the sudden, unprecedented expansion in numbers at Oxford and Cambridge that took place in the early 1860's: the mass entrance of new wealth into the citadels of clerical and aristocratic privilege. This conclusion, however, by no means solves the question of the part played by the public schools in the problem of social change in Victorian Cambridge and like the matter of social mobility in the grammar schools deserves re-examination.

EDUCATIONAL COSTS, SOCIAL MOBILITY

The original public schools, nine in number, were grammar schools that drew their students from the same range of social classes as less renowned institutions, but at some point–conceivably in the seventeenth century, surely in the eighteenth century–they became in varying degree the preserves of the rich and influential social classes from whom they took their tone, manners and scale of values. The schools were called 'public' (the word was probably used consistently first in the sixteenth century) to distinguish them from private schools. They were supported by endowments, administered by non-private and non-local boards of governors, were not run for profit and possessed close ties with the ancient universities, dons and 'beaks', masters of colleges and headmasters forming one, educationally-homogenous group.[1] They were also called 'public' because long before the nineteenth century a large, in some schools the largest, proportion of their students came from non-local families, especially from the territorial aristocracy, gentry and clergy; City of London merchant gentlemen, barristers and bankers; nabobs and West Indian planters; and diplomats, administrators and military or naval officers serving on the continent or abroad. Sons of tradesmen, artisans and farmers frequently attended the public schools; but they were not usually respected or even encouraged, especially if they were nonconformists, as so many eighteenth-century businessmen were.

Seven of the original public schools were called Clarendon schools, after the chairman of the royal commission investigating them in the 1860's. Since a majority of the boys came from non-local families, boarding facilities were a prominent feature of the Clarendon schools, whereas St. Paul's and Merchant Taylors'–London schools founded in the Tudor period–were placed in a different category precisely because they were essentially day schools. Boarding itself was certainly common in the eighteenth century. Several of the masters even at Merchant Taylors' took boarders. Headmasters of lesser eighteenth-century schools frequently arranged board and room. Boys were

[1] The term 'public school' is discussed in the Fleming Report, Board of Education, The Public Schools and the General Educational System, Report of the Committee on Public Schools appointed by the President of the Board of Education in July 1942 (1944), pp. 8–11, 106–23.

accommodated in the homes of grammar school masters, in spare rooms above taverns or shops, in the houses of widows or other townsfolk in need of extra income. Sometimes quarters were found in lodging houses or in buildings near or adjacent to the town grammar school itself. But major differences existed between schools which took boarders and boarding schools. The Clarendon schools were not merely interested in providing accommodation for boys away from home; they sought to substitute communal for family life. One distinguishing feature of a Clarendon school was its impressive code of behaviour: rules, rituals and traditions made the school glamorous.

The most elaborate form of public school communal life was in the Winchester and Eton Colleges, sister foundations, in fact, of New College, Oxford, and King's College, Cambridge, respectively. Before 1865 only Etonians attended King's. Living in college was the privilege of students who held foundation awards – scholarships bequeathed in founders' wills. College scholars – also called collegers and foundationers – were assumed united in purpose and identity by virtue of their love of knowledge and their common housing. They were distinguished from the pensioners, commoners, or oppidans who paid their own way and lived in rooms and lodging houses outside the college, often in the town. Foremost among these non-collegiate lodgings were 'dames' houses',[1] loosely-licensed private boarding houses that grew up on the fringe of the schools. Headmasters like Thomas Arnold (Rugby) in the 1820's, Hawtrey (Eton) in the 1840's and Ridding (Winchester) after 1850 brought the dames' houses under the authority of the public school by replacing the 'dames' with assistant masters and by allowing the houses – through the introduction of distinctive dress and customs – to develop a corporate spirit similar to the colleges. Within this new setting, housemasters like Edward Bowen at Harrow and Oscar Browning at Eton began to express themselves, their ideals and their ambitions through the lives of their students.

In the second quarter of the nineteenth century the nine public schools were joined by a group of new schools. Cheltenham (1841), the first public school to be founded in over two

---

[1] E. Gambier-Parry, *Annals of an Eton House* (London, 1907), is an account of the last of the dames' houses in Eton. In time the word 'dame' came to designate a house headed by either a man or woman.

hundred years, was soon followed by Marlborough (1843), Rossall (1844), Bradfield (1850), St. John's, Leatherhead (1851), Victoria College, Jersey (1852), Ardingley (1858), Wellington College (1853), Birkenhead (1860), Beaumont (1861), Clifton (1862), Haileybury (1862), Cranleigh (1863), Malvern (1865), Trent College (1866). Two schools–Trinity College, Glenalmond (opened 1847) and Fettes College near Edinburgh (1886)–were Scottish versions of the English public schools; and Campbell College, Belfast (1894), was a similar experiment in Ireland. In addition to these new foundations, grammar schools and private institutions re-established or re-organized themselves to conform with the trends. Some of these were Berkhamsted School (1841), Durham School (1842), St. Peter's School at York (1844), Sir William Turner's School at Coatham (1868), Dorchester Grammar (1882), Repton, Sherborne, Sedbergh, Uppingham and Oundle.[1] As the century advanced famous grammar schools like Manchester, as well as others like Nottingham which had fallen on evil days, reformed their curricula, their standards and pretensions and were for-mally admitted to the public school ranks.

The great public schools were an historical fact. Emulation was one means of capturing their success. Throughout the century headmasters who went from the older to the newer public schools brought with them typical public school symbols and institutions: prefects in mortar-boards, school songs, caps, hats, foundation day ceremonies and speeches.[2] The gothic revival was a convenient means of erasing a recent origin, but some of the new foundations actually managed to acquire renowned buildings. Dover College, founded in 1871, was especially pleased with 'The antiquity of its buildings, which formed part of the old Priory of St. Martin [and] has given to the College from the first the appearance and tone of an ancient foundation.'[3] Haileybury, founded mainly to train boys for the

---

[1] Fuller lists are given in J. A. Banks, *Prosperity and Parenthood* (London, 1954), pp. 228–30. Trinity College, Glenalmond, claimed to 'embrace objects not attainable in any public foundation hitherto established in Scotland, viz., the combination of general education with domestic discipline and systematic religious superintendence.' *PSYB* (1889), p. 57.

[2] Sir Ernest Barker, *Age and Youth* (Oxford, 1953), pp. 267–8.

[3] *PSYB* (1889), p. 40.

India Civil Service, acquired the buildings which formerly belonged to the East India Company.

The proliferation of schools claiming identity with the older and more famous public schools led to a meeting of twelve prominent headmasters in 1869 at the home of Edward Thring, headmaster of Uppingham. The purpose of the meeting was to determine the criteria for a 'public school'. A year later representatives of thirty-four schools met at Sherborne and formed the Headmasters' Conference of Public Schools. The first edition of the *Public Schools Year Book*—the public schools' publicity organ—was issued in 1889 and listed thirty schools[1] which the editors hoped would be considered the élite schools of Britain. By 1914 the list had grown to one hundred and thirteen.[2]

There is no satisfactory general definition of a 'public school' which covers the many types of schools represented in the Headmasters' Conference. Editors of the *Public Schools Year Book* acknowledged the difficulty in the preface to the 1904 edition: 'When the *Public Schools Year Book* was first projected, it was the intention of the Editors to include only the great historical Public Schools along with the more important Victorian schools, which have so ably maintained the traditions of the earlier foundations. It was from the first recognized that the only line which could be drawn must be an arbitrary one. The term "public school" is in itself nothing more than a popular misnomer, and it was clear that guidance must be sought not so much from what the term denotes as from what it connotes. Hence, in determining the inclusion of any particular school, the Editors asked themselves such questions as the following: Does the school possess the "public school spirit"? Are its pupils entitled to be called the "public school men"? Is it of more than local interest? What are its numbers, standard of teaching and governing body?

'Although opinions were drawn from various sources and every effort was made to apply these tests in a conscientious and impartial manner, it must be acknowledged that the attempt was, from its very nature, incapable of complete success.'[3]

When the editors of the *Public Schools Year Book* spoke of numbers as a criterion for determining a public school, they wished to know if the school were of good size and of stable

[1] *PSYB* (1889).   [2] *PSYB* (1914).   [3] *PSYB* (1904), p. (64).

enrolment; when they spoke of the governing body they wanted to know the amount of community or national support a school received and, incidentally, what public figures associated their names with it; when they mentioned teaching standards they were asking if the school drew its masters from Oxford or Cambridge, sometimes Trinity College, Dublin. All of these questions implied a concern for the financial condition of the school and its ability to provide scholarship and eleemosynary assistance. But when the editors spoke about 'public school spirit' and 'public school men' they enveloped the public schools in an air of mystery in order to distinguish them from state-supported institutions and isolate them from criticism.

At least one of the Victorian public schools, Wellington, founded to educate the orphaned sons of army officers, was essentially an aristocratic school; but most can be described as schools of the middle classes, especially the town grammar schools. 'Middle classes' or 'middle class', however, are not altogether happy designations since they cover a wide range of incomes and occupations from clerks and actors to industrialists and clergymen. It is in fact desirable to distinguish the leading professions (clergymen, doctors, lawyers, schoolmasters) from other middle class occupations since these were the groups that most depended on secondary and university education and provided the majority of university intellectuals and public school masters.

The proportions of middle class and professional sons in the Victorian public schools varied according to the purpose and location of the school, its scholarship programme and admissions policy, and its boarding facilities. Epsom, for example, was specifically founded in 1855 to aid doctors' sons; and although sons from other occupations were admitted, only doctors' sons could hold foundation scholarships.[1] At King Edward's, Birmingham—a Tudor grammar school which James Prince Lee made into a famous public school—sons of tradesmen, manufacturers and clerks were in the majority in 1857, although there was a significant proportion of sons from professional families.[2] However, until more research is undertaken it is difficult to determine the exact social composition of each of

[1] *PSYB* (1913), pp. 108–9.
[2] David Newsome, *Godliness and Good Learning* (London, 1961), pp. 249–50.

the Victorian public schools in any period of the nineteenth century.

More is known of the social structure of the great public schools. T. W. Bamford has recently analysed the social composition of eight of the nine public schools in the first fifty years of the nineteenth century. Eton, Harrow, Rugby and St. Paul's are the only schools whose admission registers provide enough data for a detailed analysis, so Bamford's conclusions about Winchester, Shrewsbury, Charterhouse and Westminster are extrapolations. Of the four schools which figure prominently in the analysis, only St. Paul's made a practice of admitting boys from artisans', farmers', manufacturers', and shopkeepers' families. At the other three schools boys from gentry and noble families clearly predominated; clergymen's sons were prominent; and boys from professional families (to include higher civil servants, architects, artists, engineers and teachers) were consistently admitted, as were sons of bankers. Bamford's figures show that before the nineteenth century the public schools were socially exclusive and became even more selective in the period 1800 to 1850.[1] This reinforces Edward Mack's conclusion that the poor had not been going to Eton for centuries,[2] and makes Vaughan's statement about the exclusiveness of Harrow in the 1860's less novel than is sometimes supposed.[3] Bamford's most interesting conclusion refutes the familiar sentiment that Dr. Arnold successfully rebuilt Rugby on the sudden influx of manufacturers' sons; it appears that Arnold, in fact, rebuilt it on the traditional core of gentry and clergy, particularly the former.[4]

[1] T. W. Bamford, 'Public Schools and Social Class, 1801–50', *British Journal of Sociology*, XII (September, 1961), Tables 1 and 2. Without clarifying his category, Bamford classifies twenty-five per cent of the boys at the eight public schools as 'others'.

[2] Edward C. Mack, *Public Schools and British Opinion since 1860* (New York, 1941), p. 32. Eton installed the competitive scheme of entrance to the foundation in the 1840's.

[3] The headmaster of Harrow told the Clarendon Commission that 'in no instance is any son of a Harrow tradesman now a member of the great school.' Quoted in Simon, p. 314. Mack, ibid., whose argument regarding the fate of closed scholarships is similar to Simon's, says that competitive entry at Shrewsbury, Rugby and Harrow represented a radical break with the past 'in theory if not in practice'.

[4] Bamford, p. 227 and Table 1.

It has been suggested that the Clarendon schools were even more exclusive in the late Victorian period than in the first half of the nineteenth century. In 1892 an Etonian of the 1840's, Arthur Duke Coleridge, accused the aristocracy of appropriating foundation scholarships at Eton: 'The Eton Collegers of to-day are certainly not the poor lads whose education was the object of our founder. A year or two since I heard the Head Master calling "absence", and the names of "Peel, K.S." [King's Scholar] "Talbot, K.S." "Fremantle, K.S." etc., made me rub my eyes, like Rip Van Winkle. We never affected such purple blood in our time. Such associates cheek by jowl with the sons of Windsor tradesmen would no more have amalgamated than the Rhine and the Rhone. I am not likely to be tried by a baronetcy or a peerage, but I think I should pause before I claimed for my son an education *à bon marché*. I never yet knew a colleger who could indulge in the luxury of a private tutor in school-time; we were distinctly poor boys: with one single exception I never heard of a colleger succeeding to an hereditary fortune, and in that instance the property was not bequeathed by the parents. ... I am afraid the sons of Windsor and Eton tradesmen will be heavily handicapped in the Eton race if they are allowed to compete with some of the best blood in England. Democracy is forging ahead, but I think a young nobleman in a serge gown is an anomaly never contemplated by the statutes or the founder.'[1]

Coleridge's complaint extends Bamford's conclusion to the end of the nineteenth century: instead of accusing the Victorian plutocracy of appropriating foundation scholarships, Coleridge blames the aristocracy. Historians are therefore still unable to make accurate statements regarding the course of social change in the late Victorian Clarendon schools.

It may be asked, however, whether the collegers of the 1840's were 'distinctly poor boys'. Bamford unfortunately does not provide an analysis of scholarship holders at the great public schools, but simply states in passing that the middle class entry in the years 1800–50 was severely restricted to boys on the foundation. Since he demonstrates that few boys from artisan or business families were in attendance at Eton, Harrow and Rugby, the foundationers must have come mainly from families

[1] Arthur Duke Coleridge, *Reminiscences* (London, 1921), pp. 79–80.

in privileged or comfortable circumstances. It is entirely possible that Arthur Coleridge himself was an 'anomaly never contemplated by the statutes or the founder.'[1] A member of the Devon Coleridges, a large and prominent family of clergymen, scholars and lawyers, Coleridge numbered among his uncles an Eton clergyman-master and Sir John Taylor Coleridge, Eton colleger and judge of the Queen's Bench, 1835–59. Coleridge's grandfather was a colonel and a county J.P., and his father was a solicitor. Arthur did not become a colleger immediately upon entering Eton. He was an oppidan for 'several happy years' and probably spent as much as £200 per annum for tuition and board; as a scholar his expenses very likely still came to approximately £80 a year.[2] Therefore, although he was certainly not a nobleman in a serge gown, he was also not a Windsor tradesman's son dependent solely on the generosity of King Henry VI.

2. Public School Costs

Historians connect the unprecedented increase in Cambridge matriculations throughout the latter half of the nineteenth century with the admission of boys from new and old public schools; but they cannot explain the immediate cause of the sudden increase in college enrolments in 1860, some years before the Taunton and Clarendon Commissions completed their reform of English secondary education. And historians

[1] The statutes of the founder required the scholars of Eton to be 'poor and needy boys of good character' and stipulated that they be 'chosen, firstly from the natives of the parishes in which either Eton or King's College hold property; secondly from natives of the counties of Buckingham and Cambridge; and failing these, from natives of the realm of England generally.' See Henry Charles Maxwell-Lyte, *A History of Eton College* (London, 1889), p. 499. It was only the first clause that could be distinctly interpreted in favour of the lower social classes. In the long run geographical restrictions were too broad to be of any genuine importance—except perhaps to favour the rural clergy, since the income of the colleges was solidly based on land until the twentieth century. On page 291 Maxwell-Lyte makes the fascinating point that after the abandonment of celibacy restrictions at Eton in the late seventeenth century fellows began to marry into one another's families with the consequence that 'Before the days of genuine examinations, the members of certain families looked upon Scholarships at Eton, and Fellowships at King's, almost as part of their birthright.'

[2] Coleridge, pp. 9, 20, 49.

have yet to determine the exact proportion of boys coming from each of the social classes. The statistical samplings of social backgrounds and schools of Cambridge students are too incomplete, imprecise and amateurish to be decisive. Information on decadal change is only available for Sidney Sussex College.[1] In connection with other information, however, the available statistical data can be used to indicate some of the possible answers to the vexed question of demographic change.

One study of the social backgrounds of Cambridge students estimates that the numbers of students attending Cambridge from what may be called the twenty-three foremost public schools rose from 43 per cent in the second half of the eighteenth century, to 46 per cent in the first half of the nineteenth century, to 52 per cent in the second half of the nineteenth century.[2] The twenty-three schools include the nine original public schools, five ancient grammar schools (Tonbridge, Oundle, Repton, Sherborne, Uppingham), and nine Victorian foundations (Cheltenham, Clifton, Fettes, Haileybury, Loretto, Malvern, Marlborough, Radley, Rossall). However, since the nine Victorian schools did not come into existence until the railway boom, there were actually only fourteen foremost schools in the pre-1840 period, which indicates that proportionately there were probably more Cambridge boys from the great public schools before 1850 than after. Other public schools supplied Cambridge with 19 per cent of its undergraduates in the period 1752–99, 27 per cent in the first half of the nineteenth century, and 30 per cent in the second half of the nineteenth century. The Headmasters' Conference therefore accounted for 62 per cent of Cambridge students in the second half of the eighteenth century, 73 per cent in the next fifty years, and 82 per cent in the second half of the nineteenth century.

The twenty-three foremost schools charged high boarding fees, usually over 80 guineas per annum. But even in the days of Nicholas Carlisle major secondary schools like Oundle, Repton, Sherborne and Uppingham had been expensive, asking 33–40 guineas per annum. Board was even higher in 1889. West-

---

[1] Appendix II: A.

[2] Hester Jenkins and David Caradog Jones, 'Social Class of Cambridge University', *British Journal of Sociology*, I (1950), p. 102. The authors use the 1943 edition of the *PSYB* to select public schools.

minster, however, still charged £65, the same as in 1818. Boarding fees at some of the grammar schools could be as high as £138, the same as at a great public school like Harrow, but most charged £80–110. In 1889 the minimum tuition charges for a day student at fourteen of the twenty-three public schools varied from £13 at Rugby to £60 at Fettes, the mean being £25–30. Charterhouse, Loretto, Oundle, Radley, Rossall and Winchester do not appear to have admitted day students in the second half of the nineteenth century; and Repton and Harrow admitted only a few.

Headmasters' Conference schools not included among the twenty-three foremost public schools made comparable charges. In 1889 Bedford Grammar School charged £12 for day students and £78 for board and tuition. Schools like Dover College charged £22 for day students and £85 for boarders; but Brighton College, Lancing and Wellington College asked £100 or more for a year's board and instruction. A large number of schools with lesser fees also supplied Cambridge with undergraduates. By 1913, fifty-eight grammar schools or similar foundations (including the five mentioned in the twenty-three foremost schools) were included in the one hundred and sixteen schools of the Headmasters' Conference: seven did not take day boys, but all of the remainder except two charged day fees under £30 and usually under £20; boarding fees generally totalled £50–70.[1]

Besides board and tuition, Headmasters' Conference schools levied fees for books, sports and gratuities; use of the library, laboratory, or workshop; for optional subjects like painting or music; and for incidentals like linen and admission. As Banks noted, these incidental fees could raise the costs of education by a third or more.[2] However, the total costs of a secondary education in a Headmasters' Conference school could be reduced by an elaborate schedule of exemptions and reductions according to means, nomination, social class, or straitened circumstances; and there were numerous scholarships and awards to help defray expenses.

Nothing conclusive about the private resources and social background of Cambridge students, therefore, can be gathered from a heterogenous category like twenty-three foremost public

[1] Appendix I.   [2] Banks. p. 189.

schools, unless the historian divides the students in these schools into day boys and boarders and calculates the degree to which educational expenditure was defrayed by exhibitions, scholarships, special categories of admission, prizes and other awards. Even this procedure would have to take into account wealthy students who attended expensive public schools as day boys.[1]

The Royal Commission appointed in 1919 attempted to classify Oxford and Cambridge students according to their expenditure on secondary education instead of the prestige of their schools. The Commission concluded that in the two years before World War I, 'out of a total number of 892 Scholarships and Exhibitions awarded at Oxford and Cambridge ... to boys from schools in the United Kingdom, no fewer than 425, or nearly 50 per cent, were won by boys from the cheaper boarding schools (with fees not exceeding £80 a year) or from day schools with fees exceeding £10 a year but providing education, nevertheless, at a very moderate cost, while 157, or not far short of 20 per cent, were won by boys from the cheapest day schools with either no fees at all or fees not exceeding £10 a year. In addition, 606 boys from the former list of schools and 237 from the latter list went up to Oxford and Cambridge in the same years as Commoners. No doubt all the boys from the former list were not poor in the strict sense of the word; but nearly all of them were probably the sons of parents whose means were at any rate moderate, and a considerable proportion must have come from poor or fairly poor homes. Practically all the boys on the latter list must have been sons of poor parents.'[2]

The Royal Commission summary can be compared with the returns of Cambridge scholarship holders compiled in 1893–4 by the Bryce Commission on Secondary Education.[3] Out of a total of six hundred and seventy-five scholarships awarded in that year, three hundred and sixty-six or 54 per cent went to boys from fifty-two Headmasters' Conference schools, excluding

[1] e.g., Walter Leaf. See *Some Chapters of Autobiography* (London, 1932).

[2] Royal Commission on Oxford and Cambridge Universities (1922), Report, p. 132.

[3] Royal Commission on Secondary Education (Bryce Commission), 1895 (c. 7862), xlix, Appendix pp. 426–7. The returns do not include Peterhouse, a small college of perhaps fifty students in the early 1890's.

the Clarendon schools; forty-five of the fifty-two schools were endowed or grammar schools. The Clarendon schools accounted for 10 per cent or sixty-six scholarships. One hundred and thirty-five or 20 per cent of the scholarships were held by boys from seventy-seven endowed schools, thirteen proprietary schools and seventy-three private schools not part of the Headmasters' Conference, the endowed schools providing three-fifths of the students in this category. Sixteen per cent of the scholarships were held by students from the Celtic fringe, from the empire and abroad, from training colleges, technical schools, public elementary schools (higher grade board schools[1]), pupil teacher centres, or by students educated in the home. The percentage of all students—award holders and pensioners—coming from various categories of schools in 1893–4 are as follows:

Clarendon	13%
Headmasters' Conference	40%
Endowed, proprietary, private	18%
Private tuition or home	18%
Remainder	11%

The Bryce returns are ultimately inconclusive because they do not differentiate between day and boarding students, but they certainly cannot substantiate any charge that nineteenth-century wealth progressively bought its way into the university and displaced poorer boys accustomed to receiving a Cambridge education. Boys from the Clarendon schools, the most exclusive of the secondary schools, were no more in evidence in Cambridge in 1893–4 than earlier in the century; and the grammar schools, endowed and private schools—representing a great many occupations and incomes—were the major sources of university scholars and provided Cambridge with most of its students.

3. Restricted Scholarships: School and University

Most public school boys did not enter the universities, since the public schools were the main vocational channels to the higher professions (except positions in the Church, university and secondary teaching), the services, domestic and imperial ad-

[1] Local authority elementary schools providing some secondary instruction.

ministration, most technical posts and clerical-secretarial positions in finance, industry and commerce. Boys preparing for the university generally read classics, the subject of college scholarship examinations, but others could choose from 'modern' or 'English' sides geared directly to business, or army, engineering and civil service sides. To a certain extent the designation of a side as classical, mathematical or modern was misleading, for subjects from one side were frequently included in another. Boys reading for the civil service examinations, for example, had to study Greek; and until the end of the century Latin was necessary for admission to the military academies of Woolwich and Sandhurst. In general, however, the name of a side indicated its primary emphasis.

Mid-Victorian headmasters, mainly clergymen, reluctantly accepted the non-classical sides but realized that the idea of a specialized side allowed them the opportunity to continue classical teaching. A bright but hesitant student might be pressured into studying Latin and Greek, especially if a university scholarship could be offered as reward. Coercion was more difficult for grammar school masters than masters in the aristocratic and heavily-endowed Clarendon schools. Dr. Gow of Nottingham High recalled that the headmaster of a grammar school could not say to a 'recalcitrant parent,' 'My friend, these subjects are taught in this school, and if you do not like them you may take your boy away.... [This] was not "business" to the Grammar-school Master. His business was to keep a civil tongue, to keep the boy in the school, and to keep his own way.'[1] It was probably easier for masters to coerce working-class boys with no family experience in secondary education than boys from business families. At least the famous Roman historian Samuel Dill had no difficulty persuading Ernest Barker to read classics instead of modern languages when the newly-arrived villager entered Manchester Grammar School in order to become a business foreign correspondence clerk.[2]

Ernest Barker's experiences at Manchester Grammar are especially interesting because he was one of the very few working-class boys in grammar schools before 1902. Masters had mainly

---

[1] Discussion of the First Report of the Studies and Examinations Syndicate, *Cambridge University Reporter* (December 17, 1904), p. 361.

[2] Barker, p. 257.

to contend with sons from business and professional families; of the two, they preferred the latter, particularly clergymen's sons. Whenever possible special privileges were accorded the sons of doctors, lawyers, clergymen, or 'gentlemen'. Thus in 1889 such members of the Headmasters' Conference as Bradfield College, Berkshire, admitted only orphans and sons of poor clergy and gentlemen to the foundation, while Brighton College awarded a number of scholarships to sons of gentlemen resident in Sussex and to sons of army officers. Trinity College, Glenalmond, a school which received Gladstone's support, gave exhibitions to sons of clergymen. Haileybury and Rossall reduced fees for the sons of clergymen, and Marlborough provided seventy scholarships of £30 per annum for clergymen's sons. Loretto, founded as a private school, had several places on the foundation for needy sons of gentlemen as well as two musical scholarships for sons of Oxford and Cambridge graduates. Wellington College received only sons of deceased military and naval officers on the foundation.[1] Mill Hill, a school in the north London suburbs founded by nonconformists, provided exhibitions only for sons of Christian ministers; Monmouth Grammar School gave exhibitions to the sons of clergymen and army-navy officers; and Epsom reduced charges to physicians' and surgeons' sons, admitting only the orphans or needy sons of doctors to the foundation.[2] In 1862 Chigwell Grammar School in Essex provided a scholarship for clergymen's sons which reduced tuition and board to 25 guineas per annum.[3]

While masters at the newer foundations introduced the system of preferences characteristic of the older public schools, Cambridge, as historians emphasize, opened some–perhaps most–of its restricted scholarships to general competition about 1860. At the same time, however, closed exhibitions were introduced in order to continue the association between Cambridge and the older grammar or public schools. Trinity College, for example, substituted three exhibitions of £40 for three scholarships restricted to Westminster students.[4] At St. John's two

[1] *PSYB* (1889), pp. 10, 17, 57–8, 62, 82, 93–4, 114, 154.

[2] *PSYB* (1913), p. 349; *PSYB* (1914), pp. 108–9.

[3] *The Oxford, Cambridge, Bar, Public School and Middle Class Reporter*, IV (January, 1862), p. 1.

[4] Report of the Cambridge University Commissioners (Graham Commission), 1861, xx, p. 9.

scholarships traditionally reserved for Shrewsbury students were converted into an exhibition for Shrewsbury, and scholarships customarily awarded to Sedbergh students were replaced by six exhibitions, also for Sedbergh students with priority to be given to a native of the parish of Sedbergh.[1] All exhibitions were tenable with other awards, and in addition Sedbergh had second claim to the Bishop Otway Scholarship at Christ's.[2] Other conversions and modifications were introduced. Three Pembroke scholarships for students from St. Bee's Grammar School in Cumberland were replaced by a grant of £200 per annum to the Governors of St. Bee's for school-leaving exhibitions to any Cambridge college.[3] Students of the twin foundations of Uppingham and Oakham were preferred for sixteen £30-exhibitions awarded by St. John's, Emmanuel, Sidney and Clare.[4] In the late 1850's King's opened twelve of its twenty-four Etonian scholarships to general competition–but without prejudice to Eton. As Austen Leigh, Provost of King's, explained to John Neville Keynes on the occasion of Maynard Keynes' election to an open scholarship in 1901, when an Etonian won an open scholarship, the emoluments were increased and tuition and rooms included–'at any rate for a time'.[5]

Cambridge was particularly anxious to assist clergymen, the class which sent the university one-third of its undergraduates. The Rustat Scholarships at Jesus College remained restricted to orphans and sons of clergymen,[6] and students reading divinity were preferred for the Jeston Exhibitions at Trinity College.[7] For most of the nineteenth century the university mainly awarded Bell and Abbot Scholarships to needy sons of clergymen;[8] and six exhibitions for non-collegiate students proposing to take holy orders were founded in the latter half of the century

[1] 1859 (sess. 2), xix, vol. pp. 205–11.
[2] *PSYB* (1904), p. 265. In 1889 Shrewsbury also had a £45 exhibition to Trinity and other awards as well.
[3] Graham Commission (1861), pp. 9–10.
[4] *PSYB* (1889), p. 152.
[5] Austen Leigh to John Neville Keynes, December 16, 1901, C.U.L., Add. 7562.
[6] *University Reporter* (February 26, 1884), p. 490.
[7] Trinity College Library, Minutes of Meetings of the Sizarship Committee, Rec. 24.1, entry for June 1910.
[8] *Student's Guide to the University of Cambridge* (Cambridge, 1880), pp. 46–7.

by the Clothworkers' Company.[1] Three small exhibitions restricted to sons of clergymen educated at Sidney Sussex were provided in 1906 when the charity commissioners and college officials reinterpreted the provisions of a college trust.[2] Other assistance was available informally or through societies specifically formed to aid future parsons or deserving sons of clergymen. The Cambridge Clerical Education Society, for example, was formed in 1838 and remained in existence until 1927. From 1839 to 1904 college tutors acting on behalf of the Society distributed financial aid ranging from seven guineas to £40 to two hundred and ninety-two out of four hundred and forty-one applicants.[3]

A preference for clergymen's sons or boys intent on ordination definitely existed in several Cambridge colleges. Royal commissions reviewing university policy from 1850–80 respected each college's right to determine its own criteria for undergraduate admissions; and short of imposing a common academic standard for university entrance, it is difficult to see how a uniform admissions policy could have been enforced. In small colleges admissions was the function of the tutor or master; and entrance criteria were not as subject to argument and controversy as in larger colleges where educational policy was heatedly debated and where more than one tutor was independently responsible for selecting students. Furthermore, the smaller colleges had to contend with the longevity of certain dons who held the most important collegiate positions and acted as a brake on proposals designed to accelerate social change in the university. Jesus and Corpus Christi Colleges are good examples. During the mastership of Corrie (1849–85), the son of a Lincolnshire parson, nearly one-third of the undergraduates of Jesus came from clerical families and over one-third entered the Church. Under Corrie's successor, H. A. Morgan (1885–1912), another clergyman's son, over one-fifth of the undergraduates

[1] John Willis Clark, *Endowments of the University of Cambridge* (Cambridge, 1904), p. 443.
[2] Sidney Sussex College, Minutes of College Meetings, 1876–95, June 18, 1906.
[3] Reports of the Cambridge Clerical Education Society, 1838–1903, C.U.L. Cam. b. 21.16.1; Minute Book of the Cambridge Clerical Education Society, C.U.L. Add 6984 (E).

in the period 1885–1900 entered the Church – more than entered any other single occupation.[1]

The reputation of Corpus as a training college for priests began in 1822 when John Lamb, the son of a clergyman, assumed the mastership. Two successive masters maintained the reputation: James Pulling, the son of an admiral, and E. H. Perowne, the son of an Anglican missionary. There are indications that Perowne tried to keep dissenters out of the college even after the abolition of the Tests Act in order to maintain the quasi-seminary character of Corpus. From 1822 to about 1880 the majority of Corpus undergraduates took orders, and the college educated more priests than at any other comparable period in its history. Eleven of the men entering Corpus in the first seventeen years of Perowne's mastership became bishops [2]

Other masters may have also favoured students preparing for clerical careers. The Reverend Dr. Charles Edward Searle, the seventh son of a Hackney gentleman, became master of Pembroke in 1880, and according to a fellow of the College who was an undergraduate at the time, Searle was an old-fashioned evangelical of narrow views and great natural shrewdness who attracted a considerable number of evangelicals to the College. More than half of the fifty freshmen entering Pembroke in 1882 were destined for holy orders, 'and the Master was hard on those who changed their mind.'[3]

4. The Costs of a University Education

Cambridge, a residential university, had always been costly. Fathers were frequently dismayed or discouraged by the extraordinary university expenses, and clergymen or small country

---

[1] Arthur Gray and Frederick Brittain, *A History of Jesus College* (London, 1960), pp. 174–90. In the thirty-six years of Corrie's mastership about 15 per cent of the undergraduates came from Clarendon schools. This compares with the 13 per cent derived from the Bryce returns for the university as a whole in 1893–4.

[2] John Patrick Tuer Bury, *A History of Corpus Christi College, 1882–1952* (Cambridge, 1952), pp. 50–85, also p. 98. The author states that most of the boys came from smaller public schools or grammar schools and that there were only a few wealthy students in the college.

[3] Leonard Whibley Papers, Pembroke College Library, 356.12.1. There is no indication when the fragment was written.

gentlemen were quick to notice any rise in costs. In 1784 Thomas Malthus' father, a gentleman of moderate means, paid £100 to have his son educated at Jesus College and remarked in passing that if costs rose any higher, the clergy would have to send their sons to Leipzig where a university education could be obtained for only £25.[1] The costs of a Cambridge education appear to have risen considerably in the next three decades. Early in the nineteenth century William Airy, father of the future Plumian Professor of Anatomy and a farmer who at one time held a minor post in the Excise, was astounded to learn that £200 per annum was required to send his son to Cambridge,[2] and this rough estimate is confirmed by the records of an undergraduate who kept scrupulous account of his expenditures. John William Whittaker, the son of a Bradford gentleman, entered St. John's in 1810, subsequently becoming a scholar and fellow and eventually taking holy orders. His first year expenses, including £15 refundable caution money and £16 for clothes, came to approximately £150, as did his expenses for the third year. He spent most in his second year, just over £200, of which £42 went for private tuition. Additional sums went for meals in restaurants, for wine, mathematical instruments, transportation and for the purchase of silver eating utensils.[3] In the following century total Cambridge expenses, necessary and social, did not change as drastically as they had in the latter part of the reign of George III and in actuality remained quite stable, if still prohibitive. Various editions of *The Student's Guide to the University of Cambridge* and *The Student's Handbook to the University of Cambridge* give the following estimates of total university costs in the second half of the nineteenth century:

1862	1874	1893	1902–13
£192–357	£205–402	£219–403	£155–326

These estimates, as the *Guides* and *Handbooks* admit, do not

---

[1] John Maynard Keynes, *Essays in Biography* (London, 1961), p. 91.

[2] Sir George Biddell Airy, *Autobiography*, ed. Wilfrid Airy (Cambridge, 1896), pp. 14–24. Airy went to Colchester Grammar School and entered Trinity as a sizar despite the fact that Colchester had a restricted scholarship at St. John's. Both sides of his family were yeoman farmers; his maternal grandfather is described as 'well to do'.

[3] C.U.L. Add. 7457.

represent absolute minimum costs, since personal and social expenditures were almost completely at the discretion of the student. In 1867 several tutors thought that pensioners might manage on £125–150 necessary annual expenses, with most students, even at a small college, spending £180–210.[1] One sizar at St. John's in 1880 found that £130 or £140 per annum, 'an amount which, though it may seem to some rather short allowance, is at Cambridge sufficient with economy to enable a man to meet the necessary expenses of college life.'[2] Others agreed that economy was possible.[3]

One Cambridge student left a detailed record of his university and college expenses which supports the contention that annual costs, even in a fashionable college, could be kept below £200. Sir Arthur Eddington, the philosopher and scientist, spent a total of £553 or £184 a year while a student at Trinity (his

[1] Special Report from the Select Committee on the Oxford and Cambridge Universities Education Bill, together with the proceedings of the Committee, Minutes of Evidence and Appendix (Ewart Committee), 1867, xiii, Evidence, pp. 91, 99. At Oxford Jowett believed that £100 or £120 was the absolute minimum and that £200–300 was a more realistic average. 'The Universities can never become National Institutions while they are confined to persons who can provide an income of from £100 to £200 a-year.' Royal Commission on Oxford (1852), xxii, Evidence, p. 32.

[2] *Cambridge Review* (April 28, 1880), pp. 34–5.

[3] 'Economy at College', *Cambridge Review* (February 22, 1882), p. 183, claimed his itemized expenses for 1880–1, his first year, came to just under £90, including coals, lamps, caution money, entrance, matriculation and Previous Examination fees, but excluding private tuition, books, academicals, clothing and subscriptions. James Bryce, *The Future of the English Universities* (London, 1883), p. 391, gives £140–200 per annum as the minimum for the full benefits of collegiate life (his article was first published in the *Fortnightly Review* for March 1883). Charles Tennyson, who was admitted to King's in 1899, felt that it was possible to live a conventional collegiate life on £180–200 a year, excluding vacations. *Cambridge from Within* (London, 1913), p. 56. A university report of 1909 states that the careful student could live on £120 per annum, excluding vacations, clothes and travel. Laboratory fees meant an additional £20 a year. Report of the Committee on the Relations of the Colleges to the University and to One Another, 1909, p. 16, C.U.L. Cam.b.909.10. On the basis of detailed returns from the colleges, the Royal Commission on Oxford and Cambridge, appointed in 1919, Report, p. 140, gave the following as Cambridge expenses for 1919–20:

Cheapest College	£123
Dearest College	172
Average of all Colleges	145

figures include clothes and vacation travel, expenses not usually provided in estimates):[1]

1902–3: £240 2s. 6d. (includes £15 caution money refundable upon taking degree)
1903–4: £163 7s. 0d.
1904–5: £150 1s. 2d.

TOTAL £553 10s. 8d.

These figures are especially significant because Eddington was a boy of decidedly modest means. His father was the headmaster of a Quaker school in Somerset and died when his son was two. Eddington attended private school until he obtained a Somerset County Scholarship at age fifteen, enabling him to enter Owen's College, Manchester. He matriculated at Trinity in Michaelmas 1902 after winning an entrance scholarship in the previous December.

In terms of necessary costs the most expensive period in the history of nineteenth-century Cambridge was approximately 1830 to 1870 when private tuition or coaching became virtually indispensable to any student anxious to succeed in his examinations. Coaching increased the necessary costs of a Cambridge education by one fifth to one third. The average student spent £24–30 per annum, but amounts as high as £70 or £100 were not uncommon, especially if the student paid 'whole' or 'full tuition' for daily coaching or if he engaged a private tutor in the Long Vacation.[2] By 1860 'full tuition' was becoming rarer, and

[1] T.C.L., Add. b.48.
[2] Ewart Committee, Evidence, pp. 91, 105, 235. Francis Galton enthusiastically wrote home in the 1840's that William Hopkins, the famous mathematics coach, charged 'only £72 per annum instead of £100 as currently reported: this will make a jolly difference to my finances.' Karl Pearson, The Life, Letters, and Labours of Francis Galton (Cambridge, 1914–30), I, p. 163. The costs of coaching also appear in Charles Astor Bristed, Five Years in an English University (New York, 1852), I, p. 214; Sir Joseph John Thomson, Recollections and Reflections (London, 1936), p. 42 et seq; William Emerton Heitland, After Many Years (Cambridge, 1926), p. 129; Thomas George Bonney, Memories of a Long Life (Cambridge, 1921), p. 16; G. G. Coulton, Fourscore Years (Cambridge, 1943), p. 115; Henry Jackson, 'Cambridge Fifty Years Ago', Cambridge Review (June 2, 1910), p. 449; in various editions of the student Guides and Handbooks; and in the Royal Commission on Cambridge (Graham Commission), 1852–3 (1559), xliv, Index, pp. 130–4.

after 1870 coaching in general began to decline, first in classics and later in mathematics. The decline in coaching greatly benefitted the poorer student who had always found the additional expense an extraordinary trial; but this measure of financial relief was partially offset by a slight rise in college tuition fees in the 1880's and by the necessity to pay fees for laboratories and special lectures like those for the India Civil Service examinations.

From 1870 to 1914 various measures were taken to reduce necessary costs in order to bring more students to Cambridge and extend the influence of the university. One of the most notable experiments was Fitzwilliam House, founded in 1869 as a non-collegiate institution for students unable to afford the more expensive college life. Fitzwilliam House did not possess a large staff of teachers and domestics, did not provide a full programme of studies, did not develop a system of tutorial teaching and had few scholarships or exhibitions to award. Students attended intercollegiate or university lectures. At no point before the First World War could Fitzwilliam House be considered an educational success, for it provided none of the emotional or social satisfactions deemed by many to be the most important aspect of the ancient universities. Its maximum nineteenth-century enrolment was in 1881 when two hundred and fifty-four students affiliated, but these numbers were not reached again until 1920 when two hundred and fifty-two students entered. Migrations were sometimes as much as one-half or one-third of the number of students resident in a given year: in order to improve their career opportunities the best students migrated to colleges as soon as they received scholarships.[1] As an educational experiment Fitzwilliam House was a failure, but as a means for enabling students of limited means to attend Cambridge, it was moderately successful. This does

[1] Migrations are given in the reports of the Non-Collegiate Students Board published in the *Cambridge University Reporter*. See also C. J. B. Gaskoin and J. L. Kirby, 'Fitzwilliam House', in John Roach, ed., *The Victoria History of the County of Cambridge and the Isle of Ely*, III (London, 1954), p. 497, and Memorandum submitted to Royal Commission of 1919, C.U.L. Box VI, folder 4, c. 82, June 11, 1920. In the 1890's the Master of Balliol College, Oxford, made the interesting point that employment opportunities for non-collegiates were not as good as for collegiates. Bryce Commission, xlvii, p. 152.

not mean that working-class boys attended Cambridge by matriculating at Fitzwilliam. Although Fitzwilliam House succeeded in reducing university costs to an unprecedented minimum, it is unlikely that boys who matriculated at Fitzwilliam came from different social backgrounds than the collegiates; the only major difference was their reduced circumstances.[1]

Another experiment in cheaper university residence was a revival of the hostel system which began in 1860. The hostel was a compromise between lodgings in town and collegiate life. The most famous hostel was Selwyn, founded in the late 1870's. The founders of Selwyn intended their society to be a college, and one of their principal objectives was to attract poor sons of clergymen by reducing residential costs. Those who predicted that Selwyn would be unable to lower costs much below other colleges appear to have been correct;[2] but from 1902 to 1914 Selwyn at least advertised room, board and instruction at £100 to £110 per annum.[3] At the turn of the century older colleges countered with similar plans. Emmanuel established a hostel for thirty-two students whose university expenses were to be met by a fixed and inclusive payment of £75–90 per annum; Queens' adopted a prepayment system which required no caution money and came to about £100; St. Catharine's and Downing Colleges, small, weakly endowed and of low reputation, advertised schemes similar to the others.[4] Technically the colleges were not supposed to profit from the maintenance of undergraduates, but it was well known that poorly-endowed colleges sometimes profitted. It is not unlikely that wealthy students were offered rooms and accommodations at higher prices in order to offset possible losses under economy plans or at least to keep college income

[1] This was certainly the case at Oxford. The Censor of the Oxford Noncollegiate students stated in the 1890's that while many non-collegiates were the sons of small shopkeepers and a few the sons of artisans, the majority were sons of professional men. Bryce Commission, xlvii, p. 210. Expenses for the non-collegiate arts student at Cambridge were £75–80 per annum, or half the amount spent by a careful college pensioner.

[2] *Cambridge Review* (February 22, 1882), p. 183, and Royal Commission on Oxford and Cambridge (1922), Appendices, pp. 187, 189, 191–2. In evidence submitted to the Commissioners officials of Selwyn explained that as the College had remained underendowed, undergraduates had to pay more than the founders hoped. C.U.L. Box V, folder 23.

[3] *Student's Handbook* (1902), pp. 72–6 and (1913–14), pp. 74–9.   [4] Ibid.

stable,[1] especially as college income fell during the agrarian depression at the end of the century.

The most ambitious hostel plan in Cambridge was launched by Cavendish College in the early 1880's but lasted only ten years. The experiment was remarkable because it sought to reduce expenditure in two ways: by providing a corporate life for about 80 guineas a year, including a short period of residence in the Long Vacation; and by admitting boys a year or two younger than was customary, thus reducing the amount of money required for a secondary education.[2] Since boys matriculated and graduated earlier, it was expected that Cavendish students would also enter the employment market at an earlier age. The experiment was abortive, and Cavendish was eventually absorbed into the Homerton teachers' training college.

Undoubtedly more could have been done for students if the colleges had put their affairs on a more businesslike basis or if the late Victorians had been willing to adjust their notions of personal comfort. R. H. Tawney mentioned some possible economies in 1919, although dons had noted these earlier. He suggested that utilities be more strictly controlled, that more meals be taken in common instead of individually in rooms, that a solitary student occupy a bed-sitter rather than a two-room suite, and that poorer students be allowed to forgo the services of college menials like the gyp and scout. He also advised the colleges to cease contracting for certain services they could perform themselves more cheaply. Butlers frequently purveyed butter and distributed letters for a fee, and throughout the nineteenth century cooks and butlers were independent businessmen who charged prices high enough to compensate for vacation periods when students were not in residence. Tawney pointed out that the small savings he advocated would make a great deal of difference to boys of limited means: he specifically named sons of clergymen and doctors, 'whose parents can afford £120 a year but not £170.'[3]

It was always possible to blame part of the high cost of a

---

[1] Memoranda submitted to Royal Commission of 1919, C.U.L. Box II, folder 23, p. 11, and Box VI, folder 5, p. 18.

[2] *Student's Guide* (1880), pp. 116–17 and 116 n.

[3] Memorandum and evidence submitted to Royal Commission of 1919, C.U.L. Box VI, folder 11, pp. 2–5, and Box III, folder 2, p. 9. Possible

university education on student extravagance. The Graham Commission was not satisfied that parents checked expensive habits learned at school;[1] and the university appeared to agree. Although an early edition of *The Student's Guide* stated that sumptuary measures were unnecessary,[2] Cambridge had always attempted some form of regulation. Undergraduates were required to inform tutors of indebtedness to wine merchants, and there was a specified limit to the amount of beverage that could be charged to college accounts. Tradesmen were directed to inform tutors of student expenditures, and dinners and parties in town lodgings or inns were forbidden without the tutor's prior consent. These regulations were not always enforced, but some limit to student spending was definitely considered desirable and necessary.

In the 1860's it was becoming less possible for dons to blame student extravagance on the faineant aristocracy of Cambridge, those young men of birth and fortune who did not work for an honours degree, who 'disdained to adorn a noble lineage with the graceful addition of academic honours.'[3] The conduct of this small group of extremely wealthy boys was generally reprehensible. Their standard of living was extremely high, frequently envied and sometimes infectious. They entered Cambridge as noblemen and fellow-commoners, wore distinctive academic dress, and dined with the dons at high table. Shortly after mid-century they were reduced to a handful. There might have been a momentary revival in their numbers when the Prince of Wales matriculated at Trinity College in 1861, but most dons considered them a vanishing race.[4] Banished from the high table and no longer distinguished by special dress, they formed a distinct social community, their extravagant habits quarantined. Walter Leaf, himself a wealthy manufacturer's son, recalled the 'real fine gentlemen' and their Beefsteak Club.[5]

---

economies resulting from changes in the standard of personal comfort had been discussed at various times in the second half of the nineteenth century. See Ewart Committee, Evidence, p. 35, and *Cambridge Review* (May 12, 1880), p. 72.

[1] Graham Commission (1852), Report, p. 147.   [2] *Guide* (1862), p. 49.
[3] Quoted in EVC, p. 415.
[4] Ibid., Ewart Committee, Evidence, p. 50.
[5] Leaf, p. 81. John William Strutt, the third Baron Rayleigh, was not

EDUCATIONAL COSTS, SOCIAL MOBILITY

At almost the same time that the young aristocrats ceased to tempt other students into extravagance, the suggestion was made that luxurious habits were nevertheless spreading throughout Cambridge, that undergraduates were spending more on recreation and entertainment than had been customary. The reason, it was said, was that some students were remaining longer in the sixth forms and were coming to Cambridge at an older age entrusted by their parents with more money to spend.[1] In the 1860's few dons noticed the change that was beginning to occur in the student standard of living – the trend was not sufficiently advanced to attract comment – but by 1880 the alterations were unmistakable. Protracted wine parties, sherry or port, in which students or dons dared each other to immoderate drink in order to miss chapel, the long, vigorous walks and heavy, late afternoon meal – activities to consume the excessive leisure of the 'old college system' – were giving way to a new and varied social and cultural world. The parochial, county tone of Cambridge social life had vanished, one consequence of the unprecedented rise in middle-class and professional incomes in the palmy decades after 1850. Secular music, organized athletics, theatricals, clubs, student publications, balls and picnics assumed a new place in Cambridge life. A few of these activities had existed before, but by the 1880's they were far more conspicuous and essential to collegiate life. In 1882 Henry Latham of Trinity Hall disapprovingly described the new conditions and looked back to the simpler and less self-indulgent habits of preceding decades: 'It has been observed, that either from the increased wealth of the country or the greater attention paid to material comforts within the last few years, there has been a general increase in the scale of living in the upper and middle ranks of society. People think themselves entitled to greater indulgences, and to a larger share of enjoyment and amusement than they did a few years back. This change is sensible, in some degree, at the Universities. What

---

altogether pleased with some of the changes. Entered as a fellow-commoner in 1861, he felt the privileges should have been retained. 'He valued the opportunity of social intercourse with the Dons.' Robert John Strutt, Fourth Baron Rayleigh, *John William Strutt, Third Baron Rayleigh* (London, 1924), p. 25.

[1] Ewart Committee, Evidence, p. 112.

were formerly considered luxuries or indulgences, are coming to be regarded as necessaries: more animal food is taken, which at the present prices materially increases the expense of living. The Colleges have generally yielded to the desire to put the dinner-hour later, and luncheon has, in consequence, become a more substantial meal. The cost of amusements has also increased. The great encouragement given in society generally to all kinds of games and athletic sports has led to a considerable expenditure under this head. Such pursuits are carried on in a more expensive style than they formerly were, a rage has sprung up for prizes in various kinds of sports, and the cost of prize cups and medals is a new item of most needless expense. The introduction of prizes of pecuniary value is exercising a pernicious effect. The moral qualities called out in athletic sports are valuable when the sports are followed for their own sake in friendly contests, but the whole spirit of the contention is deteriorated by the introduction of prizes having considerable money value. Subscriptions to the clubs are often imperfectly collected, and an unfair burden is thus thrown on those who pay punctually. These matters can be set right by the Undergraduates themselves, and it is to be hoped that some rising financier will turn his attention to the auditing of the accounts of the various Clubs. Freemasons' or Odd Fellows' Lodges, and all merely convivial societies should be avoided as causing a waste of money and time.

Friends visiting Cambridge cause serious disturbance and expense to Undergraduates. It was said of one of the Professors that our young men would be studious and simple enough in their habits if their parents would suffer them to be so. The gaieties lately introduced in the Easter Term have largely increased the expenditure of a considerable number of men. Visitors will stay a week or more, breakfasting, lunching, and supping–not only with their sons for whom they pay themselves –but with the whole circle of their sons' friends.

Again, persons do not always consider that to urge a Student to pay a guinea or more in order to go with their party to a public ball or concert, is doing him a doubtful service.'[1]

Although Latham was certainly correct in warning that the higher standard of living could easily raise the costs of residence

[1] *Student's Guide* (1880), pp. 99–101.

in Cambridge, the changes in student patterns of recreation and leisure did not mean that either total or necessary expenses rose. As certain categories of expenditure increased, others fell. Economy was still possible, and both the deflationary movement of prices and the efforts made by colleges to aid deserving students were checks on mounting costs. Estimates of university expenses and records of student spending indicate that in 1880 or in 1900 a Cambridge education could still be had for approximately the same amount as earlier in the century.

5. *Scholarships*

In the 1850's the colleges, with the assistance and sometimes the prodding of the royal commissioners, consolidated a number of minor or 'bye' fellowships and scholarships in order to provide more realistic pecuniary assistance to students; at the same time some foundation scholarships were augmented in value and number. Many restricted scholarships were opened to general competition on the grounds that scholarships were a reward for past excellence, a stimulus to future efforts, and 'an important influence upon the public schools and other places of education throughout the kingdom.'[1] The laissez-faire theory of competition and advancement by merit, however, was not fully accepted. Important remnants of the older attitude remained, and some pecuniary assistance continued to be granted on the basis of social background, school or limited means.[2] Financial need continued to be associated with sizarships and lesser scholarships known as exhibitions. By 1914 some exhibitions were still awarded on a basis of financial need, but others had become simply minor scholarships awarded for academic excellence. It is difficult to distinguish purely eleemosynary exhibitions from academic exhibitions because college records are confusing. Sizarships and subsizarships, however, definitely remained awards for students of limited income.

The statutes of Trinity College provided for sixteen sizars to be selected by examination from a group of subsizars chosen by

[1] Graham Commission (1861), p. 26.

[2] Section 33 of the Cambridge University Act (19 and 20 Victoria, cap. 88) allowed a college to retain closed and restricted emoluments for any school which could prove that closed scholarships were essential to its function as a place of learning and education.

a means test. In 1866 some fellows of the college proposed a change in the nature of sizarships when they introduced a resolution which would have abolished the category of subsizar. Their argument was that subsizars performed badly in examinations and lowered the academic standards of the college. James Lemprière Hammond, a noted Trinity tutor, opposed the resolution on the grounds that the abolition of subsizarships would change Trinity into a rich man's college, 'not likely to be remarkable either for discipline or learning. But the existence of an order of sub-sizars not only introduces a certain appreciable element of confessedly poor men, but also materially strengthens the position of a still larger body of pensioners, who being men of moderate means can nevertheless by the exercise of some self-control pay their own way in the midst of wealthier and more extravagant neighbours. I believe therefore that the abolition of sub-sizars would be followed by a rise in the average rate of expenditure among the pensioners, and by a corresponding decline in the general standard of academical success in the College.'[1]

Hammond's warning had medieval echoes: the poor must guide the rich and shore up the weak. The echoes were apparently heeded for the offending resolution was withdrawn, and the procedure for selecting the sixteen sizars of Trinity remained unchanged. Matriculants who could prove genuine need were admitted to the college as subsizars and proceeded by examination to vacancies in sizarships. The best sizars then obtained major scholarships worth no more than sizarships but essential for election to fellowships. But although the sizars were confessedly poor men, they did not come from the 'poor classes' of society: they were, like scholars or exhibitioners, mainly the sons of professional men, especially the sons of clergymen. Of the sizars of 1875[2] whose social origins can be determined from Venn, six were sons of clergymen, including one son of a clergyman-schoolmaster; three were sons of dissenting ministers; two came from naval officer families; one was probably the son of a

[1] Flysheet, December, 1866 (J. L. Hammond), p. 3. Cam.c.866.19. In 1852 there were one hundred and forty-three sizars and subsizars in Cambridge out of a total enrolment of perhaps sixteen hundred students. Distribution varied radically: St. John's had fifty-four sizars and subsizars while some colleges had none. Graham Commission (1852), Report, p. 195.

[2] Meetings of Tutors and Lecturers, May 21, 1868–79, T.C.L., Rec.16.1, contains the names of the sizars.

London 'gentleman'. The professions chosen by the twelve sizars are in keeping with the university's traditional orientation: two became teachers and two entered academic life; five took holy orders; two were called to the bar; and one entered medicine. Seven of the sixteen sizars had brothers who matriculated at Cambridge colleges; seven brothers entered the Church of England (an eighth brother died before actually leaving the university).

By 1900 the class character of Trinity sizars and others in receipt of eleemosynary assistance had not changed. Twenty-eight students were listed in the Minutes of the Meetings of the Sizarship Committee of Trinity College as having received sizarships, certain special exhibitions and small grants in 1899 and 1900 when the famous Henry Jackson was chairman of the committee.[1] The social backgrounds of eleven can be determined: three were sons of clergymen and two of dissenting ministers; one was the son of a doctor; one the son of a banker; one sizar's father was employed in a secretarial position; one was a schoolmaster; one a farmer; and one subsizar was the son of a major-general. They came to Cambridge from the following schools:

Grammar	11
Clarendon	3
Proprietary and lesser public schools	4
Abroad	1
Other	3
	22/28

This group of students entered virtually the same professions as their predecessors in the 1870's:

Academic	7
Law	2
Teaching	2
Church	3
Civil Service	2
Medicine	2
Clergy-schoolmaster	1
Army doctor	1
Engineer	1
	21/28

[1] Minutes of Meetings of Sizarship Committee, June 17, 1899–July 29, 1926. T.C.L. Rec. 24.1.

An analysis of the social backgrounds of Sidney Sussex students, a less fashionable group than at Trinity, strengthens the conclusion that throughout the nineteenth century the majority of sizars, scholars and exhibitioners came from professional, especially clerical, families and could claim some degree of financial need.[1] The distribution of rewards in Sidney remained significantly uniform, indicating that sons of professional men preserved their historic advantage in obtaining awards. In the seventy years before the outbreak of World War I, of those students whose backgrounds are known, sons of anglican clergymen accounted for approximately one-third of all sizarships, one-quarter of all scholarships and half of all exhibitions awarded in the college. The college appears to have given few scholarships before the first of the reform periods, several students even migrating in seach of assistance; but in the critical decade of the 1860's, when open awards were first instituted, sons of clergymen obtained over half the college scholarships and exhibitions. In each of the last three decades of the nineteenth century clergymen's sons held approximately half the sizarships, one-quarter of the scholarships and half or all of the exhibitions. Sons of professional men other than the anglican clergy received one-third of the sizarships and scholarships in the 1860's, one-third of the scholarships in the 1870's, 43 per cent of the scholarships in the 1880's, and nearly half the scholarships and 40 per cent of the exhibitions in the 1890's. Only in the Edwardian period is it possible to find a change in this pattern, with sons of businessmen – very broadly defined to include salaried, self-employed and owners of capital – taking as many scholarships as sons of clergymen, although fewer exhibitions.

In the 1890's more boys from lower middle class backgrounds and an occasional working-class boy began to attend Cambridge with the assistance of local authorities. The Technical Instruction Act of 1889 as amended in 1891 authorized county councils to award residents scholarships tenable at schools outside county jurisdiction. The Local Taxation Act of 1890 was another measure in support of university education: part of the beer and spirits duties collected under the act could be diverted into education. Some of the councils used the money in relief of rates, but others chose to assist students of limited means. At

[1] See Appendix II.

least twenty-six male undergraduates (and one female) aided by local authorities attended Cambridge colleges between 1896 and 1899.[1] Venn provides the following information on their social backgrounds:

Schoolmaster	1
Clergyman-schoolmaster	1
Fruiterer	1
Shopkeeper	1
Innkeeper and sometime police sergeant	1
Bootmaker	1
Farmer	2
Civil service clerk	1
Chemist	1
Tailor	1
Wharf foreman	1
Compositor	1
Doctor	2
Clothier	1
Bridle cutter	1
Brewer's manager	1
Business agent	1
Civil engineer	1

20/26

Nine of the twenty were craftsmen or shopkeepers, while the wharf foreman was from the higher ranks of the working classes. The list suggests that all of the county council scholarship winners justifiably claimed financial need. Six of the county council scholars were admitted as sizars or subsizars, one held an exhibition, and eleven received Cambridge scholarships. Support available from the counties varied considerably from the £30 per annum for three years provided by Leicester to the more realistic £90 a year from London. At least nineteen students came from Headmasters' Conference schools or grammar schools that were soon to be designated public schools. Both doctors' sons had been to Shrewsbury, but they were the only

[1] County Council Scholarships, England and Wales, 1896–9. 1900, lxxiii, vol. pp. 59–154.

boys from Clarendon schools. Of the others, two graduated from St. Paul's–the tailor's son and the civil service clerk's son; one had gone to Wellington College–a farmer's son; and the other farmer's son had attended Denstone, a Victorian public school. The son of the wharf foreman attended the City of London School, while only Humphrey Owen Jones, the son of a shopkeeper and a future fellow of Clare, had been to a university college. The most illustrious future represented is that of Owen W. Richardson, the son of a woollen manufacturer's agent. Richardson was successively scholar and fellow of Trinity, Professor of Physics at Princeton and Nobel prize winner in 1928. The county council scholarship holders followed professional occupations. One entered medicine, and two were called to the bar; nine became schoolmasters, one took holy orders, four entered academic life, and four became civil servants–two of them school inspectors.

The poor boy's success in meeting Cambridge costs depended on the number of awards he accumulated, as it was possible to combine school-leaving exhibitions, university prizes and scholarships. In some colleges exhibitions could be held jointly with sizarships. Small grants from special funds and informal aid were additional possibilities.[1] Sometimes boys received awards from town corporations and grants from the great London guilds. By the end of the century county awards, matriculation examination scholarships and Board of Education grants for prospective elementary teachers were also available. There were a few small awards for special purposes, like the scholarships established at Cambridge in the 1890's to assist boys in the Day Training College for Teachers.[2] Few poor boys could have matched Eddington's pluralism; from 1898 to 1905 he received a total of £862 10s. in scholarships, excluding Cambridge prizes:

[1] In 1886 King's established a Supplementary Exhibition Fund to aid students of limited means. The Fund is still in existence. In 1881 the Master of St. John's gave his college a small sum out of which were to be paid the lecture fees of students attending certain lectures in other colleges. *The Eagle*, XI (1881), p. 471. At Oxford it was estimated that the colleges in the early twentieth century maintained a discretionary fund of at least £3000 per annum which they could use to assist poor students. Lord Curzon, *Principles and Methods of University Reform* (Oxford, 1909), p. 81.

[2] *University Reporter* (November 8, 1892), p. 154.

		£	s.
1.	Somerset Senior County Council Scholarship,		
	£60 × 3 years (June, 1898)	180	0
2.	London Matriculation,		
	£15 × 2 (June, 1899)	30	0
3.	Victoria University Preliminary – Gilchrist		
	Scholarship, £50 × 3 (June, 1900)	150	0
4.	Heginbotham Physical Scholarship		
	(June, 1900)	15	0
5.	Victoria University Scholarship, B.Sc.		
	(June, 1902)	25	0
6.	Trinity College Scholarships		
	(natural science and mathematics)	312	10
7.	London University Scholarship,		
	£50 × 3 (November, 1903)	150	0
		862	10

From 1902–5 Eddington earned enough in scholarships and prizes to meet more than four-fifths of his Cambridge expenses; in his fourth year he took private students and found 'good pupils remarkably easy to get; mainly because [Sir James] Jean's departure to America had left Cambridge almost without an applied mathematician.'[1]

The occasional boy from a working-class family was almost totally dependent on scholarships. Sir Ernest Barker was poor socially and economically. His mother had worked in a cotton mill, and his father was a farm and quarry labourer, earning perhaps 18s. a week, an income of under £50 a year. Barker was sent from a Church of England village school in north-east Cheshire to Manchester Grammar School, a distance of ten miles. In an earlier age he would have been a boarder, but the railways made it possible for him to attend as a day boy. Ashamed of his speech and dress, he persevered; learned his Greek from a generous master who tutored him without charge during vacations; accumulated several money prizes to ease the financial strain on his family; and finally went up to Balliol in 1893 with an £80 foundation scholarship and a £45 leaving exhibition from Manchester, a total of £125 per annum which still could not meet his needs. He added an additional £40 per annum for two years by winning the Craven. An interest-free

---

[1] Eddington, Journal, p. 29.

loan from his mother's grocer enabled him to meet the expenses of coming into residence, especially caution money. Food costs were reduced by abstention from hall dinner two or three nights a week, but in retrospect Barker called it a foolish economy which might have impaired his health.[1]

It was possible for the exceptional student, like Eddington, Barker and the sizars to whom Hammond referred in 1867,[2] to accumulate enough scholarships, prizes or school-leaving exhibitions to meet nearly all his university expenses, but the average scholar was not usually so fortunate. At best he met half or just over half his expenses. A graduate of Pembroke College, Oxford, wrote *The Times* early in 1907 that most scholars were sons of professional men who could manage £80–100 per year for university education but no more. 'My own case is probably typical; I had an £80 scholarship, an £80 allowance, and I earned £40 by the two means open to an undergraduate, teaching and journalism. Without a scholarship, I could not have gone into residence.'[3]

Some poor boys did not become scholars, did not win exhibitions and attended colleges with few sizarships. G. G. Coulton described such a classmate at St. Catharine's in 1878: 'The best student of that year was Henry Knight, who rivalled the heroism of Scottish students like Peter Giles and James Adam. His father was an impecunious parson in North London, with three boys and two girls. His mother was from an artistic family. One of her brothers was Fred Walker, whose "Harvest Moon" is to be seen in the National Gallery, unless it has been superannuated lately; another was an organ-builder. When one of Knight's sisters died, about 1911, he said to me, "She, and my Caius [actually Selwyn] brother who was killed at football soon after his degree, were the only two of us who inherited my father's imperturbable optimism. In all our difficulties, I never saw him depressed; his spirits were always buoyant." Boys and girls alike had to make their beds, black their boots, wash up plates and knives daily before they could trudge off to a rather distant day school. The second son became Bishop of Rangoon and Principal of St. Augustine's, Canterbury. Henry, the eldest,

---

[1] Barker, pp. 244–300, 317–18.
[2] Ewart Committee, Evidence, p. 50.
[3] *The Times* (January 8, 1907), p. 6.

was an enthusiastic cricketer, but never touched bat or ball at Cambridge: he couldn't afford it. He slept in an attic on the Library staircase, without a fire except in the coldest winter weather; and nothing ever kept him for an hour from his alotted time of daily reading. In later life, he found that even music took him too much from his work, and seldom indulged in a concert. The majority of us, the unregenerate, looked upon his perfection as rather discouraging: it was obviously impossible to live up to Knight's standard, yet of course nothing short of that was the right and proper thing to be done for one's parents' and for one's own credit. I used to watch him come in from the "Grantchester Grind" and climb up to that garret with something of the same feelings with which, almost daily after breakfast, I used to walk through Queens' to the Backs, and look in for a moment at Erasmus' portrait in the Hall.'[1]

Henry Knight eventually became Bishop of Gibraltar, and Coulton's tale of an heroic, humble and deserving student ended happily, if somewhat mysteriously. For the romance of Henry Knight and his brothers has its unknown and intriguing dimensions, and part of their story surely remains untold. Coulton did not explain – it would be instructive to know why – how an impecunious parson in North London managed to support three sons at Cambridge, two at the same time, when it can be shown from Venn that none of them held scholarships or exhibitions and all were formally matriculated as pensioners. Abstemiousness is not the whole answer.

Yet the story of Knight and his brothers certainly calls attention to the importance of family and class traditions of education and helps explain a fundamental fact in the relationship between Cambridge University and the Victorian clergy. The son of a country vicar or curate or the son of a parson serving in slum parishes was expected to attend the university and receive the education appropriate to his station and future. He could go to Durham where his necessary expenses would be only half that of the ancient universities; but if he chose Oxford or Cambridge an enormous financial burden was placed upon his father, especially as the general prosperity which at mid-century raised the standard of living of other professional men did not conspicuously help vicars, rectors and curates. They were the

[1] Coulton, pp. 121–2.

least able to afford a Cambridge education for their sons. The basic income of beneficed clergy was assumed to be at least £100 by the Commutation Act of 1836, but from then until 1916 the average value of the tithe-rent-charge was only £92, although there were some years in which it went above par.[1] Clergymen derived additional income from rental of the glebe, from the performance of marriages and burials, from private teaching and various chaplaincies; but nevertheless it is apparent that many parsons were still precariously dependent upon private sources of income. Even these, it seems, were disappearing in the second half of the nineteenth century; at least it was noticed that the financial position of ordinands was beginning to fall by mid-century.[2]

These disturbing trends did not escape the attention of Victorian dons. Often themselves members of clerical families or in holy orders, dons were sensitive to the discomfort caused clergymen's sons by the exceptionally high costs of a Cambridge education. They knew of the Henry Knights who sacrificed many of the social and physical amenities of collegiate life and for the sake of a Cambridge education risked going heavily into debt.[3] Wherever possible they tried to assist the group of students whose connexion with Cambridge stretched back to its foundation. Loans were advanced, special eleemosynary funds were collected, plans for reducing collegiate costs were made and closed awards were either reintroduced or retained, all in the hope that the student from a clerical home or the student preparing for a pastoral career would still find it possible to attend Cambridge in the new and more competitive age.

In the nineteenth and early twentieth centuries dons were

---

[1] The Chronicle of Convocation (London 1918), Report Number 513, Tithe-Rent-Charge.

[2] Charles Kenneth Francis Brown, *A History of the English Clergy, 1800–1900* (London, 1953), pp. 185–7, 235. In the 1860's Jowett agreed with the opinion that the fall in clerical income could be partly attributed to the fact that 'men who now enter orders . . . come from a somewhat lower class of society than was usual 25 years ago.' Ewart Committee, Evidence, pp. 139 and 147.

[3] One Cambridge graduate, the son of a very small farmer and grandson of a curate, left Cambridge owing his tutor the appalling sum of £200. [S. Atkinson], 'Struggles of a Poor Student Through Cambridge,' *The London Magazine*, n.s., I (April, 1825).

usually satisfied that scholars and exhibitioners could legitimately claim financial need, being sons of widows, younger sons of gentlemen of limited means or professional men in reduced circumstances. The definition of needy was sometimes very generous. It was implicitly conceded that a professional man and his son had to live in a certain style which it would be unfortunate to alter. They were prepared to argue that even a father in relatively comfortable circumstances would have to husband his resources against possible catastrophe. Nevertheless, dons were not altogether comfortable when occasionally boys from obviously wealthy families held scholarships, although no one could be certain how many such boys there were. The colleges kept faulty records, and the estimates of individual dons varied so much as to be virtually meaningless. Not until 1919 was precise information on the financial need of scholars and exhibitioners requested. The colleges reported to the Royal Commission on Oxford and Cambridge that nearly all the scholars and exhibitioners could claim some degree of financial need, and the Royal Commission was satisfied that 'in most cases, though not yet in all, Scholarship emoluments are now enjoyed by students who are in actual need of the financial assistance granted to them.'[1]

In the 1890's Henry Montagu Butler, Master of Trinity, argued that wealthy boys should have honours without money.[2] Possibly some Cambridge colleges tried to provide for the voluntary resignation of scholarships, although probably without publicizing their action. The question of scholarships and financial need does not appear to have received public attention until 1907 when Bishop Gore of Birmingham accused Oxford and Cambridge of exclusiveness. A year later the fellows of Sidney Sussex College, in response to a letter from the heads of Balliol, New, and Magdalen Colleges, Oxford, and Trinity College, Cambridge, unanimously agreed to inform parents and guardians that the whole or any part of the emoluments of a scholarship could be resigned, the money to be used for poorer students, 'and it was also unanimously agreed that the proposal

---

[1] Royal Commission on Oxford and Cambridge (1922), Report, p. 135; Appendices, p. 201.
[2] Bryce Commission, xlvii, pp. 145–6.

to exact a statement of the financial position of any elected scholar was both unnecessary and undesirable.'[1] Provision for the voluntary surrender of emoluments appears to have been the general Oxford-Cambridge answer to the question of the wealthy scholar. Lord Curzon, Chancellor of Oxford, probably spoke for both universities in 1909 when he argued against other alternatives. He believed that poverty clauses or any other means test would be difficult to apply and would lower standards. He feared that any attempt to establish a category of honorary scholarships would only renew social distinctions based on wealth or discourage clever boys with means. He thought too that students would not compete for scholarships if they believed the money settlement arbitrary or uncertain. The total revival of closed scholarships, in the form today called special opportunity scholarships, he regarded as impractical.[2] After Curzon, little thought appears to have been given by either of the two ancient universities to the problem of the wealthy scholar until the introduction of state scholarships in 1920, a temporary measure, but the forerunner of a policy which in principle survives today.

6. *The Professional Man and the Professional Ideal*

In the nineteenth century dons did not expect unusual or sudden changes in the social structure of Cambridge; and none occurred, at least none that can support a causal explanation of reform. The available evidence regarding the social composition of the university and its colleges points to a remarkable continuity in the social background of undergraduates. Professional families, and especially clerical families, continued to supply Cambridge with the majority of its undergraduates. Compare the statistics compiled from the admissions books of Sidney Sussex College with the sample for the university as a whole made by Jenkins and Jones:[3]

---

[1] Minute Book of Sidney Sussex College, May 20, 1908.

[2] Curzon, pp. 82–7. Interestingly enough, the Franks Committee also rejected the idea of closed awards, arguing that this was a class solution to a problem rooted in the structure of secondary education. See Franks Report, I, pp. 77–8.

[3] Appendix II; Jenkins and Jones, p. 99.

Occupation	Sidney Sussex, 1843–1914	Cambridge, 1800–1850 (Jenkins and Jones)	Cambridge, 1850–1900 (Jenkins and Jones)
	%	%	%
Anglican clergy	25	32	31
Professional men (excluding services)	25	21	26
Landed classes	5	31	19
Businessmen	15–19 (but only 10% in 1860's and 1890's)	6	15

The proportion of students from clerical and professional homes does not appear to have changed significantly in the course of the nineteenth century; they comprised at least half the university. The percentage of students from landed families–never important in Sidney Sussex–declined, but only by 12 per cent and over a period of half a century.

The pivotal figures relate to students from families in business. The numbers of businessmen's sons at Sidney Sussex fluctuated, but never rose above 19 per cent; in two of the decades, including the controversial period of the 1860's, the percentage fell to only 10 per cent. In the university as a whole they more than doubled in the course of the nineteenth century, but still remained proportionately small. These figures, combined with information on the structure and distribution of university awards, suggest that the problem of social change in Cambridge is not the dispossession of the proletariat but the relative exclusion of new wealth and influence. Surely it is remarkable that the industrial and commercial wealth so conspicuous in social and political life outside the university did not achieve greater representation within.

Why did England's prominent and successful capitalists fail to gain more recognition from the ancient institutions along the River Cam? The explanation lies in a modified version of the theory of class or group conflict. In the birth of modern Cambridge factors of class competition and rivalry are present, although the nature of the competition and the rivalry, as well as the identity of the rivals must be redefined. Cambridge did indeed desire to accommodate the needs or interests of certain groups within English society. Dons had their favourites. One of the primary objects of the great nineteenth-century reforms was to guarantee that Cambridge did not lose its traditional connexion with the professions and professional men, especially clergymen. Dons planned to preserve the connexion and to enhance it by strengthening the university's ties to the liberal professions and by bringing under university influence newer professions developing outside Cambridge. This does not mean that dons wished to definitely close the university to non-professional groups; merely that they had no intention of making Cambridge in any way attractive to students from non-professional families who might prefer a career in business, or who were unprepared to accept Cambridge values and style.

In the 1860's dons were asked by the Ewart Committee of the House of Commons which social groups were most likely to benefit from a reduction in the costs of a Cambridge education. Their customary answer was that reduced expenses would of course greatly assist the sons of clergy; but among groups without any experience of a university education, students interested in the lesser professions or raised in professional families would be the principal beneficiaries. Students preparing for careers as schoolmasters, attorneys and civil servants, they said, were willing to make the necessary financial sacrifices in order to acquire a collegiate education. The lesser professions themselves appeared anxious to enter into closer association with the university. Solicitors had reduced the required period of articled clerkships by two years in order to attract graduates, and there was hope that similar or other preferential arrangements could be made with the civil service or even major professions like the bar.[1] There was talk of a mutually advantageous arrangement with the Institute of Civil Engineers, but dons doubted whether major firms would employ enough university graduates to justify an investment in an engineering staff and facilities.[2] Dons were even more pessimistic about the chances of attracting a larger number of sons from commercial families. Students

[1] Ewart Committee, Evidence, pp. 92, 100.
[2] Ibid., p. 240. Apparently there was some question as to the status of engineering for Ewart told the House of Commons that engineering was now both a science and a profession. H. C. Deb., 3rd ser., clxxxvii (June 5, 1867), col. 1616.

preparing for commercial careers, they said, were not accustomed to lowering their standard of living in order to acquire a university education, especially as no commercial advantage could be gained by residence in Cambridge. Stated bluntly by the Tutor of Queens' College, merchants would not consider a Cambridge education appropriate for a Liverpool office.[1]

There was an odd confusion and curious evasion in the answers given the Ewart Committee by dons. They assumed that sons were inclined to follow the occupations of their fathers, that a Liverpool merchant's son would want to enter the family firm and had little to gain by a Cambridge education (even that he would find Cambridge uncomfortable and inhospitable) and that only sons from professional families were genuinely interested in professional careers. Dons frequently spoke as if there were hereditary tendencies within the professions that Cambridge ought to respect and promote. This is one important reason why dons worried so much about the sons of the impoverished £100 curate, or the sons of country vicars and rectors who formed the largest single group within Cambridge in both halves of the nineteenth century. This is why dons were so eager to assist the younger sons of professional men, why George Murray Humphrey, Professor of Anatomy at Cambridge from 1866 to 1883, could be described as 'poor and without influence' even though he was the third son of a Sudbury barrister and entered Cambridge in the expensive category of fellow-commoner.[2] Sons of professional men were expected to enter the professions, even to follow the career of their fathers; and dons, for the most part professional men from professional families, believed the university had an historical obligation to see that these enterprising sons were not forsaken.[3]

The supposition that Cambridge was attractive only to sons

---

[1] Ewart Committee, Evidence, p. 239, also p. 38. Ewart himself was the second son of a Liverpool merchant, but after Eton and Christ Church, Oxford, he entered the bar and subsequently politics. One purpose of the bill he introduced into parliament in 1867 was to extend professional education in the universities by promoting subjects like engineering, agricultural chemistry, practical geology—subjects, he said, which were useful to the large numbers of youth who were emigrating. H. C. Deb., 3rd ser., clxxxvii (June 5, 1867), col. 1616.

[2] DNB.

[3] Hereditary tendencies within the professions are discernible before the

of professional men suggests there was something special about a student preparing for the professions, that he possessed certain qualities of education–perhaps of social background–that distinguished him from the student preparing for a career in commerce. In fact a distinction between professional men and businessmen had been developing throughout the early nineteenth century as the two groups found themselves loosely competitive, and the former began to see themselves as in a special sense the descendants of the landed aristocracy and the new gentlemen of English society.[1] Especially was this true of clergymen whose role and function within English society had become obscured after lengthy association with the landed aristocracy. The clergymen had been country gentlemen, but in the middle of the nineteenth century they were becoming professional men; and Cambridge was particularly anxious to aid them in the transformation, since the university also was gradually unburdening itself of what was now regarded as an embarrassing association with the landed aristocracy.

When Cambridge announced its support for professional men, including the sons of professional men, it must be understood that the word 'professional' was being used both in a general and in a unique way. When dons spoke of professional men or of professionalization they meant actual, designated occupations or careers including their own, for they were now distressingly aware of the fact that university teaching had hitherto not been regarded as a legitimate and permanent career. Dons could not however agree on the proper training or education

---

nineteenth century. Just before 1650 about a quarter of the clergymen in several counties came from clerical families. At Glasgow University in the eighteenth and nineteenth centuries a high proportion of the sons of ministers, doctors and lawyers followed their fathers' occupations, as high as 69 per cent over a period of a century in medicine. See Lawrence Stone, 'Social Mobility in England, 1500–1700', *Past and Present*, Number 33 (April, 1966), p. 48; W. M. Mathew, 'Glasgow Students, 1740–1839', ibid., pp. 80–90. The anonymous author of *A History of the Society of Writers to Her Majesty's Signet* (Edinburgh, 1890), lx, noted that 'The continuance of a family for three generations in the society is so common as hardly to attract attention.'

[1] See the discussions in G. S. R. Kitson Clark, *The Making of Victorian England*, pp. 258–74, and in W. L. Burn, *The Age of Equipoise* (London, 1964), pp. 253–66.

for professional careers, the extent to which professional education should be utilitarian and practical or vaguely preparatory and general, even liberal; and so their use of the word professional could not be in most cases fixed to a definite course of university instruction and was to a certain extent conveniently publicistic. Nor was confusion over the meaning of professional in any way dispelled when dons also used the word to refer to a particular style of social, domestic life, a pattern of work and leisure that would suggest gentility. The precise meaning of the word professional became even more confused when it began to connote a particular social role that was not merely occupational but in fact profoundly moral; and it was at this point that dons began to exploit the status ambiguity of the designation professional and to emphasize the idea of professional behaviour, of compliance with a high ethical, altruistic standard as the predominant characteristic of a professional man.[1] To feed this conception dons drew freely from multiple social and intellectual sources, from the responsibility to society professed by the aristocrat and the clergymen, from religious ethics restimulated by evangelicalism and stressed in high church, broad church and christian socialism movements, and from the example of the new state bureaucrats who were re-working the machinery of social administration. This donnish conception of a professional man and of his responsibility towards society resulted in an ideal of service that was sharply brought to bear against the Victorian businessman; and the businessman, whether in finance, retailing, international trade or industry, predictably was found wanting.

The professional man, it was argued by those who distrusted and feared the ethical implications of the acquisitive aspects of industrialism, thought more of duty than of profit. The gratitude of his client rather than the market defined his reward, and

[1] For the varied usage of the word 'professional' see inter alia Geoffrey Millerson, *The Qualifying Associations* (London, 1964), pp. 1–25; Kenneth Prandy, *Professional Employees: a Study of Scientists and Engineers* (London, 1965), pp. 15–47. See also E. H. Pitcairn, ed., *Unwritten Laws and Ideals of Active Careers* (London, 1899), especially the sections on physicians and barristers. For professionalization as the antidote to social alienation and as a socio-moral obligation see Melvin Richter, 'Intellectual and Class Alienation: Oxford Idealist Diagnoses and Prescriptions', *European Journal of Sociology*, VII (1966) and *The Politics of Conscience* (London, 1964).

technically he was not paid but granted an *honorarium*. He earned his reputation by discretion, tact and expert knowledge rather than by advertising and financial success. He was a learned man, and his education was broad and comprehensive. Unlike the businessman, who operated within an impersonal market situation, the professional man was involved with his clients at a personal, intimate level. Ideally, he did not have to compete with others of the same profession, at least not to the same extent as the businessman. The professional society, with its principles of restricted entry, embodied in the professional examination and the *numerus clausus*, insulated him from the severer pressures of supply and demand. There was, therefore, a certain self-restraint in his manner, a gentlemanly quality which distinguished him from the brash and aggressive industrialists of the midlands and the north.

In practice the distinction between a professional man and a businessman were by no means as decisive as dons made them, and the two roles were often interchangeable or overlapping with physicians, for example, appearing as railway directors. Certainly in the context of its own history the professional ideal of service is ambiguous, but it was made a significant factor in the social history of the ancient universities when dons linked the ideal to a tradition of protest against the theory of economic competition and the profit motive that had been generating from almost the first decades of the take-off into industrialization.[1] The ancient universities with their aristocratic and clerical heritage joined in the reaction to the values of industrialism, insisted on the static ideal types and successfully kept alive the conflict between service and profit motives, ranking the former as morally superior to the latter.

R. H. Tawney, once an Oxford don, can be said to be the direct heir of some of the essential elements of the professional ideal. He also brings the university definition of service to a logical close. For Tawney, deeply sensitive to Ruskin's censure of the 'Bourbons of industry' and the 'usurer's trade', the economic man stood in the way of a socialist and democratic future. Only if the businessman and industrialist accepted the controlling moral idea of professional service, could democracy be built. Industry had to be given a social rather than a private

[1] See Raymond Williams, *Culture and Society*, any edition.

function, and the businessman had to 'be subordinated to the community in such a way as to offer the best service technically possible. . . . those who offer faithful service should be honourably paid, and . . . those who offer no service should not be paid at all.'[1] When the businessman learned the principle of self-renunciation, he would become a professional man. The last obstacle to the creation of the service society, built like the medieval community around a moral ideal, would finally be removed.

To understand the relationship between Cambridge University and society in the nineteenth century and to discover the reason behind the professional ideal, it is important to analyse the cultural as well as sociographical factors in the history of Cambridge. It is necessary to catch the dons at a precise moment of time in their lives as, within an institutional setting that was to influence their decisions, they sought to realize the professional ideal by redefining their roles and the proper function of a university. It is necessary to enter into the thinking of this vital portion of the Victorian intellectual aristocracy,[2] to recover the anxieties and establish the structure of values which made dons act. Two important figures of the mid-Victorian period, John Stuart Mill and Matthew Arnold, may be allowed to present the dilemmas of the dons by setting out the alternatives and by summarizing the possible responses to the crisis of the 1860's. Mill, not a don but well known to Cambridge through writings and acquaintances, opens the mid-Victorian search for a new definition of role with a remark he once dropped in connexion with Bentham and Coleridge. When comparing great thinkers, he said, it was as necessary to determine the extent of their agreement on secondary ends as their disagreement on ultimate questions of moral metaphysics. It is to both but especially to secondary ends that we must now turn.

[1] R. H. Tawney, *The Radical Tradition* (Harmondsworth, 1966), pp. 44, 49–54, and *The Acquisitive Society*, any edition.
[2] The phrase is Noël Annan's. See his *Leslie Stephen* (London, 1951), and 'The Intellectual Aristocracy', in J. H. Plumb, ed., *Studies in Social History* (London, 1955), pp. 241–87.

PART TWO

THE PROBLEM RESOLVED

CHAPTER 3

SECONDARY ENDS

1.

In 1836 John Stuart Mill assumed the editorship of *The London and Westminster Review* and wrote Edward Bulwer, from whom he was soliciting contributions, that Bentham's death–no doubt much to be regretted–had made it possible for the *Review* to free itself of a perverse inheritance. 'I hope you will believe,' Mill continued, 'that if the Review has hitherto been too much in the old style of Radical-Utilitarianism with which you cannot possibly sympathize very strongly (nor I either), it is because the only persons who could be depended upon as writers, were those whose writings would not tend to give it any other tone. My object will now be to draw together a body of writers resembling the old school of Radicals only in being on the movement side, in philosophy, morality, and art as well as in politics and socialities, and to keep the remnant of the old school (it is dying out) in their proper place, by letting them write only about the things which they understand.'[1]

The things the remnant of the old school understood best were the environmental basis of conduct, the relativistic character of social morality and the necessity for comprehensive social and political change when past institutional arrangements were no longer useful. The old school did not understand the nature of historical experience, the need for self-cultivation, the emotional and aesthetic requirements of human nature or the meaning of cultural standards. In short, the palaeo-utilitarians

[1] Victor Alexander George Robert Bulwer Lytton, *The Life of Edward Bulwer, First Lord Lytton* (London, 1913), I, pp. 509–10.

who posited pleasure as the end of human conduct understood little of what made men happy.

In his famous period of apostasy during the 1830's Mill over-turned one by one the basic principles of philosophic radicalism by which English society was to be reconstructed. They seemed dated and mischievous in almost every instance. It was frightening rather than gratifying that the millennium of the greatest happiness of the greatest number might actually occur. Perhaps critics were correct in deriding utilitarianism as selfish, hedonistic, materialist and neo-epicurean; for upon the incomplete and negligent principle of expediency, a society might be raised which derided the moral and intellectual values to which Mill, after the experience of his nervous collapse ten years before, almost desperately clung.

Since that 'melancholy winter' of 1826–7, Mill had sought assistance from every quarter: Marmontel's *Memoires*, romantic poetry, the Saint-Simonians, the young men of the London Debating Society. While exposure to new and fascinating ideas unquestionably gave him a greater appreciation of the intellectual and emotional limitations of his earlier educational experience, it could not solve any of his fundamental worries about the future of English society and culture. Despite his confidence that the old radicals were dying out and his brave words about keeping them in their place, Mill was almost helplessly tied to the ethics of the selfish philosophy. Only in utilitarianism and the eighteenth-century psychology of sensations attached to it could he find a far-reaching philosophy of social and intellectual reform.

Mill's problems were two-fold and contradictory: how could individualism best be preserved and how could the philosopher determine the moral and cultural standards required for leadership. Both problems arose directly from the hedonistic paradox. The older school of utilitarians, arguing by analogy from the theory of the self-regulating market, asserted that in the long run individual self-interest and public interest coincided. Precisely because individual happiness depended upon general social happiness, it was inconceivable that an individual would act contrary to the wishes of society, regarded as the will of the numerical majority. Truly selfish behaviour by definition could never produce pleasure, only pain. In the 1830's Mill was no longer convinced by the arguments for the hedonistic paradox, and he increasingly feared that minority or individual interests could not survive in a society where normative behaviour alone was sanctioned.

Mill's second problem was closely related to the first. If the numerical majority alone defined the ends of conduct, on what basis was leadership, any kind of leadership, possible? Society, the total sum of individual desires, respected only those values or beliefs with which it was in perfect agreement. No statesman or public official could possibly adopt a position at variance from what society designated the greatest good for the greatest number. The statesman accepted the standards which society offered him, and only by risking pain would he attempt to impose his own value system or make decisions independent of public opinion. The leader, in effect, was always a follower.

Mill's dilemmas were acute because he agreed that the utilitarian theory of leadership was absolutely necessary. Bentham had to make his way against a value system which favoured the minority and handicapped the majority. 'Religious or aristocratic, ascetic or chivalrous morality',[1] had formed the basis for oligarchical rule in the eighteenth century. Rules and laws were formulated by a landed aristocracy for its own benefit. If major political and legal reforms were to have any chance of success, a democratic majority had to decide the laws and establish the standards. If Bentham's principles were followed, a minority would no longer impose its wishes on the majority or reserve special privileges for itself. One code and standard determined by universal male franchise and applicable to all would replace the liberties and peculiars of the English aristocracy. A privileged élite would no longer define good or bad solely on the basis of premises derived from its own class interest.

The Benthamites discarded all the contrivances used by the eighteenth-century aristocracy to maintain existing authority and to support its claims to leadership. Absent from utilitarian theory were concepts of Christian humility and self-sacrifice, deductions from an inherent or essential human nature; also absent were social deductions from cosmology, from natural

[1] Elie Halévy, *The Growth of Philosophical Radicalism* (London, 1952), p. 477. Quoted from Bentham's *Deontology*.

99

order, from the existence of a world independent of sense experience and all theories purporting original contracts or alliances
between governing and governed. Bentham dismissed the
theory that it was 'natural' for one class to rule another or that
society could be divided into 'natural' inferiors and superiors;
he did not believe that one class more than another possessed
a notion of right or correct behaviour, or that rights and obligations were fixed and unchanging. Decisions, Bentham insisted,
were always made according to self or class interest, and no
particular man's interest was inherently superior to another's.
The man who acted from motives of charity deserved no more
praise than the man who acted from the interests of commerce.
Both motives came under the designation self-interest, the pursuit of pleasure and avoidance of pain. 'To say either that man
should, or that he should not, take pleasure in one thing, dis-
pleasure in another, appeared to him as much an act of despot-
ism in the moralist as in the political ruler.'[1] On the basis of
Bentham's ethical theories, which rejected in any form the
concept of an absolute hierarchy of values, there was no logical
reason to favour aristocratic or established institutions over any
others society might devise.

Bentham was primarily a legal philosopher, and he left to
James Mill the task of formulating the psychological and epistemological bases for utilitarian morality. In 1829 James Mill
produced the required treatise, *An Analysis of the Phenomena of
the Human Mind*, a work which has been described as opening
the third stage in the historical development of the doctrine of
association psychology.[2] Mill retained the experiential principle
of Locke and Hume. Sensation, the process of receiving stimuli,
always preceded ideation, the process of forming ideas. An
idea was always, if not simply, the copy or image of a sensation.
In a special Berkeleyan sense association psychology described
an ideal world of phenomena, always changing according to
one's perception or experience of it. There was no reality beyond
stimuli, no natural, cosmological or spiritual order which
existed apart from material sensation and no way in which
knowledge could be acquired except through the senses.

[1] John Stuart Mill, *On Bentham and Coleridge* (New York, 1962), p. 68.
[2] Howard C. Warren, *A History of the Association Psychology* (New York,
1921), p. 16.

Association psychology was the perfect complement to Bentham's legal and political relativism. The net result of the combination of utility and association psychology was the social or environmental man, totally the product of circumstances and motivated solely by egoism. Gone were the notion of an absolute hierarchy of values and the concept of a natural or essential man. Society could establish and change whatever standards it deemed the most useful; and society could make whatever kind of man it chose, since to it alone were reserved the coercive instruments of pleasure and pain, reward and punishment, laws, prisons and social sanctions to enforce and encourage good behaviour. In the face of such a display of authority, the individual was as helpless as was John Mill himself in the depressing winter of his nervous breakdown.

After his recovery, Mill cast about for alternatives to utility. While several of the rival doctrines possessed appealing features, none guaranteed change, which was the cardinal advantage of utilitarianism. Most competing theories appeared subtle or obvious manifestations of conservative political theory. Mill therefore found himself in the impossible position of defending a patrimony against which he was in revolt and attacking doctrines with which he was in partial sympathy, or which at least answered his needs more satisfactorily than the experiential philosophy.

The doctrines which appeared to remedy the defects in Mill's intellectual upbringing belonged to intuitional or nativist philosophy as interpreted by the Cambridge professoriate, Adam Sedgwick and William Whewell, and the Scottish school of common sense as represented by Sir William Hamilton, the Edinburgh logician and metaphysician. None of the philosophical positions taken by these noted men were purely nativist, as Mill acknowledged in his *Autobiography* when he defined Cambridge intuitionism and Scottish common sense as 'the more moderate forms of the intuitional philosophy;'[1] but each seemed to compromise the belief in progressive reform given Mill by his father and Bentham.

The first of the intuitionists whom Mill debated was Sedgwick. His *Discourse on the Studies of Cambridge* appeared in the early 1830's and contained a casual refutation of utilitarian

[1] John Stuart Mill, *Autobiography* (London, 1958), p. 233.

epistemological assumptions. Like Whewell, whose interpretation of German philosophy undoubtedly influenced him, Sedgwick derived his theory of the understanding from Kant's categories and fundamental ideas and from mathematical demonstrations of the meaning of necessary or *a priori* truth. In the *Discourse* Sedgwick immediately conceded that the mind possessed no innate knowledge, as that phrase was commonly understood, but he insisted nevertheless, that sensory experience alone could never provide a suitable standard of moral behaviour. Material or phenomenal experience required the assistance or intervention of certain innate powers, inherent moral capacities or faculties, a 'sentient principle within.'[1] Conscience was such a faculty. When excited by sensation, conscience provided intuitive distinctions between right and wrong. The resulting moral ideas, although not innate ideas *per se*, could not be dismissed as merely imitations of sensation or copies of stimuli. Experience was a condition of their existence, not their prototype or cause, and could never produce their verification. Fourteen years later, when Sedgwick produced the fifth edition of his *Discourse*, his argument was virtually unchanged. The mind he wrote, in refutation of tabula rasa psychology, was not so much a blank sheet of paper upon which almost anything from sensible experience could be written as it was a sheet of paper 'prepared by chemical skill, which shews some picture or design the moment the light is made to shine upon it';[2] a design, as he explained in 1835, prepared by a celestial hand.[3] The mind gave form, colour, attributes and powers to the stimuli it received from the external world of matter and projected the transformed sensations back 'to create ... the outer world anew.'[4]

Sedgwick's nearly rapturous sermonizing on innate capacities especially piqued Mill; it did so because, as he acknowledged, Sedgwick was not only a respected Cambridge professor, but also one of the more liberal members of the university and a proponent of educational reform. If a well-known clergyman-scientist undertook a criticism of Cambridge studies, his views were almost automatically guaranteed a wide reception.

---

[1] Adam Sedgwick, *A Discourse on the Studies of the University of Cambridge* (London and Cambridge, 1850), p. 47.

[2] Ibid., cxciii.   [3] Ibid., p. 53.   [4] Ibid., clxxxii.

There was no damage like the damage a liberal reformer could do to the cause of liberal reform, especially if he were an intuitionist and his proposals were accompanied by a general denunciation of utility doctrine. Mill's rejoinder to Sedgwick, his very first contribution to the *London and Westminster Review* in 1835, was therefore especially pungent. Sedgwick's views were dismissed as trivial and erroneous, his attempt to understand the pleasure principle pronounced a complete failure. In a closing acerbic comment, Mill credited the popularity of Sedgwick's views to their appeal to 'a lower class of capacities'; he invited the defenders of utility to 'join battle in the field of popular controversy with every antagonist of name and reputation, even when, as in the present case, his name and reputation are his only claims to be heard on such a subject.'[1]

In 1867 Mill alluded to the 'asperity of tone' which his criticism of Sedgwick contained, but there was no regret in the allusion and no attempt to disown this departure from his customary style of disputation. Mill explained his almost personal attack on Sedgwick by saying that he was defending maligned doctrines and individuals against persons well able to hold their own in debate;[2] and later, in his *Autobiography*, he called Sedgwick's criticism an 'unjust attack'. Even at the end of his life, Mill continued to question Sedgwick's competence in philosophy.[3]

When in 1852 Mill undertook a review of Whewell's moral theories, he found an opponent who could not so easily be dismissed from the realm of philosophy. Whewell's attempt to unite the history and philosophy of science in a *History of the Inductive Sciences* was invaluable to Mill in his own *A System of Logic*. Whewell was not only abreast of much of the new scientific knowledge but was also an important contributor to that new knowledge. He produced a monumental study of tides, invented an anemometer for measuring the force and direction of wind, and he was acknowledged England's leading authority in the coinage of new scientific words. Mill admitted that Whewell's work deserved special commendation and that he had done almost all that one man could in removing from the ancient universities the reproach that they neglected 'the higher regions

---

[1] John Stuart Mill, *Dissertations and Discussions* (London, 1859), I, p. 159.
[2] Ibid., v.   [3] Mill, *Autobiography*, p. 170.

of philosophy.'[1] This praise, however, was given grudgingly; for Mill prepared to demonstrate that the tendency, if not the intention, of Whewell's philosophic efforts was to uphold Cambridge's role as a defender of conservative ideas and institutions.

Mill knew that within Cambridge Whewell was widely respected but also regarded as imperious by students and younger dons. Even Sedgwick, one of his closest friends and vice-master of Trinity, had to submit to Whewell's craving for authority.[2] Whewell was not exactly a stern, unbending tory. In politics he may have shared some of Peel's ideas,[3] and in education many of his views were progressive. Doubtless his personality more than any other single factor established his reputation as an uncompromising conservative. He was temperamental and intermittently vain, perhaps through nervousness;[4] and it was natural for critics like Mill to confuse his ethical theories and personal characteristics.

In fairness to Whewell it should be noted that his moral philosophy was not as straightforward an apology for existing political arrangements as may be supposed from Mill's criticism. In fairness to Mill and to some of Whewell's other critics, it should be said that Whewell's arguments were in a process of development and not always lucidly presented. His basic problem was to work out a coherent philosophy of discovery rather than a philosophy of proof. He wished to determine the exact basis upon which truths were actually known. Like Sedgwick, Whewell began with the phenomenological assumption that knowledge could never be acquired solely without experience;[5] but this did not mean that knowledge could always be traced back to experience. Sensory phenomena did not yield knowledge or truth until they were shaped or formed by a fundamental idea–space, number, cause, likeness–which alone could give

[1] Mill, *Dissertations* (London, 1859), II, p. 450.
[2] R. Robson, 'William Whewell, F.R.S., Academic Life,' *Notes and Records of the Royal Society of London*, XIX (December, 1964), p. 171.
[3] Ibid.   [4] Ibid., p. 174.
[5] For Whewell's intuitionism I follow the explanation in Robert E. Butts, 'Necessary Truth in Whewell's Theory of Science', *American Philosophical Quarterly*, II (July, 1965), pp. 1–21. See also Walter F. Cannon, 'Scientists and Broad Churchmen: An Early Victorian Intellectual Network', *The Journal of British Studies*, IV (November, 1964), pp. 65–88.

meaning or validity. Fundamental and necessary truths were not arbitrary intuitions as the utilitarians claimed, conveniently summoned up to justify beliefs already held. Necessary truths, said Whewell, were derived over a period of time and could only be intuited by a mind prepared by culture and education to receive them. Furthermore, they had to be mutually supporting and capable of soliciting further truths. Finally, necessary truths did not comprise a fixed and closed body of knowledge. At no point was there a body of necessary truths known completely: new truths always developed in time.

In his criticism Mill attempted to prove that Whewell's nativistic philosophy was an illogical compound of the experiential principle of Bentham and the older theories of received and *a priori* truth. Despite its alleged modifications the Kantian theory of necessary truth was essentially still another defence of orthodoxy. But what else could be expected of a clergyman in an ecclesiastical institution, Mill concluded, than a 'catalogue of received opinions.'[1]

In the 1860's, close to the end of his life, Mill was still combatting bits and pieces of intuitionism. In 1865 he published a lengthy refutation of the Scottish school of common sense theory of the independence of higher ideas usually called belief. Mill's last major effort of logic was a conventional sensationalism. Belief, he said, resulted from ideas arising from sensation which became confused with other ideas arising from still other sensations. The mind, unable to distinguish each of the separate, sensations, mistakenly assumed the higher idea or particular belief to be an original datum of consciousness.[2]

Frederick Denison Maurice knew Mill well. Usually polite and generous in intellectual dispute, Mill was a man of vehement convictions, desirous but incapable of entering into the mind of an opponent.[3] On the intuitionist question Mill was absolutely adamant. The 'asperity of tone', which he hinted was so uncharacteristic of his polemical manners, appeared whenever he thought he saw the doctrine of innate ideas. To admit the

[1] Mill, *Dissertations*, II, pp. 454, 451–2.
[2] Mill, *An Examination of Sir William Hamilton's Philosophy* (New York, 1873), I, chapters 11 and 12.
[3] Frederick Denison Maurice, *The Life of F. D. Maurice*, ed. Frederick Maurice (London, 1884), II, p. 610.

existence of an inherent moral instinct or moral sense; to speak of conscience or consciousness independent of phenomena; to grant even the remotest possibility of a native sense of shame or guilt; or to maintain that the activity of the mind itself could impose form on sensory impressions—even if the mind worked in strict subordination to the laws of its own existence—was to admit that utility was not the best determinant of right and wrong and to reinstate an oppressive authority. The difference between Intuition and Experience, Mill wrote in his *Autobiography*, 'is not a mere matter of abstract speculation; it is full of practical consequences, and lies at the foundation of all the greatest differences of practical opinion in an age of progress. The practical reformer has continually to demand that changes be made in things which are supported by powerful and widely-spread feelings, or to question the apparent necessity and indefeasibleness of established facts; and it is often an indispensable part of his argument to show, how those powerful feelings had their origin, and how those facts came to seem necessary and indefeasible. There is therefore a natural hostility between him and a philosophy which discourages the explanation of feelings and moral facts by circumstances and association, and prefers to treat them as ultimate elements of human nature; a philosophy which is addicted to holding up favourite doctrines as intuitive truths, and deems intuition to be the voice of Nature and of God, speaking with an authority higher than that of our reason.'[1]

Mill frequently wrote as if intuitionism was a more influential philosophical theory than utility. His replies to opponents carry the tone of a man who is certain the cause of reform is in imminent danger. In view of the actual influence of utilitarianism in his own time, Mill's anxiety seems unwarranted and excessive, unless it indicates another and greater fear. Despite his attacks on philosophical Germanizing, Mill had almost to concede that Kantian philosophy solved the problems which disturbed him the most. Paradoxically the intuitionist definition of conscience yielded free will; in the Victorian debate this meant freedom from pure experience and from society, if not freedom from divine will and intention. The utilitarian definition of

[1] Mill, *Autobiography*, p. 232.

conscience produced a state of conformity and dependence. Conscience, wrote the utilitarian Alexander Bain, is an idea which derives from sensation, 'an imitation within ourselves of the government without us . . . conscience . . . reproduces, in the maturity of the mind a facsimile of the systems of government as practiced around.' External authority was 'the genuine type and original of moral authority within.'[1] In this conclusion lay the other half of utilitarian theory, the neglected argument of Bentham's *Deontology* with its stress on normative behaviour,[2] forgotten or muted in the more exhilarating task of devising revolutionary programmes. Intuitional morality might very well be one support of conservative philosophy, but Mill still suspected that the mental laws governing duplex and complex associations were by no means as perfect a guarantee of individual liberty as he had been led to suppose.

Doubts weighed upon Mill's mind and blunted his zeal. Even when he wrote his youthful, caustic article answering Sedgwick he had mixed feelings. In a draft of the reply he included several pages of comment on the mistakes of the utilitarian moralists, but his father considered these personally damaging and persuaded him to omit them.[3] The suspicions could not be suppressed, however, and they emerged unmistakenly in the outburst of 1838 when Mill claimed that Bentham, in his desire to establish a political democracy, had 'exhausted all the resources of ingenuity in devising means for riveting the yoke of public opinion closer and closer around the necks of all public functionaries.'[4] Clearly there were things the old school of radicals did not understand.

Mill's doubts about philosophic radicalism, his decision to modernize the school and update its doctrines, were the direct consequences of his personal failure to find emotional satisfaction in the harsh intellectuality of his father's teachings. Still

---

[1] Quoted in Jerome B. Schneewind, 'Moral Problems and Moral Philosophy', *Victorian Studies Supplement*, IX (September, 1965), p. 37 n.

[2] Sheldon Wolin, *Politics and Vision* (London, 1961), p. 346. In his criticism of Whewell, Mill claimed that Bentham did not write the *Deontology*; but even if not, the compilers produced a legitimate deduction from utilitarian premises.

[3] Jack Stillinger, ed., *The Early Draft of John Stuart Mill's Autobiography* (Urbana, 1961), pp. 158 and 158 n.

[4] Mill, *On Bentham and Coleridge*, pp. 87–8.

more, they were the direct result of the changing social and political character of England, its movement away from an agrarian economy and aristocratic institutions to an industrial society. The world which Bentham had set about to reform was vanishing, there could be no doubt of it. To be sure, aristocrats could still be influential in government, a whig theory of leadership was perfectly compatible with utility; but it was certainly no longer possible for an aristocracy to rule simply in its own class interest. The guiding principle had to be the greatest happiness for the greatest number.

When Mill stepped out into the London intellectual world after the first reform bill, he no longer saw the aristocracy as a threat to progress. Landed families still dominated politics, but the tendency, he thought, was for their influence to decrease. A democratic electorate and a representative parliament were a long way from realization, but Mill was inclined to regard their appearance as almost momentary. His thoughts were drawn to the manufacturers and businessmen who were getting and spending. To them were allotted the tasks of defining liberty, of providing leaders and of raising the general cultural standard.

Mill invariably became depressed when he reflected on the qualifications for guidance and leadership that the new public possessed. He began to discover within himself sentiments which a utilitarian should have instantly disowned. The aristocracy, he sentimentalized, had achieved a certain high standard of aesthetic refinement, a certain sensitivity of behaviour from centuries of experience. By contrast—he was prone to generalize —the middle classes were too newly risen, had come into social and economic influence too quickly to possess a sense of the possibilities of social improvement. Aesthetic, ethical and social qualities became at times totally confused in Mill's mind; artistic and literary refinement were almost equated with moral tolerance and broad-mindedness. Even in the *Autobiography*, which looked back in partial detachment to the formative influences of his life, Mill could not dismiss the mood of the thirties. He recalled Bentham's sojourn at Ford Abbey in Devonshire—'the spacious and lofty rooms, of this fine old place' —and he could not resist a comparison to 'the mean and cramped externals of English middle class life'. The old buildings 'gave the sentiment of a larger and freer existence'. Nothing, he was finally led on to say, 'contributes more to nourish elevation of sentiment in a people, than the large and free character of their habitations.'[1] The aristocracy ceased to be tyrants. Liberty was jeopardized and cultural standards threatened by the middle classes. Armed with Bentham's ethical theories, push-pin being as good as poetry, they were certain to place a Saul among the prophets.

Utilitarians, however, were accustomed to thinking in terms of paradoxes. If push-pin as good as poetry invalidated the idea of a hierarchy of cultural values, it was at the same time a possible solution to Mill's dilemmas. There was, he realized, a saving relativism implicit in association psychology. In the sensational theory, individual differences were as numerous and varied as the experiences or education or history of the individual himself. The spectre of a unified public opinion could successfully be prevented if each individual's environmental experiences were satisfactorily diversified.

Environment—what made men happy or caused them pain—was the source of all Mill's difficulties. It was environment that decided behaviour, it was environment that determined belief and accounted for change. It was environment that produced a society of free and independent men or a society of conformists and slaves. Whoever controlled environment controlled behaviour.

There was nothing particularly new in the realization that environmental influences were the sole determinants of conduct. All the theorists of association psychology had established environment as the foundation of utility doctrine, yet few had examined environmental ramifications to Mill's satisfaction. His troubled state of mind and his fears that an advancing mass mediocrity would cancel the highest achievements of civilization did not leave him content with environmental theory as it had been taught him. The explanations of association psychology which posited the absolute tyranny of environment were no more comforting to Mill than the arguments for innate capacities and fundamental categories. He was in a hopeless middle position, needing and fearing environment at one and the same time.

[1] Mill, *Autobiography*, pp. 46–7.

This impasse dictated his next logical move. He would re-examine the problem of how environment conditioned behaviour. He would try to determine the extent to which external influences formed individual and collective character. He would attempt to decide how likely it was that the actual course of behaviour could be predicted and what decisions would encourage behaviour most in agreement with society's goals. It was entirely possible that previous utilitarian theorists had neglected important ingredients of experiential doctrine, perhaps over-estimating the degree of social control possible under environmentalism; perhaps he had exaggerated the conformist tendencies which he thought characteristic of the middle classes. He would, however, have to be careful; he had to be certain that his possible revision of environmentalism did not leave an opening to the intuitionists. He had to be sure that nothing was conceded to his opponents and their seductive élitist position.

It was in *A System of Logic*, published in 1843, that Mill commenced a systematic analysis of the limits of environment on behaviour. He had to dispose of two problems about which little was known but which might—precisely because utilitarians could not easily explain them—offer scientific support to intuitional philosophy. The problems involved behaviour conditioned by neurophysiological factors and behaviour classified as instinct. In his discussions of the laws of mind, Mill took up the question of physiological or bodily differences which could not be attributed to sensualism. Although he had to admit that there was a general state of ignorance about neurology, he dismissed its possible effects on behaviour by a rigid sensational argument. Organic or bodily differences, he maintained, affected the intensity of an idea rather than the actual quality of the idea. Although it was possible that the intensity of an experience itself might even lead to 'different *qualities* of mind, different types of mental character,'[1] it could never be proven that the ideas which were intensified by bodily experiences were in themselves generated by physiological operations.

Neurology was a problem which had come to the attention of utilitarians before and upon which a body of speculation existed; but when Mill turned to the problem of instincts he

[1] John Stuart Mill, *A System of Logic* (London, 1843), II, pp. 507–8.

found a category of 'mental facts' for which association psychology by itself provided no satisfactory explanation. He supposed instincts to be phenomena of the body similar to those described in neurology; and no doubt he would have left the subject alone had he not engaged in a curious debate with Samuel Bailey, a businessman, economist and banker who produced in 1842 an extensive critique of Berkeley's theory of vision in lower animals. Bailey appeared to be a phenomenalist like the utilitarians, but Mill suspected after his experiences with Sedgwick that any attack on Berkeley was probably inspired by a lurking intuitionism. He spared no pains to discredit Bailey's theories. Ironically enough, in refuting Bailey Mill came dangerously close to erecting his own theory of innate ideas, almost suggesting that animals possessed a prior notion or idea of the identity of an object whose distance was deceptive.[1] Rather clumsy in his handling of Bailey, Mill virtually avoided the problem of instincts in the first edition of his *Logic*. In subsequent editions he dismissed the subject with the dogmatic statement that it was an 'indisputable fact' that instincts could be modified or entirely conquered in human beings as well as in some animals 'by other mental influences, and by education.'[2]

Mill next commenced a discussion of the influence of environment on character formation. In his reply to Sedgwick in 1835 he had called for the establishment of ethology, the science of education, the scientific study of behaviour, collective and individual. In the *Logic* he could do little more for ethology than sketch its dimensions, since the precise data ethology required were unobtainable at that time. Two general conclusions seemed warranted by his discussion of ethology. The first was that the course of individual or collective behaviour could never be predicted with ideal, scientific accuracy. Provided the social scientists had some knowledge of a man's individual character and some knowledge of the causes or circumstances acting upon him, prediction at best would only indicate *tendencies* of conduct.[3]

---

[1] Nicholas Pastore, 'Samuel Bailey's Critique of Berkeley's Theory of Vision', *Journal of the History of the Behavioral Sciences*, I (October, 1965), pp. 334–5, 334 n. Mill was equally at a loss on other occasions when he attempted to refute the intuitional theory of mathematics and found that he could not substitute a convincing experiential theory. See R. P. Anschutz, *The Philosophy of John Stuart Mill* (Oxford, 1953), pp. 157–63.

[2] Mill, *Logic* (London, 1851), II, p. 431.   [3] Ibid. (1843), II, p. 523.

Mill's second general conclusion was that environment was not the absolute tyrant he had supposed. The individual possessed a certain power to alter his own character; he was an intermediate agent in his own development. In confronting his environment, the individual acquired a sense of himself and his capacities and participated in his maturation.[1]

Both conclusions offered some relief from what, using Tocqueville's phrase, Mill was inclined to call the tyranny of the majority. And yet he had only won a Pyrrhic victory. For if he had shown that environmental influence might in some degree be resisted or that the course of human conduct was unpredictable enough to frustrate the attempts that might be made to channel it, he had not come appreciably closer to solving the other half of his dilemma. He had not derived from experientialism a means for deciding how superior intellectual and ethical standards could be recognized. Too much of his attention had been diverted to refuting the only theories that offered a solution to the problems of culture and leadership.

One other area of thought was open to him. Mill turned from logic to history, from experience regarded as material sensation to experience defined as cultural continuity. History for Mill was a convenient digression. It allowed him to avoid answering directly the question of how high standards were to be recognized by drawing his attention away from geometrical reasoning—deductions from first principles, man and society as logical constructs—to the analysis of man and society as dynamic and changing elements. Mill began to think more in terms of tradition, of the accumulation and preservation of values, than in terms of establishing institutions and values absolutely anew from philosophical principles. To create anew was the method of the older school of radicals. To preserve, to adapt, to modify, to incorporate into the happiness principle anything old or lasting that might be useful, was the method of the new.

The advantages of the historical approach to behaviour and change lay in a verification of the relativism of utility. The survival of institutions and beliefs, the multiple experiences bequeathed the present by the past, increased the number of sensational experiences that went into the formation of char-

[1] Ibid., p. 485. See also John Stuart Mill, *Utilitarianism, Liberty, and Representative Government* (New York and London, 1951), p. 158.

acter. Mill had worried about the revolutionary implications of utilitarianism. He now understood that the survival of the past was a factor which made the reconstruction and reform of society a complicated task and sufficiently subtle to vex the efforts of the most zealous reformer.

Two schools of historical thought were available to Mill. The first, the romantic school, descended from Burke to Coleridge where it had acquired important German ingredients. It had also gained popularity from the writings of tory novelists. The disadvantage of the romantic school, the factor which had rendered it alien to the older school of philosophic radicals, was its political conservatism. The romantics stressed historical experience at the expense of the present in order to discredit reform. Past arrangements were seen to embody a collective and cumulative wisdom with which it was foolish to tamper.

The second, the sociological or positive school, derived from the St. Simonians and Comte and seemed for a time very promising to Mill. History was defined as the laws of behaviour which were indispensable to the statesman who sought guidance for the future. The French school, with its emphasis on stages of historical experience, seemed to Mill more progressive than the romantic, until he discovered that the tendency of their efforts was to re-establish dogmatic authority with the assistance of a science of history. He became more wary of Comtean ideology, amending successive editions of the *Logic* in order to de-emphasize Comte's influence. As Mill's familiarity with historical thinking increased, he began to share some of the suspicions of his utilitarian predecessors who had found history such an obstacle to reform. He stopped short of abandoning history altogether. History had given him some assurance that the reformer ignored tradition at his own peril; but he would not go so far as to grant history equal status with utility doctrine. On several occasions he repeated that history could only corroborate and never independently establish the foundations of ethology.

It is well known that Coleridge's historiography especially intrigued the youthful Mill. From Coleridge Mill derived the fascinating notion that cultural continuity and reform might be combined in such a way as to provide a means for maintaining high standards of behaviour. Unlike Bentham, Coleridge looked to the form or idea of an institution before he looked to its practical deficiencies. It was an obviously conservative device, but attractive. Before Coleridge would destroy an institution, he would seek out its historical rather than its logical importance. 'What mode is there of determining whether a thing is fit to exist, without first considering what purposes it exists for, and whether it be still capable of fulfilling them?' was his formula.[1] Later Newman would apply this approach to the university, but the example which most intrigued Mill was the Anglican Church.

For Coleridge the Church was an historical idea and possessed an historical function: its purpose was to support and advance minority opinion, the 'arts against arms, or the serf against the signeur, peace against war, or spiritual principles and powers against the domination of animal force.'[2] It was true that the Church had once been the right arm of the monarchy and later the protégé of the aristocracy; but this departure from its true or historical function could be corrected. In the industrial age as in the feudal age the Church could be used to preserve traditional values or advance new ideas, even those certain to be unpopular. It could protect the dissident, yet assure his loyalty to society. The essence of the Church was independence, not political servility. Its endowments could be used to support and protect an intellectual élite whose function it was to set and preserve high cultural standards and criticize the shortcomings of society. The clergymen of the past would become the clerisy of the present—if need be, the *clercs* of the future.

In the 1830's, when Mill felt especially stifled by utilitarianism and its peculiar mixture of democracy and authoritarianism, the idea of an established, national institution, insulated from public opinion and free of specific class or religious interest was especially attractive. The clerisy seemed to be an ideal solution to the problem of leadership and standards. As he grew older, however, Mill toned down his youthful apostasy and became less interested in the clerisy *per se*. The idea of a special institution to house and protect the best educated people fell away as Mill saw the dangers of uniting all intellectuals in one easily-isolated institution. In *On Liberty*, his most famous state-

[1] Mill, *On Bentham and Coleridge*, pp. 140–1.
[2] Ibid., p. 135.

ment regarding unorthodox and even eccentric opinion, he advocated a plural solution to the problem of nonconformist behaviour. He scattered educated men throughout all the principal institutions, public and private, of Victorian society, so that none would suffer from want of talent, and so that all would check and balance each other's claims through the principle of competition.

The solution which guaranteed the liberty of minority opinion, however, destroyed the possibility of a satisfactory answer to Mill's second major problem. Having established a society of plural institutions as the best guarantee of free expression, Mill had given even more support to the utilitarian notion of the relativity of values. Checks and balances could not produce an élitist culture clearly recognized by all to have the highest standard of values. Intellectuals or the best educated would form only one group, provide only one standard, in a society composed of many groups professing many standards. Contained in his own theoretical framework, Mill could do little more with the problem of leadership than tinker with fancy franchises, a confession that he had come to a logical impasse. Indeed, his final and favourite argument for élitist values only underscores his failure to affirm on any absolute ground the cultural and ethical values he believed superior to those held by the greater mass of society. Heterodoxy, he had noted, had to be tolerated because one day it might become orthodoxy. This was a perfectly utilitarian solution; heterodox values possessed no intrinsic merit: they could be justified only by the notion that at some unknown point in the future they might become the values of the greatest number.

Mill claimed that he had remained a faithful utilitarian, but his loyalty had certainly been compromised by forty years of doubts, vacillation and ambivalence. He did not outgrow his youthful hesitations and continued to revise or re-examine utilitarian principles, sometimes to the annoyance of other utilitarians who did not find the same difficulties. Bain could never understand, for example, why Mill fussed so much over the exact philosophical character of memory.[1] Actually, as has been stated in a valuable work, Mill's utilitarianism had little

[1] Michael St. John Packe, *The Life of John Stuart Mill* (London, 1954), p. 441.

to do with happiness and nothing at all to do with pleasure.[1] Despite the doctrine of expediency, he had come to believe in the necessity for disinterested action, for duty and self-sacrifice as ends, conceivably painful ends, in themselves.[2] While disinterested self-sacrifice undertaken in the name of general happiness might seem in one sense to preserve utility as the standard, in actuality it contradicted the corollary of an identity of interests between the individual and society. No man, the older utilitarians had argued, ever behaved from truly altruistic motives, for no man could possibly be happy if his views profoundly differed from society's. The old school of radicals, Mill concluded, professed to understand happiness. By their social and political doctrines, however, they had helped create a situation which made happiness difficult to obtain. By their theories of behaviour they had almost made the necessity for pain a secondary end.

2.

In the 1850's and 1860's, as Mill continued to struggle with some of the more unsettling implications of utilitarianism, Matthew Arnold, Professor of Poetry at Oxford from 1857 to 1867, joined in the warning that material prosperity did not automatically yield high cultural values. Unlike Mill, Arnold did not have to disentangle his values from a utilitarian past. His father, Dr. Arnold, the great Rugby headmaster and Oxford professor, detested utilitarianism and took care to see that his sons were spared its contagion. In Newman's Oxford, Matthew had been almost completely insulated from philosophical radicalism. He never had to reconcile its internal contradictions. Cultural and ethical relativism, therefore, had never frustrated him as it frustrated Mill. Arnold knew which values were superior and which qualities were suited to leadership, 'the best that has been thought and known,' he said. His ideal was the holistic principle of eighteenth-century society, where standards of behaviour were set by the aristocracy and where the doors to acceptance were closed against martyrs, saints, don quixotes and other fanatics mounted on hobby-horses likely to disrupt established ties and delude sensible men. Mill, com-

[1] Anschutz, p. 18. [2] *Logic* (1851), II, pp. 526–7.

mitted to a philosophical doctrine which guaranteed him at least half of his goals, inevitably settled for compromise. If moral relativism prevented him from forming an élite responsible for identifying and preserving the highest achievements of civilization, it also prevented others from establishing the rule of unquestioned authority. If relativism bestowed value upon mediocrity, it also ensured the survival of unpopular opinion.

Arnold was neither attracted by the relativity of values nor pleased by the joint appearance of mediocrity and excellence. Compromise, in his opinion, was failure; anything less than excellence was tantamount to decadence. Mill at least had found a place for the individual in the plural society; intellectuals like himself could play a role, if not the foremost role. Arnold rejected this solution. If intellectuals could not play the foremost role, there was no other role worth having, there was no other place suited to their qualifications. Exile was the only alternative.

Arnold expressed this conclusion in his poetry of the 1850's. In the 'Stanzas from the Grande Chartreuse' he had sensed his distance from the modern world, placing himself among the children beneath the abbey wall who were unsuited for the life of 'action and pleasure' required by contemporary society.[1] The theme of estrangement, set off by images of darkness, helplessness and finally hysteria, was continued in *Dover Beach*, the most widely reprinted poem in the English language. *Dover Beach* contained Arnold's statement of the imperfection of the actual or adult world. In a series of formal, poetic denials of reality he related a child's demand for a society of total perfection and security, where light would dispel darkness.[2] By 1867, the year which saw the publication of Arnold's Oxford farewell lecture, 'Culture and its Enemies'—better known as 'Sweetness and Light', the opening essay of *Culture and Anarchy*—Arnold's state of alienation from himself and from the values of mid-Victorian society was fully established. As he admitted in despair, he found no place for himself in Victorian society,

[1] David J. Delaura, 'Matthew Arnold and John Henry Newman: The "Oxford Sentiment" and the Religion of the Future', *Texas Studies in Literature and Language, Supplement*, VI (1965), p. 585.

[2] Norman N. Holland, 'Psychological Depths and "Dover Beach" ', *Victorian Studies Supplement*, IX (September, 1965), pp. 20–1, 27.

he saw no class or group with which to identify, no function he could perform which gave him satisfaction and defined his usefulness. The unsatisfactory cultural state of society, he concluded, had inevitably brought about his own decline.

English society appeared hopelessly divided into ruinous social divisions and conflicts. The pluralism which Mill accepted as a negative solution to the problems of individualism and the maintenance of high cultural standards was for Arnold symptomatic of the decay of English civilization. Plural competition only produced wasted energy, acrimonious debate, intolerance and selfish behaviour. Arnold could not see the possibilities for equilibrium contained in Mill's concept of a society in which one group or institution balanced off the claims of another. He saw only instability, disintegration and anarchy. There was no virtue in disagreement: therefore the slightest example of disorder took on the proportions of a major disturbance or indicated the presence of a malignant organism. All self-restraint had gone out of English life; all notions of duty and responsibility had suddenly become unfashionable.

No class cared any longer for the maintenance of public law and order, neither the barbarian-aristocrats, the philistine-middle classes,[1] nor the populace who were still an unknown quantity but very apt to become middle class. Arnold was thoroughly depressed by an episode in 1866 when the railings in Hyde Park were pulled down by a group of London roughs and the flower beds trampled. He exaggerated the importance of the episode and overdramatized the failure of constituted authority–'the trembling hands of our Barbarian Home Secretaries and the feeble knees of our Philistine Alderman-Colonels'[2]–to punish the offenders swiftly and surely. In addition, John Bright's demagogic campaign on behalf of franchise reform and the militancy of the Reform League convinced him that the middle classes preferred civil disobedience to stability. The 1867 franchise reform did nothing to allay his suspicions that the higher values which he advocated had no hope of immediate adoption.

[1] Matthew Arnold, *Culture and Anarchy* (Cambridge, 1961), p. 61: 'the passing generations of industrialists, forming, for the most part, the stout main body of Philistinism.'
[2] Ibid., p. 205.

The more Arnold convinced himself that England was in a state of spiritual anarchy and total disobedience, the more did he stress the need for authority, plead for individual self-restraint and deplore each man doing as he likes. As the institutions and classes responsible for the maintenance of public order proved increasingly helpless, Arnold cast about for a new sovereign authority which would end anarchy, discredit each man doing as he likes, put down the warring classes and heal the social divisions. Only under a new, absolute authority would England regain a sense of national purpose and recover her unity. Without absolute authority, without 'a firm and settled course of public order', it was impossible for 'man . . . to bring to maturity anything precious and lasting now, or to found anything precious and lasting for the future.'[1] The restoration of the holistic ideal and the ressurection of high moral and cultural values depended upon the re-establishment of authority.

Having spoken of the need for authority, however, it remained for Arnold to demonstrate how authority was to be regained, where it was to be found, how it was to be installed. Where was 'the firm and intelligible law of things' so necessary to the urgent task of national recovery? Church and State were the usual categories in which political theorists of the Coleridgean tradition spoke of authority. Church and State together throughout the eighteenth century had constituted the socio-moral bases of English society. Church and State contained, in Coleridgean language, the ideas or principles of authority. Where were Church and State now in the era of liberals, nonconformists, industrialists and philistines?

The Church had established authority through comprehension and unity. At one time the Anglican Church had been national in character, containing under one roof a wide variety of religious disagreement and opinion. 'One may say,' Arnold observed, 'that to be reared a member of a national Church is in itself a lesson of religious moderation.'[2] Moderation in turn removed the need to defend particularistic interests, encouraged the relaxed frame of mind which enabled men to look beyond their immediate concerns and selfish aims to a fuller meaning of existence, to see life clearly and see it whole: 'The great works by which, not only in literature, art and

[1] Ibid., p. 204.　　　　　　　　　[2] Ibid., p. 15.

science generally, but in religion itself, the human spirit has manifested its approaches to totality, and to a full, harmonious, perfection, and by which it stimulates and helps forward the world's general perfection, come . . . from men who either belong to Establishments or have been trained in them. . . . The fruitful men of English Puritanism and Nonconformity are men who were trained within the pale of the Establishment, – Milton, Baxter, Wesley. A generation or two outside the Establishment, and Puritanism produces men of national mark no more. With the same doctrine and discipline, men of national mark are produced in Scotland; but in an Establishment.'[1]

The future of establishments looked bleak in the England of the 1860's. When *Culture and Anarchy* appeared, the Protestant church in Ireland had been disestablished due to the influence of John Bright's nonconformists – 'the strength of the Liberal majority in the House of Commons.' The national mind, Arnold said, had declared itself in favour of religious toleration and freedom of conscience; but the disestablishment of the Irish Church revealed its true character. Reason and justice demanded, and religious toleration required, that the property of the Irish Church be fairly apportioned among the principal religious communions of the island, or that the major religion of Ireland be endowed and established. Reason, justice and toleration required that the Catholics receive 'their fair and reasonable share of Church property;' but reason, justice and toleration were not considerations that moved the dissenting conscience or concerned the national mind.[2]

Disestablishment, in fact, was just as much a symptom of anarchy – as much the destruction of recognized and permanent authority – as broken park railings and unsafe streets. Unfortunately there was no longer any possibility that authority might come from religion and the Church. Religion had ceased rendering any service to civilization. Religion had raised man from savage to human, had tamed his animality by repressing his instinctual passions and controlling his libidinous urges. This historical function performed, religion changed from a civilizing to a destructive force. Religion in general and sectarian protestantism in particular had made men querulous and opinionated. Sectarian conflict prevented the establishment of a unified

---

[1] Ibid., p. 13, also pp. 20–1.   [2] Ibid., pp. 166–9.

system of national education and led to Hebraised behaviour – a sense of sin and strictness of conscience.

At first Arnold spoke of Hebraised behaviour or Hebraism with praise. He was, he said, in absolute accord with its final aim, no less than man's perfection or salvation. On two separate, critical occasions in the history of the western world – in antiquity and in the renaissance – Hebraism had served as a necessary check to spiritual unbalance. As he continued to discuss Hebraism, however, all the while maintaining that its aim and end were august and admirable, Arnold began to connect Hebraism with the fundamental problems of decay and disorder in his own time. We want fire and strength, the Cambridge philosopher Henry Sidgwick had replied to Arnold's plea for reasonableness in 'Sweetness and Light'. Yes, answered Arnold, but not at this time. The historical moment for fire and strength had passed. 'The law and science . . . of things as they really are' could not be learned from Hebraism, as reason, justice and toleration could not be learned from nonconformity. Hebraism, in fact, turned out to be a side stream checking 'the main stream of man's advance,' contravening 'the natural order,' and producing, 'as such contravention always must produce, a certain confusion and false movement, of which we are now beginning to feel, in almost every direction, the inconvenience.'[1]

Arnold had assured his Hebraic reader that the end of Hebraism was perfection; but it was no such thing. It was a digression, it was unnatural, finally it must produce imperfection itself. It is only necessary to read Arnold's discussion of the concept of sin to understand why the end of Hebraism could never be perfection. Hebraism operated through a sense of sin and guilt. Ostensibly sin was the means by which perfection was to be reached, for how else could the sinner be made to amend his ways and pursue the path of right conduct which would lead to salvation? But Hebraism, by continually reiterating the sinfulness of man, succeeded only in making perfection remote and unobtainable. Was it Carlyle who said that Socrates was terribly at ease in Zion? No matter, Arnold answered. The saying, whether or not Carlyle's, suggested another: 'Hebraism . . . has always been severely pre-occupied with an awful sense of the impossibility of being at ease in Zion; of the difficulties which

[1] Ibid., p. 143.

oppose themselves to man's pursuit or attainment of that perfection of which Socrates talks so hopefully, and, as from this point of view one might almost say, so glibly.'[1] The reader had certainly been misled. Hebraism was not the means to perfection at all but rather, in Dr. Pusey's loathesome image, 'a hideous hunchback seated on our shoulders, and which it is the main business of our lives to hate and oppose.'[2]

There was a final irony in Arnold's description of Hebraism. He had said that Hebraism contained the principle of obedience, that the purpose of sin and strictness of conscience was to control behaviour, prevent excess and teach balance. If this were true, then how could Arnold connect anarchy, disobedience, trampled flower beds, loss of self-restraint and social conflict with nonconformists who were the principal inheritors of the Hebraic conscience? Surely he had been right at the outset when he said that the end and aim of Hebraism were perfection, for perfection in Arnold's view was no less than obedience and authority. The irony lay in the fact that Hebraism had substituted means for ends. Hebraism did not regard obedience as a means to obtaining perfection but as an end in itself, much as sin and guilt were no longer a means to salvation but a total preoccupation. Obedience in Hebraism meant adherence to a narrow code of conduct, to a set of rules which were known, and unlike perfection, did not have to be sought. Perfection, Arnold reiterated, was a process of growth and self-realization involving a continuous reappraisal of standards. Hebraism did not advocate the pursuit of perfection, for Hebraism professed to know already what perfection was. As rules and obedience to rules were the strict aims of Hebraism, intolerance and a disputatious temper were the inevitable products, for the Hebraic conscience would never admit that any other definition of conduct or any other rules possessed validity. Dogmatic opinions, fixed moral laws, a passionate conviction of being right, leading in the long run to purely mechanical conduct, had become the historical characteristics of Hebraism and the reasons why Hebraism, once a means to perfection, was itself a cause of imperfection and a source of England's spiritual decay. Hebraism was no defence against 'the growth of commercial immorality in our serious middle class, of the melting away of habits of strict

[1] Ibid., p. 135   [2] Ibid., p. 159.

probity before the temptation to get quickly rich and to cut a figure in the world.'[1] Hebraism began as authority but ended as anarchy.

Arnold proposed an alternative to Hebraism, the other means to perfection. It was to complement Hebraism, but since he had invalidated Hebraism completely, it was really an antidote and replacement. The alternative was Hellenism, or really Atticism, since Sparticism had been taken over by the public schools after the Crimean War; and Arnold had grave reservations about public schools. Unlike Hebraism, which demanded obedience and thus led man away from nature and, Arnold implied, natural behaviour, Hellenism produced 'that irresistible return of humanity to nature and to seeing things as they are.'[2] Hebraism was strictness of conscience; but Hellenism was spontaneity of consciousness, the discovery of self and the liberation of natural feelings, 'the letting a free play of thought live and flow around all our activity, the indisposition to allow one side of our activity to stand as so all important and all sufficing that it makes other sides indifferent.'[3]

Arnold's Hellene was no other than the renaissance man which European writers of the 1860's like Burckhardt had discovered and opposed to the *homo oeconomicus* of the machine age; he was the Italian of the quattrocento who had discovered himself and sought his own cultural perfection. Sonneteer, artist, parodist, biographer, scientist, musician, courtier, an aristocratic gentleman rather than a feudal warrior, he had sprung to life in the mid-nineteenth century as quickly as he was imagined to have burst upon the slow, hesitant, anonymous medieval world. He was the symbol of the man reborn and regenerated, not after death as Hebraism stipulated, but in life, with perfection an immediate and attainable end rather than an eschatological reward. The Hellene or renaissance man was not a moral, nonconformist gentleman, laced to duty by a sense of sin and obedience; he was a man who had to experience sin to understand perfection.

Arnold had opposed Hellenism to Hebraism, and he had in the course of his argument virtually identified Hebraism with anarchy. With the agonistic, or really eristic method of his argument, Hellenism—the opposite of Hebraism—had actually

---

[1] Ibid.   [2] Ibid., p. 141.   [3] Ibid., p. 158.

come to stand for the principle of authority. But Arnold had called his famous book *Culture and Anarchy*, not *Authority and Anarchy*. It would appear he was speaking about a particular kind of authority which he called culture. As he developed his critique of English values, culture came to be the same as Hellenism, for which he devised a long string of synonyms: 'right reason and the will of God,' 'sweetness and light' (which he took from Swift and which Newman too had used), 'the firm and intelligible law of things,' 'the best that has been thought and known.'

Culture had to be sought, and it was the search rather than the end which distinguished the liberal and critical intelligence. Mill had spoken in the same vein when he stated that the best the intelligent man could do was follow the argument withersoever it went, the stress being on the process rather than on its conclusion. To stop at this point, however, would be to miss the implications of Arnold's argument. He had started from the assumption that England was in a condition of spiritual anarchy which tended to produce social anarchy, and that the remedy to degeneration was to be found in authority. Arnold defined culture as an on-going process, he spoke about the *pursuit* of perfection, but his mind was on perfection as an end, that is, the pursuit of perfection was to yield authority. Means and ends were as confused in Arnold's Hellenism as he said they were in Hebraism. *Culture and Anarchy* was the name of his book, but *Authority and Anarchy* was what he meant. Part of a passage which he suppressed in subsequent editions of his book[1] reveals his mind: 'I remember my father, in one of his unpublished letters written more than forty years ago, when the political and social state of the country was gloomy and troubled, and there were riots in many places, goes on, after strongly insisting on the badness and foolishness of the government, and on the harm and dangerousness of our feudal and aristocratical constitution of society, and ends thus: "As for rioting, the old Roman way of dealing with *that* is always the right one; flog the rank and file, and fling the ringleaders from the Tarpeian Rock!" And this opinion we can never forsake, however our Liberal friends may think a little rioting, and what they call popular demonstrations, useful sometimes to their own interests and to the interests of the

[1] Lionel Trilling, *Matthew Arnold* (New York, 1939), p. 278.

valuable practical operations they have in hand, and however they may preach the right of an Englishman to be left to do as far as possible what he likes, and the duty of his government to indulge him and connive as much as possible and abstain from all harshness of repression. And even when they artfully show us operations which are undoubtedly precious, such as the abolition of the slave-trade, and ask us if, for their sake, foolish and obstinate governments may not wholesomely be frightened by a little disturbance, the good design in view and the difficulty of overcoming opposition to it being considered,—still we say no, and that monster processions in the streets and forcible irruptions into the parks, even in professed support of this good design, ought to be unflinchingly forbidden and repressed; and that far more is lost than is gained by permitting them.'[1]

'We want an authority,' Arnold wrote, 'and we find nothing but jealous classes, checks, and a deadlock.'[2] Where was an authority to be found? If not in the Church, there was only one other place, the State. 'Culture,' Arnold continued, 'suggests the idea of *the State*.'[3]

The idea of the State, the principle of authority—the language was Coleridgean. Culture *suggests* the idea of the State, but culture was no less than the State itself. It had once been customary for thinkers to speak of religious values as sacred; but religion, in Arnold's eyes, had been profaned by Hebraism and did not deserve men's worship. For Arnold the mystery that religion had once conveyed, the sense of the awful and wonderful which worship entailed, the power of regeneration and rebirth with which religion had once been equipped, was now transferred to the State. 'In our eyes, the very framework and exterior of the State . . . is sacred.'[4]

When speaking of the State, however, Arnold temporarily forgot that the selfsame nonconformists whose motto was the dissidence of dissent and whose anarchic handiwork could be seen in the disestablishment of the Irish Church were a fundamental part of the State. The State, and 'whoever may administer the State, is sacred; and culture is the most resolute enemy of anarchy, because of the great hopes and designs for the State

---

[1] *Culture and Anarchy*, pp. 203–4.   [2] Ibid., p. 96.
[3] Ibid.   [4] Ibid., p. 204.

which culture teaches us to nourish.'[1] Perfection, right reason, culture, Hellenism were finally no less than the State. Arnold could write about 'spontaneity of consciousness,' the liberation of the natural self, the free play of the mind; but when he wrote of the 'idea of a *State*, of the nation in its collective and corporate character,' he spoke of it as 'controlling, as government, the free swing of this or that of one of its members in the name of the higher reason of all of them, his own as well as that of others.'[2] The 'free swing of this or that' was not, after all, the solution to anarchy, for that was simply each man doing as he likes.

Arnold's equation of culture, perfection, authority and the State was the psychological result of the projection of his own alienated state of mind into the social situation. Having lost his class identity and having withdrawn from the religious and moral authority under which he had been raised, Arnold merged his own personality with an abstraction called the State. The State was classless, nondenominational, unified. The State was totally the opposite of anarchy. In identifying culture as the State, Arnold had ended his search for a new absolute authority; he had recreated the adult world to gain the perfection it lacked, and he had set at rest the warring halves within him.

The unity which Arnold sought for English society exactly duplicated the unity he sought for himself. The struggle between nonconformists and Anglicans, philistines and barbarians, industrialists and landed aristocrats, was also a struggle between the best and the worst qualities in each class; this was repeated as a struggle within Arnold himself between an 'ordinary self' and a 'best self' as he called them. By 'ordinary self' Arnold meant private judgment, individualism, class consciousness and class interests, which he contrasted to the best, cultivated or classless self which looked to standards and values outside itself.[3] Each class within English society contained best and ordinary selves, and no class had succeeded in liberating the best selves within it. The barbarians had come closest (Arnold had a special affection for them; as a Balliol undergraduate he had affected an aristocratic style, earning a reputation as a dandy)

[1] Ibid.   [2] Ibid., p. 81.   [3] Ibid., pp. 105–9.

but they were really triflers, possessing sweetness but not light, only the 'shadow of true refinement'.[1] The aristocratic style 'consisted principally in outward gifts and graces, in looks, manners, accomplishments, prowess. The chief inward gifts which had part in it were the most exterior, so to speak, of inward gifts, those which come nearest to outward ones; they were courage, a high spirit, self-confidence. Far within, and unawakened, lay a whole range of powers of thought and feeling, to which these interesting productions of nature had, from the circumstances of their life, no access.'[2] To this Dr. Arnold might have added that by retaining some semblance of the chivalric code of individual honour and personal glory, the barbarians, for all their sweetness, were convicted of encouraging anarchy.[3]

Deeply ambivalent, Arnold alternated between a sense of impotence—culture was defeated, even the working classes, the hope of the future, would become philistines[4]—and a sense of omnipotence–John Henry Newman's Oxford, 'in defeat, in isolation, in want of hold upon the modern world,' had nevertheless undermined 'the hideous and grotesque illusions of middle-class Protestantism'[5] to prepare the way for the new, democratic challenge. The hope of the future lay in those men of every class who were like Arnold himself, *aliens* he called them, 'persons who are mainly led, not by their class spirit, but by a general *humane* spirit, by the love of human perfection,'[6] who struggled with their ordinary self and waited for the new powerful authority of the State to transform their alien self into a best self, to move them out of a class into a classless society where they would no longer be alone. If the individual identified himself with the State–'or organ of our collective best self, or our national right reason'[7]–instead of a particular class, if through culture he replaced his Hebraic or anarchic conscience with an internal 'firm State power,' then the self and the nation would no longer be divided. 'By our every-day selves . . . we are separate, personal, at war. . . . But by our *best self* we are united, impersonal, at harmony.'[8]

Behind Arnold's best self lay Newman's *beau ideal*, the gentleman of spiritual balance and moderate temper. The

---

[1] Ibid., p. 83. [2] Ibid., p. 103. [3] Trilling, p.54.
[4] *Culture and Anarchy*, p. 65. [5] Ibid., p. 63. [6] Ibid., p. 109.
[7] Ibid., p. 97. [8] Ibid., p. 95.

gentleman is modest and self-effacing, tolerant, patient, re-signed, courteous, gracious, dispassionate, a man of Hellenic contemplation rather than Hebraic action: 'Nowhere shall we find greater candour, consideration, indulgence: he throws himself into the minds of his opponents, he accounts for their mistakes. He knows the weakness of human reason as well as its strength, its province and its limits. If he be an unbeliever, he will be too profound and large-minded to ridicule religion or to act against it; he is too wise to be a dogmatist or fanatic in his infidelity. . . . He is a friend of religious toleration, and that, not only because his philosophy has taught him to look on all forms of faith with an impartial eye, but also from the gentle-ness and effeminacy of feeling, which is the attendant on civiliza-tion.'[1]

The gentleman restrains his impulses and resists the tempta-tion to do as he likes, for even if he has no formal religion or cannot accept the Christian God, he acknowledges the principle of a higher authority which religion suggests and submits to the edifying influence of a greater truth: 'His religion is one of imagination and sentiment; it is the embodiment of those ideas of the sublime, majestic, and beautiful, without which there can be no large philosophy. Sometimes he acknowledges the being of God, sometimes he invests an unknown principle or quality with the attributes of perfection.'[2]

Newman's concept of the gentleman was a defensive mechan-ism, a means by which the reality of liberal, philistine, industrial civilization might be ignored or tolerated without the alienated self losing his sense of inner security and balance. The gentle-man might be alienated, but he need not be *déraciné*. Newman's gentleman, issuing forth from the universities, was to be equipped with the qualities which would enable him to accept with quiet resignation the acrimony and wasted energy of a materialist society.[3] Sustained by the pursuit of perfection, fortified by right reason and the firm intelligible law of things,

[1] John Henry Newman, *The Idea of a University* (New York, 1962), pp. 218–19.

[2] Ibid., p. 219.

[3] 'If he engages in controversy of any kind, his disciplined intellect pre-serves him from the blundering discourtesy of better, perhaps, but less educated minds; who, like blunt weapons, tear and hack instead of cutting clean, who mistake the point in argument, waste their strength on trifles,

under no authority but the highest authority, the very idea of authority itself, Newman's gentleman could look out upon the world in calm of mind, all passion spent.

In the 1860's Arnold accepted Newman's conclusions as a defence against the disturbing tendencies of his age, and in *Culture and Anarchy* he advocated withdrawal, the philosophy of self-renouncement and consolation. He preached the need for sweetness and light, at the same time expressing his confidence that culture would eventually conquer and prove him a prophet. Accused by the positivists and utilitarians of inaction and effeminacy,[1] Arnold turned the other cheek: 'Plenty of people there will be without us–country gentlemen in search of a club, demagogues in search of a tub, lawyers in search of a place, industrialists in search of gentility,–who will come from the east and from the west, and will sit down at that Thyesteän banquet of clap-trap which English public life for these many years past has been. . . . But we are sure that the endeavour to reach, through culture, the firm intelligible law of things,– we are sure that the detaching ourselves from our stock notions and habits,–that a more free play of consciousness, an increased desire for sweetness and light . . . is the master-impulse even now of the life of our nation and of humanity,–somewhat obscurely perhaps for this actual moment, but decisively and certainly for the immediate future; and that those who work for this are the sovereign educators.'[2]

Arnold considered Mill a sovereign educator too; but Mill's solution to the crisis summarized in Arnold's muted cannibalistic image was profoundly different. Mill desired a plural society in order to put down conformity and to prevent the establishment of any absolute authority in matters of culture or politics. Because Mill feared the State as a potential tyrant, he allowed it a limited role in the organization of civil society and made it just another of the institutions in a society of checks and balances. Against his own egalitarian sentiments, he stated that

---

misconceive their adversary, and leave the question more involved than they find it.' Ibid., p. 218.

[1] Henry Sidgwick, 'The Prophet of Culture', *Macmillan's Magazine*, XVI (August, 1867), pp. 271–80; Frederic Harrison, 'Culture: a Dialogue', *The Fortnightly Review*, VIII (November, 1867), pp. 603–14.

[2] *Culture and Anarchy*, pp. 209–12.

education, the foremost ingredient in character formation, had to be in the hands of both public and private authorities, so that no single body would possess the undisputed right to impose its values on society.

Arnold wanted conformity, unity through the State, in order to put down pluralism and prevent each man doing as he likes. Arnold did not desire the free swing of this or that, for the free swing of this or that produced the dissidence of dissent and civil disobedience. For Arnold the State was the only means by which the reign of culture could be assured and the only mechanism for encouraging the pursuit of perfection. An admirer of continental systems of State-supported education, he advocated the establishment of a national system of education for the benefit of all citizens and not merely those who could pay. It would appear, then, that Arnold was less willing to compromise the democratic principle than Mill, who knew that in the circumstances of the 1860's the retention of a strong system of private education would weaken efforts to establish publicly-supported schools. But to see the Arnold of the 1860's as a democrat is to miss the peculiar character of Arnold's definition of equal opportunity. If the State was assigned the task of defining character, if the State and the best self were one and the same and Hellenism the cultural standard for both, then all individuals would be in a condition of perfect equality, for all would have lost their individual identity, none would be free to follow the argument withersoever it went. Arnold's best self, his real self, was an ideal self flourishing in a world in which everyone was a best self, since ordinary selves had ceased to exist. No longer able to sustain the psychological burden of an alienated and divided self, Arnold demanded the annihilation of class, personality and individual identity so that the State or culture might give him another self, a true self he said, but a false self Mill would have replied, unable to face reality.

Perhaps the difference between Arnold and Mill is best summarized in their views of Socrates, whom they deeply admired. For both, Socrates was the symbol of the search for truth and perfection, the embodiment of self-cultivation, the disinterested and persistent seeker of knowledge. But Arnold also regarded Socrates as a man of reflection who went to his death patiently and resignedly. It is fair to say that Mill saw

Socrates as a man of action like Pericles, able to stand in open defiance of public opinion, and even court his own death. Heroism was an active not a passive quality. 'The heroic,' Mill had once written, 'essentially consists in being ready, for a worthy object, to do and to suffer, but especially to do, what is painful or disagreeable: and whoever does not early learn to be capable of this, will never be a great character.'[1] In utter defiance of the logic of the pleasure principle, Mill concluded it was necessary not to bear pain but to seek it.

Mill and Arnold disagreed on ultimate questions of moral metaphysics. Was it possible that men of such profoundly antithetical intellectual traditions could agree on secondary ends? There were in fact notable areas of agreement between the leading representative of utilitarianism and the prophet of the new humanism. Both regarded the aristocratic domination of society as ended. Both saw the rise of industrial civilization and the rise of industrialists as a problem of culture. Both believed that standards of behaviour had fallen as a consequence of the appearance of philistines and that English society had reached a crisis stage in which the profit motive created, in Mill's phrase, 'the debilitating influences of the age'. Both were environmentalists. Believing that the individual was as good as the society which made him, that a decline in character was a telling symptom of social decay, they agreed that England required a regeneration of the individual and of society. Both agreed that education was the means by which social decay might be stopped and national rebirth accomplished. They even agreed, to a certain significant extent, on the nature of a liberal education. In the *London and Westminster Review* for April 1836, Mill stated that he doubted whether the vices of Oxford, Cambridge, Eton and Westminster, 'would be cured by bringing their studies into a closer connexion with what it is the fashion to term "the business of the world;" by dismissing the logic and classics which are still professedly taught, to substitute modern languages and experimental physics. We would have classics and logic taught far more really and deeply than at present, and we would add to them other studies more alien than any which yet exist to the "business of the world," but more germane to the great

[1] Mill, *Dissertations*, I, p. 180.

business of every rational being—the strengthening and enlarging of his own intellect and character.'[1]

In his inaugural address at St. Andrews thirty years later, Mill reiterated that the primary function of university education was to produce capable and cultivated human beings.

Here were secondary areas in which Mill and Arnold, otherwise so different, might agree. Common problems, the establishment of high moral and cultural standards, the necessity for leadership by the best educated, brought them together, as did a similar social background. Mill and Arnold were members of an intellectual aristocracy. Neither of them were men of business nor connected in any way to industrial families. Hence they spoke of philistines, the thirst of gain and the seductions of mammon. In this they resembled Cambridge dons who were also struggling with the implications of pluralism as they adjusted the university to changing social conditions.

[1] Ibid., p. 193.

CHAPTER 4

PROPHET OR SCEPTIC

1.

The era of Cambridge greatness, according to the *Scrutiny* critics, is unquestionably Henry Sidgwick's Cambridge, an era which it was their especial mission to recapture and restore. In their estimation Sidgwick's Cambridge was an heroic, undefiled and golden age which valued character and intellectual virtue to an extraordinarily high degree. By contrast the later Edwardian or Bloomsbury period is called an age of decline, in which frivolity, conceit and superficiality replaced the sensitivity and responsibility of the earlier period. Sidgwick himself is regarded as the embodiment of all that was valuable in those happier days, like *Scrutiny* in fact, the essential or pure Cambridge.[1] Such apotheosis is excessive and an oversimplification of the historical record, but there can be no doubt that *Scrutiny* is right to praise Sidgwick. He must be considered a central figure in any account of the generation of the 1860's. His hand, sometimes his inspiration, was in every major administrative or teaching reform in that critical period in which modern Cambridge was born. But of equal importance to the actual reforms Sidgwick encouraged or created, was his gentle, shy, witty and wise spirit, the unusually introspective and engaging mind which never ceased to comment on itself and on contemporaries. He has left behind a remarkable memoir, compiled from his letters and journals, which indicates–even with

[1] Q. D. Leavis, 'Henry Sidgwick's Cambridge', *Scrutiny*, XV (December, 1947), pp. 2–11. Also F. R. Leavis, 'Keynes, Lawrence and Cambridge', p. 259, and 'E. M. Forster', pp. 261–77, *The Common Pursuit* (Harmondsworth, 1962).

important biographical material undoubtedly suppressed by his wife and brother—his extraordinary self-awareness and provides one guide to the thinking and ambitions of his generation. With Sidgwick's assistance it may be possible to establish the essential tensions of the university world of the 1860's.

Sidgwick came from a clerical family. His father, the Reverend William Sidgwick, matriculated at Trinity in 1823 and subsequently became headmaster of Skipton Grammar School. His cousin, later brother-in-law, was E. W. Benson, Archbishop of Canterbury. In 1876 Sidgwick acquired still another brother-in-law of future prominence when he married Eleanor Balfour, sister of Arthur Balfour. Sidgwick was educated at Rugby during the period in which Benson was an assistant master, and Arnold's legacy of hard work and duty was still pronounced. The Rugby influence, especially as reinforced by Benson, never left him, and in Cambridge he was known to be a serious student, or in the jargon of the day, a reading man. His award was election to the Apostles, an arcane intellectual society for undergraduates considered to be the intellectual élite of Cambridge. Sidgwick's tenure as an undergraduate and junior fellow coincided with one of the most exciting intellectual periods of the nineteenth century, and he was soon completely absorbed in the writings of Mill, Comte, Spencer, Strauss, Renan, Carlyle, Matthew Arnold, George Eliot and Darwin, wandering freely from biological science to biblical scholarship, ethics and problems of proof. His extraordinary intellectual diet both stimulated and depressed him, since the questions raised by his reading could never be purely academic. Rugby had sent him into the world to be useful, but as he turned over in his mind the implications of higher criticism, neo-epicureanism, positivism and Darwinian science, little seemed left of the Rugby world of service, responsibility and certainty. If by an act of will he could still claim a duty to society, it was by no means certain what form that duty should take or on what basis it could be justified.

Philosophical definitions of duty mixed with more practical thoughts. For which career was he best suited in the new industrial and democratic age? At one time he had thought of taking holy orders as the best means of fulfilling the Rugby ideal and of staying within the family tradition, but his Christianity had been so thoroughly shaken by the disparity between religious precept and actual behaviour and by continental scholarship, that he no longer considered the priesthood a possibility. His loss of belief made the question of career even more critical because the retention of his Trinity fellowship was tied by statute to the condition of holy orders.

A career in philosophy interested Sidgwick the most, but would a nation of philistines, preferring action to thought, listen to a philosopher or be impressed with a philosopher's definition of right behaviour? Even apart from this large and vague problem and the question of holy orders, there was the question of the future of philosophy in Cambridge. The university had not given philosophy a sympathetic hearing. A moral sciences tripos had been established in 1851, but as the moral sciences were as yet outside the scholarship network, few students would read it. Consequently the colleges had little need for moral scientists. The university had one chair of philosophy—the Knightbridge Professorship of Moral Philosophy—and Sidgwick might aspire to it, but even without considering potential rivals, it was uncertain whether an unorthodox layman could hold a professorship which included the teaching of theology.

Career, psychological problems and intellectual preoccupations were further complicated by personal and family difficulties whose dimensions, in the absence of satisfactory evidence, can only be guessed. It is likely that Sidgwick was sexually impotent,[1] but whether he himself was aware of this condition in the 1860's before his marriage is not known. He was, however, fully aware of the homosexual behaviour of his brother Arthur, a young Oxford fellow and Rugby beak, who moved in the circle of John Addington Symonds, a tortured invert in a very hostile Victorian society. Several of Henry Sidgwick's closest friends from Cambridge, Roden Noel and H. G. Dakyns, were also practising homosexuals and linked to the Symonds group. Fully cognizant of the consequences of a public disclosure, Sidgwick made several attempts to force his friends to behave with greater circumspection.[2]

In the 1860's Sidgwick's thoughts of career, of the changing role of the university, of new developments in science and

[1] Kenneth Young, *Arthur James Balfour* (London, 1963), p. 40.
[2] Phyllis Grosskurth, *The Woeful Victorian* (New York, 1965), p. 128.

scholarship, of political and social change in general, and of the likelihood of his family being involved in public scandal, fused together to lend an air of urgency to every decision he had to make. Career was linked to religious belief; the question of leadership was tied to the future of democracy; ethical philosophy was related to the progress of industrialism, educational reform and pressure for change. Personal problems and social problems became virturally indistinguishable, and the resolution of personal problems became the resolution to social problems. If Sidgwick could define the nature of duty, clarify the authority upon which ethical decisions were made and thus ease his emotional burden as a Rugby sixth-former, he would at the same time solve the question of the relationship between Cambridge and society.

In the early 1860's Sidgwick vacillated between intuitionism and utility. As an undergraduate in Trinity he had been made to read Whewell's *Elements of Morality*, but this version of the nativist argument failed to satisfy him. 'It was from that book,' he noted in an autobiographical fragment, 'that I derived the impression–which long remained uneffaced–that Intuitional moralists were hopelessly loose ... in their definitions and axioms.'[1] When later he wrote his own famous treatise on ethics, Sidgwick found that he could not so readily dismiss the intuitionist position, that in fact he would have to incorporate it in his own argument. But as a young don in the 1860's, chafing under Whewell's autocratic rule and continually confronting that standoffish and astringent figure, it was natural enough for him to confuse Whewell's ethics with his personality and see both as the embodiment of the 'external and arbitrary pressure of moral rules which I had been educated to obey, and which presented themselves to me as to some extent doubtful and confused; and sometimes, even when clear, as merely dogmatic, unreasoned, incoherent.'[2]

Sidgwick turned from Whewell to utilitarianism and fell for a time under the spell of Mill, whose influence however was waning. The most important period for Mill in Cambridge was actually the forties and fifties when such different personalities and intellects as Henry Maine, Leslie Stephen and Henry

[1] Henry Sidgwick, *The Methods of Ethics* (London, 1963), xv.
[2] Ibid.

Fawcett had been excited by the *Logic*. Maine had been in Cambridge on and off for part of the fifties but was absent in India in the sixties; Stephen departed Cambridge in 1864, leaving Fawcett, named to the chair of political economy in 1863, as the leading Cambridge utilitarian. Fawcett was not the best representative utilitarianism might have. A zealous laissez-faire theorist, his attachment to the maxims of free trade and to the radicalism of Mill's *On Liberty* was narrow and partisan. In the seventies even his old college companion Leslie Stephen found him trying.[1] Fawcett's zeal was in part an overcompensation for the tragic loss of his eyes during a hunt. Having by extreme determination surmounted the terrible obstacle, he was quite naturally impressed by the efficacy of self-help doctrine. Sidgwick admired Fawcett's courageous example, perhaps too Fawcett's unequivocal commitment to a set of values and beliefs, but dogmatic utilitarianism no more than dogmatic intuitionism, was likely to appeal to his sensitive and critical mind.

It was with some relief, however, that Sidgwick turned to the *Logic*. Psychological hedonism—'the law of universal pleasure-seeking . . . attracted me by its frank naturalness.'[2] His enthusiasm for utilitarianism soon waned, however, when he pursued the implications of the hedonistic paradox. Faithful to this rendering of the invisible hand of the market place, Mill had insisted publicly that Bentham's happiness theory was not in any instance a purely selfish theory of ethics,[3] that the ends of private action and societal action were the same, that self-interest and duty were and had to be identical. Sidgwick was unconvinced. He decided finally that altruism could not be absorbed in egoism, that self-interest and duty were not harmonious but in conflict, and that Mill had cleverly masked the difficulty by substituting for the logic of his own argument an inspiring appeal for heroic self-sacrifice which he tried to justify in the name of happiness and pleasure.[4] Mill did not satisfy Sidgwick's desire to know precisely the grounds upon which he could be convinced that it was right for him to sacrifice

---

[1] Frederic W. Maitland, *The Life and Letters of Leslie Stephen* (London, 1906), p. 246.
[2] *Methods of Ethics*, ibid.   [3] Mill, *Dissertations*, II, p. 480 n.
[4] *Methods of Ethics*, xv–xvi.

his own happiness for the well-being of mankind. In 1865 Sidgwick informed a friend that he had passed the stage of unqualified approval of utilitarian morality. Mill 'will have to be destroyed, as he is becoming as intolerable as Aristeides, but when he is destroyed, we shall build him a mausoleum as big as his present temple of fame – of that I am convinced.'[1]

By the middle of the 1860's Sidgwick had reached an intellectual impasse which was also an emotional and psychological crisis. His potential value to society as well as his own self-esteem was caught, it appeared, in a philosophical conundrum. Whewell's definition of duty depended on the recognition of an arbitrary authority, a concession pernicious in its consequences. Duty was urged as an unavoidable responsibility. On the other hand Mill had entirely failed to prove, on the basis of ethical hedonism, that duty was necessary at all. At this juncture Sidgwick decided to review all the arguments again, to adjust their contexts, to bring in different spokesmen. He sought the assistance of the Reverend John Grote, brother of the more famous utilitarian historian George Grote and Whewell's successor as Knightbridge Professor; in fact he had known Grote for some years and was attracted by his 'rough thoughts', sure to be rough, Sidgwick said, and sure to be thoughts.

In the Cambridge of the 1860's a young man interested in the relationship between philosophy and social responsibility, ethical behaviour and political reform, or education and social change, would find John Grote appealing. Although a follower of Whewell's intuitional philosophy, Grote's tone was far less dogmatic and assertive. Undergraduates and younger dons likely to be put off by Whewell's authoritarian pose were impressed by Grote's accommodating and unassuming manner, and to his home in Trumpington came a few of the more promising young men of the new generation of dons: J. B. Mayor, for example, fellow and tutor of St. John's, Aldis Wright, a beginning Shakespeare scholar, John Venn, one of the first of the new generation of moral scientists, and J. R. Mozeley, fellow of King's and later Professor of Pure Mathematics at Owens College, Manchester. Their frequent meetings and attachment to Grote gave them the name 'Grote Club'.

[1] Arthur and E. M. Sidgwick, *Henry Sidgwick, A Memoir* (London, 1906), pp. 133–4, 151, 158.

Grote's assumptions were clearer than his actual arguments, which were difficult enough in themselves but made even more abstruse by an extremely awkward manner of expression. It was precisely his stumbling, however, the impression he managed to convey of a mind entangling itself in the most difficult problems of behaviour, that guaranteed him an attentive and sympathetic audience. He would openly admit that no satisfactory proof of an innate moral sense had yet been devised, he would frankly state that only a faint line separated *a priori* knowledge from general material experience; and having, with these candid remarks disarmed his listeners, who were possibly making mental comparisons of Grote and his olympian predecessor, he would raise his basic objection to utilitarianism, that it provided no standard for deciding the content of good behaviour. Utilitarians, he noted, concentrated on circumstances in order to find the exact combination of experiences which produced this or that character, but they offered no method by which it was possible to know 'what we ought to do and be, or had better do and be, and had better try to make others.'[1] In this respect intuitionism was superior to utility, for like religion it insisted that character could be improved by approximation to an ideal known through an independent soul or consciousness. The mind, he asserted, existed before sensation: 'the thing as thought, pre-contemplated by its Creator, contemplated by beings with created faculties of knowledge with such following of his thought as they can attain to, is the idea, the ideal thing, the ideal reality, the truest reality.'[2]

In 1866, shortly before his death, Grote, with the assistance of Sidgwick, wrote an interesting platonic dialogue which captures a sense of the discussions of the Grote Club in the mid-1860's and summarizes the respective arguments concerning the social implications of the experiential and intuitional concepts of duty and self-improvement. The dialogue was stimulated by an analysis of Plato's concept of justice appearing in George Grote's three-volume study of Plato published in 1865. George Grote had challenged the notion that Plato was an intuitional philosopher who had found an absolute standard of ideal justice.

[1] John Grote, *Exploratio Philosophica* (Cambridge, 1865), I, p. 198.
[2] Ibid., pp. 188–9; Grote, *A Treatise on the Moral Ideals*, ed. J. B. Mayor (Cambridge, 1876), p. 470.

George Grote's strategy was to show that Plato's doctrine of ideas had nothing to do with intuitionism but was in fact a perfectly orthodox utilitarian solution to the question of right behaviour; that is, the abstract, *a priori* conception of justice which Plato advanced was impossible of realization except in the precise societal conditions he had created for it. Plato's justice was a necessary correlate of the very structure of the platonic republic. It was the republic which defined pleasure and pain, that made the just man happy and the unjust man miserable. Whoever failed to accommodate himself to his assigned function within the platonic republic was clearly disregarding his own self-interest and could only expect to have painful experiences. Plato had created a perfectly utilitarian society, he had provided it with a concept of justice appropriate to it alone, and under no circumstances could it be claimed that platonic justice was known intuitively or was the copy of an idea whose existence was independent of material phenomena. George Grote took the argument still one step further. If the platonic conception of justice could not be universalized, if it was not a generalization applicable to all civil societies no matter when they existed, then Plato's Socrates ought not to be revered as a philosopher of scientific ethics. His conclusions were not to be regarded as the result of scientific method and careful investigation, but as undisguised preaching, a sermon on the text, 'the performance of obligations alone, without any rights, is delightful *per se*.'[1] Plato's intuitionism, Grote concluded, was nothing more than a device for imposing his own values on society. In the name of an idea of his own fabrication, Plato had falsely claimed to have discovered a superior form of justice.

In the dialogue of 1866, John Grote, assuming the character of Socrates, answered his brother's utilitarian premiss that happiness or good behaviour always in the end depended on how society, whatever society it might be, defined permissible conduct. It was true, John Grote admitted, that behaviour was in some degree influenced by the consequences that society could be reasonably expected to make in response to a given act; but not all behaviour, nor all motives for behaviour, could

[1] George Grote, *Plato and the Other Companions of Sokrates* (London, 1865), III, pp. 159, 132–59.

be traced directly to the wishes of society. Some men possessed an idea of right or just action that had little to do with the promise of award or the threat of punishment; and the happiness which attended the just act derived from the knowledge that an ideal was being followed. Sidgwick, respectfully attentive and compliant in the character of Glaucon, summarized the debate between the two brothers by saying that John Grote made improvement contingent upon the individual, whereas George Grote made it dependent on either a better society or 'a better general opinion.'[1]

2.

The dialogue of 1866 left Sidgwick exactly where he had been when he built his monument to Mill as a symbol of gratitude and disassociation. Unable to decide whether society or the individual took the lead in determining conduct, Sidgwick supposed that like John Grote, he too might remain a boy all his life, searching for answers with a refreshing openness but never coming to a conclusion. Perhaps, he wondered in a letter to Dakyns, answers eluded him because he lived in an undecided and sceptical age: 'I do not mean the frivolous scepticism of modern Philistines (I almost prefer the frivolous dogmatism of ancient ditto), but the feeling of a man who will not make up his mind till mankind has. I feel that this standpoint is ultimately indefensible, because mankind have never made up their mind except in consequence of some individual having done so. Still there seems to me to be the dilemma. In the present age an educated man must either be prophet or persistent sceptic—there seems no *media via*.'[2]

A prophet or a sceptic—there was no middle way. No doubt there were crucial differences in prophetic style—Jeremiah, Isaiah, Ezekiel were inspired differently and chose different means of expressing protest—but any prophetic role at least entailed an attempt at the moral regeneration of society, suggested a fundamental opposition of individual and societal standards and implied pain and suffering for the failure to con-

---

[1] 'A Discussion between Professor Henry Sidgwick and the Late Professor John Grote, on the Utilitarian Basis of Plato's *Republic*', *The Classical Review*, III (March, 1889), p. 102.

[2] *Memoir*, p. 158.

form. The prophet's reward came only from the knowledge he
was acting justly and that he would be vindicated at some un-
specified time in the future. Certainty was the reward for self-
sacrifice. Prophetic action seemed out of the question in 1866,
however, as Sidgwick had no philosophical means for justifying
a direct attack on society. Scepticism seemed a more feasible,
if not altogether satisfying alternative. Yielding completely to
doubt, he could relinquish the difficult attempt to set universal
standards of behaviour and take comfort in a certain detachment and objectivity, a good defence, if not a positive virtue.
In this frame of mind Sidgwick came upon a prophet, Matthew
Arnold, the 'prophet of culture,' as he entitled his critique of
Arnold's Oxford farewell lecture, indicating both his hopes and
his disappointments.

Sidgwick's encounter with 'Sweetness and Light' was sober-
ing. Certain prophetic elements were present in the essay,
notably a dogmatic self-confidence and authority; but absent
from Arnold's analysis of the failings of English society, Sidgwick thought, was a genuine belief in the efficacy of culture.
Sweetness and light could only flourish in favourable times and
were not in themselves 'a spring and source of faith and
ardour.'[1] This was not a significant improvement, therefore, on
the utilitarian position. What had started as prophecy had
ended as futility. Arnold's grand, ideal culture was at bottom
no more than a preference for traditional, exclusive, aristocratic
art and literature. Perhaps, Sidgwick reflected, Arnold was
really a sceptic–not of course the philistine sceptic unable to
distinguish between trivial and important values–but at least a
doubter, a person unwilling to make any effort to see what the
developing industrial society of England was all about. Arnold
pretended to stand aside as a sage, 'looking out with hopeless
placidity "from beneath the shelter of some wall" on the storms
and dust-clouds of blind and selfish conflict.' After reading
'Sweetness and Light' Sidgwick refused to indulge Arnold's self-
image. The prophet of culture was a prophet manqué. He did
not possess any special wisdom, and he could not be allowed to
pose as a stoic philosopher. Arnold was simply 'a cheerful
modern liberal, tempered by renouncement, shuddering aloof

[1] Henry Sidgwick, 'The Prophet of Culture', *Macmillan's Magazine*, XVI
(August, 1867), p. 273.

from the rank exhalations of vulgar enthusiasm, and holding up the pouncet-box of culture betwixt the wind and his nobility.'[1]

3.

When John Grote died in 1866 the group of young dons who met frequently in his Trumpington home continued to meet irregularly in their college rooms, with F. D. Maurice, Grote's successor as Knightbridge Professor, presiding over discussions. Maurice's connexion with Cambridge went back to 1823 when he entered Trinity College as a pensioner. He migrated to Trinity Hall, but unable in conscience to subscribe to the Thirty-Nine Articles, left Cambridge for London to edit *The Athenaeum*. Overcoming his objection to subscription, he took a first degree at Oxford in 1831, returned to London, met the young utilitarians, joined in the discussions of their London Debating Society and contributed to the *Westminster Review*. He repaid his intellectual debt to the philosophic radicals by introducing John Stuart Mill to Coleridge's thought. In a long, varied and controversial career Maurice was priest, novelist, journalist, christian socialist and professor. In Cambridge he was remembered for incorporating Coleridge's ideas into the Society of Apostles, which he had revived and influenced. It was therefore fitting that Maurice should become the unofficial head of the informal Grote Club, itself a speculative gathering in some respects similar to the Apostles. Both societies were concerned with the essentially Coleridgean task of reinterpreting tradition for the present; but the Grote Club, unlike the Apostles, was less secret, not at all ritualistic, and mainly, if not exclusively, for dons.

One famous Cambridge theologian and scholar, Fenton John Anthony Hort, once wrote another, Brooke Foss Westcott, that Maurice was 'intelligible and profitable to a person so far as that person needs him, and no farther.'[2] In the 1860's Sidgwick needed Maurice. There were extraordinary parallels in the lives of the two men, and Sidgwick very eagerly used the discussions of the Grote Club to draw from Maurice recollections that could

[1] Ibid., p. 280.

[2] W. Merlin Davies, *An Introduction to F. D. Maurice's Theology* (London, 1964), p. 17 n.

be used to guide him through his own crisis. Although separated in age by more than thirty years, both men had experienced personal religious and emotional problems during times of critical social change. Maurice had broken with the unitarianism of his family, had agonized over the decision to sign the Thirty-Nine Articles, and in the 1850's had been accused of heterodoxy by the Principal of King's College, London, a charge against which he successfully defended himself. At the same time he had devised a theology and a programme of christian socialism which he offered as a solution to the discontents caused by liberal reform, working-class protest and the landlord-industrialist dispute over the corn laws. Believing that England was disintegrating and consequently in need of manly individuals to provide leadership, he had used religion to provide a basis for national unity and guidelines for behaviour. For Sidgwick, also living in a period of major social and political disturbance, unity and leadership were critical *desiderata*. Maurice's spiritual recovery, so intimately related to his solution to the social crisis, was therefore of the keenest interest to Sidgwick. His faith in Christianity, it is true, had been shaken, but what if Christianity should prove to be the only system of ethics able to offer and justify the concepts of duty and self-sacrifice? If Maurice could make Christianity acceptable to him, the nature of duty would no longer be an intellectual difficulty, and, conveniently, his objection to taking holy orders might vanish.

Sidgwick was fascinated by Maurice's paradoxical and stimulating mind, finding relief from the continuous exchanges of utilitarians and intuitionists. But not every contemporary was so patient with Maurice's intellectual and philosophical subtleties. Matthew Arnold, for example, called Maurice 'a muddy mystic;'[1] in the 1870's, Leslie Stephen found Maurice admirable as a person, but muddle-headed, futile and bewildering as a thinker.[2] Maurice had one especially disturbing intellectual quirk. Deliberately and maddeningly, he often refused to engage in a forthright exchange of views, quickly turning discussion to categories and concepts which gave him a special momentary advantage. He had in fact acquired from the *Phaedrus* a socratic device which he used expertly. Like Socrates, who would not

[1] Ibid., p. 10.　　　[2] Maitland, *Leslie Stephen*, pp. 240, 261.

argue the possible interpretations of the myth of Boreas and Oreithyia—as life was short and allegory tiresome—Maurice avoided direct debate with either the environmentalists or nativists. The doctrine of association, the duplex and complex ideas which explained conscience, consciousness and the self as higher mental abstractions derivative from sensory phenomena, as well as the antagonist theory of innate faculties claiming the existence of knowledge outside immediate experience, were dismissed easily and disdainfully, as easily as Socrates dismissed the poets and Ionian scientists who disputed the meaning of Boreas and Oreithyia. There was a hopeless circularity to the arguments of the selfish philosophers. An awakened conscience, they said, depended upon an enlightened public opinion, but an enlightened public opinion depended upon an awakened conscience. 'Wearisome and endless see-saw! . . . Oh learn to bear the scorn of the philosophers who talk to you in this fashion!'[1] As for the intuitionists: Butler, in typical eighteenth-century language, spoke of conscience as a faculty of human nature; Whewell spoke of it as an exercise of Reason, an authority subordinate to supreme law but superior to our actions.[2] These are interesting questions and answers, but totally beside the point, essentially unimportant and ultimately insoluble. What we cannot know, it is useless to consider. 'Shall we be *happy* after death?' he was once asked. 'I do not know, I do not care to know, I do not think it is possible to know.'[3]

Discussion between the intuitionists and utilitarians had finally narrowed to the question of individual liberty, the degree to which individualism was possible, the means by which the best that was thought and known could be propagated. In both schools of thought the underlying tension was between the individual and society, between individual rights and social responsibilities—a modernized version of the theological riddle of free will and necessity. Maurice discussed the freedom of the individual from an entirely different point of view. His emphasis was neither on the autonomy of the individual or on the authority of society but rather on the actual existing relationship between individual behaviour and societal norms, the mutual, necessary obligations. The theorist could not deduce rights and

---

[1] F. D. Maurice, *The Conscience* (London and Cambridge, 1868), p. 90.
[2] Ibid., pp. 35–7.   [3] Maurice, *Life*, II, p. 559.

obligations from abstractions designated the 'individual' or 'society'. Man was born into fundamental kinship ties–first the family, next the community, thirdly the nation; and the starting point for any analysis of man had to be the fact that he was a social animal. This much accepted, it would follow that the individual was neither completely free nor completely dependent but learned 'by degrees in what sense and under what great limitations independence is possible.'[1] Morality or correct behaviour was decided by a sense of limitation on the part of both society and the individual. Complete individual autonomy was out of the question, but so was complete dependence. Authority could not be dominion and obedience could never be subjection, for otherwise immorality would result, the dissolution of those reciprocal, kinship ties between the individual and society.

Maurice's family theory of the essential organization of society produced a definition of conscience radically different from the intuitionist or utilitarian concepts. Conscience for the intuitionists was an esoteric faculty or inner sense and for the utilitarians merely a copy of sensations; but for Maurice conscience was simply the self, imperfect but aware of its imperfections. Conscience was a socratic daemon, an unrelenting prod, a continual reminder of the failure to perform social obligations. As the imperfect self, conscience could never possess authority, as it did for Butler and to a less extent for Whewell; 'its authority begins when it goes out of itself, its supremacy consists in its abdication of supremacy.'[2] For Arnold the difference between fallen nature and perfection was to be extinguished by eradicating the corrupt self, that is, by suppressing individuality and making conscience and authority identical. For Maurice the preservation of the distinction between fallen nature and perfection was essential, for only then could individual selfishness be subordinated to social good.

If conscience kept the individual properly aware of his imperfection, it also freed him from total dependence on society. In so far as man was capable of selfishness, he could never be completely at the mercy of society; but more significantly, in so far as he possessed a conscience, he realized that society had obliga-

[1] Maurice, *Social Morality* (London, 1869), xi–xii.
[2] Maurice, *Conscience*, p. 160.

tions to the individuals within it. It is not surprising, therefore, that Maurice's strongest reproof was reserved for utilitarians like Bain whom he called perhaps the first thinker to openly proclaim the complete identification of authority with punishment.[1] 'Society,' he warned in the conclusion to a series of Cambridge lectures on casuistry or conscience, 'has been used as a bugbear to frighten us; the Conscience must do what it bids or cease to be. If that is Society there are no terms to be kept with it. The Casuist's business is in the name of the Conscience to mock it and defy it. He must be more fierce in his mockery and defiance than he might have thought it necessary to be in any former age. For this theory [utilitarianism] is put forth as the last result of modern wisdom.'[2]

The hortatory nature of this conclusion derives from Maurice's fear that the kinship relationship of which he spoke, although an indisputable fact of social existence, would last only as long as men believed in it. If his intellectual opponents succeeded in convincing the majority of men that society and the individual were no more than abstract categories from which deductions about behaviour could be made, then the social unity which only the family could provide would surely disappear. In fact Maurice was convinced the process of disintegration was already well advanced. The causes were manifold – neo-epicureanism of course, but also the many forms of liberal or democratic individualism and the individualizing tendencies of sectarian religion, or laissez-faire economics with its emphasis on self-interest. Maurice believed the influence of commerce had penetrated everywhere – even into modern theology[3] – and he was certain the commercial instinct was one of the major sources of disunity in the 1860's. He equated economic self-seeking with fratricide, he called it a denial of brotherhood, the origin of murderous conflicts between labour and capital, and indicated that it must logically conclude in slavery and the slave trade.[4] His answer was always kinship, the brotherhood of man, the Sermon on the Mount, the notion of limits. He advocated the imitation of Christ and called upon educated men to follow the Christian example of inspired self-sacrifice in the name of all men. Maurice totally rejected all forms of secular or religious

---

[1] Ibid., p. 71. [2] Ibid., p. 201. [3] Maurice, *Life*, II, p. 460.
[4] Ibid., p. 459.

withdrawal and intellectual exclusiveness. He decried the existence of 'bodies of philosophical men' who had no sympathy
with vulgar people.[1] The educated man–professional man was
the phrase he had once used about himself[2]–had to take an
active lead in the restoration of social unity. The universities
too, he announced, had a special function to perform if the
drift to fratricide were to be arrested. No less than Mill the
unorthodox utilitarian, Sedgwick and Whewell the Kantian
intuitionists, and Arnold the advocate of perfection, Maurice
exhorted the universities to correct and expand the public
mind. They could not stoop to popular opinion, they ought not
to conform to the tastes and notions of the general public.[3]

A 'muddy mystic' Arnold called Maurice, but their personal
problems were in some respects identical. The search for unity
dominated the lives of both, and in both the search for national
unity was connected to the search for psychological and spiritual
unity. Maurice had experienced a period of explosive disunity
within his own family, and a sense of familial discord continued
to trouble him. Like Arnold he experienced the phenomenon of
a divided self, a disoriented personality, two halves which would
not leave him in peace until they had been united, or until the
best half triumphed over the worst. Once, in the days when he
was deciding the issue of the Thirty-Nine Articles, he had
written his mother from Oxford that, 'I have seemed to see
myself in a double mirror, one human, one divine. I could not
have seen my image in one except I had seen it also in the other.
The *self* in both was equally disgusting, but then when I could
feel a reflection back, faint comparatively in the one, strong and
permanent in the other, all became true and real again and I
have felt a happiness at times which is almost new to me.'[4]

Maurice expressed the division within him in theological
language as a struggle between good and evil; conscience
emerged to separate his evil from his good self, the former
becoming increasingly faint as the latter grew strong and permanent and even stronger as it ascended closer to God and His

[1] Davies, *Introduction*, p. 155.
[2] Maurice, *Life*, II, p. 550. Maurice also used Coleridge's word 'clerisy'.
Ibid., p. 304.
[3] H. G. Wood, *F. D. Maurice* (Cambridge, 1950), p. 134.
[4] Maurice, *Life*, I, pp. 130–1.

love. Maurice's letters do not mention the point in his life when he read Chamisso's romantic novella, *Peter Schliemiehl*, and wondered about the significance of the tale of a man who lost his shadow, but certainly the meaning of the story of a romantic double was not lost upon him. Towards the end of his life he was still thinking about the opposing self, torturing out the Socratic injunction. 'It seems to me,' he wrote in 1868, 'that the conscience with its mysterious duplicity is the very self in each man; that which is feeling after God if haply it may find him, that which, if it does not find him, must sink into selfishness and brutality and make gods after its own likeness. . . . My endeavour has been to get rid of what is called psychology and to bring each of my students to say, The conscience is not a part of my soul, but is I myself. Parting with it, I lose not like Chamisso's hero my shadow, but the substance from which my shadow is cast.'[1]

Like Arnold, Maurice sought a true or actual self, and similarly his search for psychic unity was indissolubly tied to his search for social unity. Unlike Arnold, however, who took refuge in an identification with the State, Maurice was interested in a religious—principally liturgical—answer to the Victorian crisis. Never sympathetic to exclusively doctrinaire or even theological solutions, he more than anyone else in the mid-nineteenth century supported the principle of unity contained in public worship. Devotional unity was the answer to the partisanship of the age. Forms of prayer, Maurice wrote, 'draw us out of that individuality which is our curse and ruin, and lead us, one and all, to take up our position on the same ground of being justified and redeemed in Christ.'[2] Worship was a reminder of the kinship ties which underlay social organization; it was the actual bond between men, the expression of their commonness, a community act, uniting each individual to another and ultimately to the holy family itself, the trinity in perpetual unity.

Besides his unorthodox approach to the most important problems of his day, especially those likely to interest the generation

---

[1] Ibid., II, p. 577. By psychology Maurice meant sensational psychology and physiology, the self as an invention of a man's own mind.

[2] Horton Davies, *Worship and Theology in England: From Watts and Wesley to Maurice, 1690–1850* (London, 1961), p. 299.

of the 1860's, there was one other feature of Maurice's thought that recommended him to Sidgwick. Maurice was a master in the use of paradox. Paradox enabled him to avoid synthesis—which he disliked as an unnecessary concession to opposing views—and to restate problems in such a way as to transform their content and, by a logical sleight of hand, entirely abolish them. That is, Maurice used the paradox form as a way of finding unity. His writings are full of paradoxical statements, problems rephrased, real contradictions changed into apparent ones. In the eighteenth century, he observed, the absence of enthusiasm guaranteed the stability of society and the state; in the nineteenth century, however, enthusiasm was essential to the stability of the state. Man's nature was in part brutish, began another of his more involved paradoxes, but precisely because man knew that he was part animal, he became civilized and human. 'The whole idea of recognizing theology as the permanent ground, and the consumation of thought and life in this day is anti-Comtian,' he once told Kingsley, although para-doxically supplying the Comtian demand for a higher inter-national morality.[1]

The use of paradox made Maurice a supremely socratic figure in the eyes of his admirers. He was singularly successful in defining terms and devising meanings which furthered his own argument, at the same time conveying to his listeners an appreciation of their own careless reasoning and the argument which had been concealed from them. He mastered the grand socratic gesture, imperiously refusing to enter a discussion on grounds which did not suit his conclusions and therefore by-passing problems which were very real to others. Like Socrates he was perverse and teasing, a gadfly, driven on by a daemon whom no argument could touch, confusing and finally exasper-ating others. He had once criticized Mill for failing to enter completely into sympathy with the mind of an opponent, but he was similarly guilty and could be vehement, stubborn and disregarding.[2] In one way his logic and his manner were more platonic than socratic: his discussions did not necessarily probe towards the unknown truth, encouraging others to join him in the ascent. His arguments were eristic, his conclusions already

[1] Maurice, *Life*, II, p. 553.
[2] Julia Wedgwood, *Nineteenth Century Teachers* (London, 1909), pp. 29–62.

known, his method to defeat his disputants by an intellectual brilliance which absolutely astounded Mill and made him conclude that Maurice was the most wasted talent he had known.

Maurice was difficult to follow and perhaps deliberately obscure, but in the Cambridge of the 1860's he was also refreshing, stimulating the group of young dons to move away from discussions conducted solely along lines of intuitionism and utilitarianism. In his autumnal old age he appeared to have found unity, to have healed the divisions with him, and without any sign of withdrawal. He was even a prophet with a mission: 'I was sent into the world that I might persuade men to recognize Christ as the centre of their fellowship with each other, that so they might be united in their families, their countries, and as men, not in schools and factions.'[1] Maurice's intellectual influence on Sidgwick, however, did not last. When the young Trinity scholar began his own great treatise on ethics it was along the lines of the utility-intuition controversy that he proceeded. But at least for the moment there was an answer. By his own example, if not his actual arguments, Maurice made scepticism unnecessary. There was no need to go outside society to discover an absolute authority or standard, nor were there grounds to believe that the individual could not oppose society. Maurice had re-established Jesus and Socrates as great moral and social teachers labouring in the real world. Socrates' daemon had not misled him, and Jesus was not unheroic, passive, feminine or a slave simply because he had submitted. Nor was he motivated, as the crudest utilitarians mocked, by the thought of his own happiness, enduring the cross and despising the shame 'for the joy which was set before Him.'[2] He was truly manly and courageous, and in his self-sacrifice was exhibited the cardinal principle of morality: the duty we owed society was the recognition of our humanity–the social nature of existence–and the willingness to live or die for it.

[1] Maurice, *Life*, I, p. 240.
[2] Maurice, *Social Morality*, pp. 476–7, 460–2.

4.

When Maurice's name was first proposed for the Knightbridge Professorship, Sidgwick, a supporter of Maurice, withdrew his own candidacy for the chair. He correctly surmised that the Board of Electors favoured Maurice and would not be deterred from selecting him by either the protests of Cambridge opponents or the events of Maurice's controversial career. And yet Sidgwick was not altogether certain that Maurice was the answer to Cambridge's educational problems. Apparently he worried about the tendency of the older professors to regard their chairs as freeholds, to return no significant teaching, and even fail to maintain residence in Cambridge, in which case they could have no influence over the direction of undergraduate education. Early in Michaelmas Term 1866 he wrote his mother that someone from the 'new school' of professors would probably be a better choice than Maurice, someone who regarded himself 'as much bound to teach and to write as any other salaried functionary is bound to discharge the duties for which he is paid.'[1]

Maurice put these fears to rest. He was an Apostle who had returned to Cambridge especially to guide the new generation. At that time of his life he preferred a Cambridge chair of philosophy or theology to all other possible distinctions he might receive, and he definitely looked upon the Knightbridge Professorship as virtually a calling.[2] Maurice considered teaching and writing absolutely essential requirements of a professor, and shortly after arriving in Cambridge he even asked his old friend Charles Kingsley, then Regius Professor of History, to spend more time in Cambridge.[3] The request was very relevant. Kingsley had been elected to the chair of history in 1860, but as he also held a living in Eversley, in the county of Hampshire, he had to maintain a dual residence, moving back and forth between Eversley and Cambridge. When the financial strain proved too great, he parted with his Cambridge house and took up full residence in Eversley, going up to Cambridge twice yearly in order to examine for degrees and deliver approximately a dozen lectures. He found even this arrangement taxing;

[1] Sidgwick, *Memoir*, p. 153.   [2] Maurice, *Life*, II, pp. 542, 552.
[3] Ibid., p. 552.

he had difficulty meeting his expenses, and in 1867 offered to resign, but was persuaded to remain until 1869.[1]

In one way Kingsley's presence in Cambridge might have been more desirable than Maurice's, for in a sense the Regius Professor was becoming a more important appointment than the Knightbridge Professor. Student interest in history was greater than in philosophy, and there was a better chance for a teacher to reach a wider audience through history than philosophy. In Cambridge in the 1860's the very air seemed full of Comtianism, an unhappy Kingsley wrote Maurice.[2] Historical method was replacing the older science of human nature with its stress on psychology and logic. Biblical and classical scholarship had become increasingly historical-minded; and anthropology and sociology too, emphasizing the state of social organization and belief in the past, helped draw attention to historical method.

Typically, Sidgwick was also momentarily attracted to history. He had never been thoroughly sympathetic to Comte— at times he even reacted violently to Comtian dogma—but he was intrigued by the new importance positivism attached to religion, even if the religion were not Christian. Before long, however, he concluded, as Mill before him, that historical method by itself was incapable of furnishing the substance of ethical ideals and was less satisfactory than philosophy. By 1865 his interest in Comte's historical science had shifted to an interest in Comte's mind or intellectual qualities. At the same time he was drawn to the history of religion itself, to problems of myth and ecstasy, or as was becoming fashionable, to the origins of belief and institutions. In 1867 he actually began to teach history as part of his responsibilities as college lecturer in moral sciences, to which he had been appointed in the same year; but shortly thereafter history was removed from the moral sciences, and Sidgwick restricted his history teaching to students reading for the ordinary degree. He took some interest in English ecclesiastical history, mainly because of his personal doubts about religion, but he found history in general dull and full of wearisome detail. He only worked at the subject if his

---

[1] Charles Kingsley, *His Letters and Memories of His Life*, ed. by his wife (London, 1877), II, pp. 153, 293.
[2] Ibid., p. 274.

students showed marked interest and managed to infect him with their enthusiasm. He continued to regard history as inferior to philosophy, until finally in 1868 he admitted that he should never have attempted to teach history in the first place. He supposed the experience was not a total loss. He had learned something, his sympathies had been widened, his curiosity indulged; but in general he concluded that he was simply not an historian. Time would partially correct this self-verdict, but in the late 1860's Sidgwick was convinced that history required special qualities which he did not possess. 'History is *par excellence* a subject which ought to be taught with enthusiasm and from a full mind.'[1] He had been unable to give history this commitment, nor was he able to charge it with the ethical importance which made the study of philosophy so necessary. The task of using history to establish standards of behaviour had to be given to another, a member of the 'new school' of Cambridge professors.

[1] Sidgwick, *Memoir*, p. 179.

CHAPTER 5

ECCE HOMO

1.

In 1869 John Robert Seeley, Professor of Latin at University College, London, and anonymous author of the controversial book, *Ecce Homo*, returned to Cambridge to take up the duties of the Regius Professor of History. Biographer and historian; writer on theology, education and politics, he is known today mainly for the romantic conception of empire that he promoted in the 1880's. Popularizer in the best sense, it is nevertheless true that during most of his lifetime he was scarcely known outside Cambridge. At his death in 1895 he was rediscovered by the press. He received an impressive string of notices and appreciations, but soon after fell into comparative obscurity once again. In many respects a conventional great Victorian, he has not to this day received the tribute of a conventional life and letters. Only a few brief biographical sketches remain. And yet the contribution Seeley made to the history of Cambridge is remarkable. As a don and professor his achievements were no less important than those of other, more celebrated reformers, his contemporaries (and Oxford heroes) Jowett and Pattison, for examples, with whom his efforts compare.

Seeley came from a family of intellectuals and professionals who were only one generation removed from being artisans and tradesmen. His grandfather moved to London and established himself as a bookseller and publisher in 1784. In 1826 his father, an evangelical churchman, took control of the publishing end of the business, finding time as well to write leaders for *The Times* and engage in various religious, social and philanthropic activities, among them the agitation for a shorter working day.

His more important literary contributions included a biography of Hannah More (1838) and an article, 'Essays on the Church, by a Layman', in which he affirmed the unity of the Anglican Communion.[1]

Seeley was educated at private schools and the City of London School before following his elder brother—a fellow of Trinity and a barrister—to Cambridge. He entered Christ's College in 1852, in time to profit from the reforming spirit of John Graham's mastership and from the example of Graham himself. Translated to the see of Chester in 1848, Graham returned to Cambridge as head of the first royal commission ever to inquire into the university and its colleges. Darwin had found the college intellectually sterile in the 1820's, but Christ's under Graham was known to be a reforming and even a radical society. During his mastership the college proposed to admit dissenters and allow fellows to marry, but both reforms were opposed by some of the fellows and vetoed by the Visitor.[2]

Seeley entered Christ's just after the beginning of the long tutorship of William Mandell Gunson, one of those remarkable personalities of whom little is known. Gunson was partly responsible for improving the quality of the college, and he held the tutorship until a quarrel with Graham's successor led to his resignation in 1870. Among those destined for fame who entered under Gunson in the 1850's were John Peile, Charles Stuart Calverley, Walter William Skeat, Walter Joseph Sendall and Walter Besant. Little is known of the undergraduate activities of this exceptionally able group; more is known of their later careers. For the actual history of Cambridge, Peile was the most important. He became tutor and master of Christ's, Vice-Chancellor of the university, and he was a champion of university education for women and a reformer in general. Nothing appears known of his social background. Calverley and Sendall, both from clerical families, pursued professional careers. Calverley earned a wide reputation as a wit and parodist before being called to the bar in 1865; Sendall proceeded to an eminent career in the civil service. Skeat, the son of an architect, took holy orders in 1860 and subsequently became Professor of

---

[1] DNB and John Robert Seeley, *The Growth of British Policy*, with an introductory memoir by George W. Prothero (Cambridge, 1895), I.

[2] H. Rackham, 'Christ's College', in VCH, III, ed. J. P. C. Roach, p. 435.

Anglo-Saxon in the university. Besant, the third son of a merchant, made his reputation as a man of letters after trying his hand as a mathematics master in the public schools.

All of the problems which absorbed Sidgwick throughout the 1860's wholly occupied Seeley as well and appeared in his first book, *Ecce Homo*, published anonymously by Macmillan in 1865. Seeley dwelt on the need for enthusiasm as the alternative to scepticism and relativism, the end to alienation, self-sacrifice, duty, the place of religion in contemporary society, the relationship between history and philosophy, science and ethics, ideal and normative behaviour, the responsibilities of the teacher and the meaning of leadership. Ostensibly the book was yet another interpretation of the meaning of Christ's life – although not biblical scholarship in the strictest sense – but *Ecce Homo* was really an attempt to define the social role of élites. Its grand theme was that changes in the social and political organization of civil life required a corresponding change in moral values and behaviour. The book began with a spectacular statement of the collapse of antiquity – 'The drama of ancient society had been played out; the ancient city life, with the traditions and morality belonging to it, was obsolete'[1] – but the contemporary reader was supposed to understand that Seeley was arguing by analogy to the present. The unwritten instructions to the reader were, for the 'collapse of antiquity' read the 'collapse of aristocratic society'. Intentionally *Ecce Homo* was a thoroughly topical book.

Seeley's method of argument was sociological. His concern was with the institutions responsible for social stability, and he therefore laid primary emphasis on the family, regarding it as an early form of political organization. There was nothing absolutely new in this procedure. Plato and Aristotle had discussed the origins of the polis in this manner, and on the continent Fustel de Coulanges was using a related approach; but the more immediate influences on Seeley were Maurice and Henry Maine's *Ancient Law*.[2] Both Maurice and Maine emphasized the familial origin of social and political institutions,

---

[1] John Robert Seeley, *Ecce Homo* (Boston, 1866), p. 7.
[2] There is reason to believe that the substance of *Ancient Law* was given in Maine's Cambridge lectures in the years between 1847 and 1854. J. W. Burrow, *Evolution and Society* (Cambridge, 1966), p. 140. Of course Seeley could have read Maine's book when it was published in 1861.

although with different ends in view. Maurice was afraid that the kinship basis of communal life was being neglected and would be forgotten, whereas Maine was interested in the survival of ancient institutions as evidence of the persistence of obsolete or irrational forms of conduct. His aim was to prepare the administrator, especially the imperial administrator, for the different kinds of behaviour he was likely to encounter.[1] Seeley borrowed from both thinkers, although more from Maurice than Maine. The survival of particular institutional forms interested him less than the kinship elements in political structures. His object was to prove that there was a necessary and interdependent relationship between political institutions and moral behaviour and then to indicate how a change in one called for a change in the other.

Before the Romans, Seeley wrote, morality was exclusive or ethnic, based on the principle of loyalty to family and hostility towards the outsider. The idea of the family, reinforced by the worship of ancestors and household gods, was the political and moral basis of the ancient commonwealth. In time the family grew by absorbing persons and groups whose kinship was dubious until municipal or national units formed. Ethnic morality, however, continued to be the essential strength of the commonwealth.

It was also an Achilles' heel. The survival of the ancient commonwealth depended on xenophobia, virtue was equated with battlefield heroism, gods were worshipped for their military attributes. The nations of the Mediterranean were in a continuous state of war and threatened one another with conquest. When finally they collapsed, fragmented and exhausted by protracted enmity, no resistance could be offered to the advancing Roman armies. The pax romana supplanted conflict and imperial unity replaced ethnic hostility. But the unity imposed by Rome, Seeley remarked, was premature, artificial and incomplete, being almost totally unaccompanied by a corresponding moral reformation. The Romans could supply only stoicism, a philosophy of withdrawal and consolation, when a moral dynamic was required to complement imperial rule. The people of the ancient world rejected the 'cold comfort' of stoicism— Seeley's phrase—finding that it bore no relation to the previous

[1] Ibid., p. 171.

system of familial ethics. 'So little power,' Seeley concluded, 'had any such philosophic theory to supply the place of a morality founded on usage, on filial reverence, on great and dear examples.'[1]

It was the genius of Christianity to recognize that the necessary accompaniment to imperial unity was a concept of the universal brotherhood of man, an enthusiastic regard for the moral and physical well-being of other men. Christianity retained family morality and carried it one step further. The distinction between family and stranger was discarded: all mankind was regarded as in a state of essential kinship and bound together in reciprocal love.

The superiority of Christianity over ethnic morality was demonstrated when Rome lost its military and political hegemony to the barbarians, a circumstance that Seeley attributed to population decline. 'The Empire perished for want of men,' not from moral or spiritual degeneration as moralists supposed.[2] The ancient commonwealths disintegrated when they ceased to be victorious in war; but the Roman Empire survived long after the barbarian conquests: 'Bereft of her legions, and abandoned by the Caesar, she enrolled an army of priests and reigned on in the name of Peter.'[3] The barbarian military triumph utterly failed to dislodge the moral code which had sustained Rome in her periods of greatness, because the special characteristic of Christianity, the quality which distinguished its family morality from the ethnic form of family morality, was its independence from political authority. The principle of empire survived Rome in Christianity, which became an even greater empire, the greatest, in fact, the world had seen, incorporating all the principles of civil society and in one crucial respect superior to all the states preceding it. The Christian Church, the New Jerusalem, wrote Seeley at a moment of obvious excitement, was a platonic idea, 'a commonwealth developed, as it were, from within.' Without the support of

---

[1] *Ecce Homo*, pp. 148, 145–8.

[2] John Robert Seeley, 'Roman Imperialism', in *Lectures and Essays* (London, 1870), p. 48. This lecture was delivered at the Royal Institution in 1869.

[3] John Robert Seeley, *Classical Studies as an Introduction to the Moral Sciences* (London, 1864), p. 17.

arms and armies, 'resting on no accidental aid or physical support, but on an inherent immortality,' it 'out-lasted all the states which were existing at the time of its foundation.'[1] In *Ecce Homo* Seeley suggested that Christianity survived 'the enmity of ancient civilization, the brutality of mediaeval barbarism' and is secure 'under the present universal empire of public opinion',[2] because it had rendered itself independent of secular authority, emphasized moral revelation rather than theological doctrine and possessed a constitution so plastic that it adjusted with vigour to new conditions. Provided Christianity continued faithful to the moral revelation that created it and placed the brotherhood of man above all other motives, social, political or intellectual, the Christian Church would continue to astonish the world with its extraordinary vitality and endurance, remaining in all transformations essentially what Christ had made it. But once led astray by its pretensions, forgetting its simple but positive goal of brotherhood, Christianity and the Church became open to corruption and disgrace.

In *Ecce Homo* Seeley displayed the expert technique that inspired all his writings, whether of occasional or scholarly origin, to derive the fundamental principle or justification underlying an institution. In this he resembled other nineteenth-century intellectuals, Coleridge, Newman, Maurice and Mill, for examples, who in varying degrees found it necessary to formulate solutions to national problems by establishing controlling and guiding explanations. From the deceptively simple and ingenious argument of *Ecce Homo* Seeley hoped several things. Disputes within the Church would cease; controversies springing up around the origins of religious belief would be seen as peripheral to the historical meaning of Christianity. It would be understood that the essential importance of Christian religion had little to do with doctrine or dogma and was not necessarily compromised by defects in the structure and organization of the Church. No other proof of the success of Christianity and the Church was required than the fact of their survival, *a fortiori*, their vigorous survival. If the branches were infected, the trunk was healthy. Nothing else mattered except to contain the infection.

Freed from pointless controversies, finally realizing that the maxims of Horace had no effect applied to such new vices as

---

[1] *Ecce Homo*, pp. 348, 349–50.　　　　[2] Ibid., p. 350.

railway profiteering and adulterated foods, the Church and its clergy would be able to address themselves to real and critical problems arising from the changing nature of English social and economic life. In his writings of the 1860's Seeley even advanced a programme for the Church which may be called a distant paraphrase of the clerisy idea. He regarded the Church as the home of an intellectual *avant-garde*, a testing ground for advanced opinions, an 'ideal society, existing within the real one . . . a sort of provisional vehicle for ideas before they have power enough to embody themselves in political and social institutions.'[1] The special responsibility of Seeley's clerisy was of course to promote the brotherhood of man and therefore to prevent class antagonism and violent revolution. Drawn from all classes clergymen were the natural mediators 'in the perpetual warfare between class and class,'[2] tribunes interceding wherever necessary on behalf of the plebians.[3] But in order to accomplish this special task they had to forget the distant past and apply themselves to understanding the present; they had to acquire a systematic knowledge of modern affairs and enter fully into the activities of the new society if they were to have any share in forming ethical principles appropriate to the times. Older practices and methods would no longer serve. 'Charitable institutions are but patchwork,' he wrote characteristically, 'We are bound, not merely to relieve distresses in the detail, but to study them, to trace them to their causes; and if we find those causes in the very groundwork or framework of society, then to labour for organic change, for the abolition of bad institutions and bad customs.'[4]

Seeley's method of argument was not unlike that of Maurice, whose solutions to national crises also depended upon shifting the grounds of debate. It may even be suggested that Seeley's discussion of Christianity was almost as disingenuous as it was ingenious for what Seeley proposed was not only that the Church should heal itself but that it should ignore the attacks of rationalists advancing in the name of the new, competitive truth called

---

[1] A Letter Written by Professor J. R. Seeley on March 23, 1868, p. 15. B.M. 4109, f. 12 (9).

[2] Seeley, 'The Church as a Teacher of Morality', in *Lectures and Essays*, pp. 245–54, 278.

[3] Seeley, *Are the Churches in Touch with the People?* (London, 1867), p. 12.

[4] Ibid., p. 13.

science with its acolyte, social science. Seeley attempted to minimize the threat. If the brotherhood of man and social unity comprised the principal message of Christianity, what objection could the devotees of positive or biological science possibly bring? Proceeding in this way Seeley introduced an additional point. The Church had nothing to fear from science because science and religious morality were complementary forms of truth, twin revelations. 'Both are true and both are essential to human happiness.'[1] In a series of discussions meant as a sequel to *Ecce Homo* published anonymously in *Macmillan's Magazine* in the mid-seventies, slightly revised and republished as a book in 1882, Seeley continued his discussion of science and religion, only this time producing his final argument. Christianity was no longer simply one of two great revelations; it was one of a number of revelations, a great step in the history of religion certainly, but only one of a number of important steps that led up to an understanding of God.[2] But what was God? No less, Seeley answered, than the idea of a higher law, regularity or universal order, proclaiming the existence of a necessity beyond ourselves, defining our duty, controlling our pride, granting us knowledge of ourselves and therefore permitting freedom. In short, Christianity and science were indistinguishable, in so far as fundamentally both could be reduced (or elevated) to the principle of higher law; to that extent both the clergyman and the scientist shared the same goal. It followed that the true polarities could never be science and religion but the higher law and all adversaries of the higher law–atheism, scepticism, philistinism, secularism, materialism.

The equation of science and religion in the principle of higher law provided Seeley with the goal of unity which he had promoted throughout *Ecce Homo*, unity without force of arms, without coercion, binding and familial. It gave him too a principle of authority such as Matthew Arnold had produced by a similar equation of culture and the State; and it is therefore not surprising that Seeley also included culture in his category of higher law, as well as Maurice's theory of worship.[3] In the

---

[1] *Ecce Homo*, p. 353.

[2] [Seeley], 'Natural Religion', *Macmillan's Magazine*, XXXIV (June, 1876), p. 156.

[3] Ibid., pp. 161–2.

absence then of science, religion or culture society possessed no stable or unifying principles, and decay, enfeeblement and immorality resulted. These were the dangers, Seeley warned, confronting industrial England with its poorly-educated philistine population. Only dimly aware of the problem, the learned classes responded with penny readings, popular lectures and working men's colleges; but these were scarcely sufficient to keep the worker from the public house and the city man from the monotonous routine of desk and counting-house. Neither the worker nor the city man understood culture as anything more than a means to success and money-making. English life, Seeley concluded, was dull, tedious and corrupting; but through the recognition of higher principles outside the individual self it would achieve a rebirth and purification: 'Religion will now, for the first time, fairly undertake that regeneration of the present life and of actual society which it always promised, yet always indefinitely postponed; and in doing so it will, as we have seen, reunite itself with those other inspiring influences from which it ought never to have been separated. Religion will once more be understood as the general name for all the worships or habitual admirations which compose the higher life.'[1] And finally when regeneration is accomplished, a knowledge of duty will result: 'of all such enthusiasms it will still be held that the highest and most precious is that which has man for its object, and which manifests itself neither in works of Art nor discoveries of Science, but in emancipations, redemptions, reconciliations, and in a high ideal of duty; and this is the religion which bears the name of Jesus of Nazareth.'[2]

Sidgwick was in two minds regarding *Ecce Homo*. He found it consistently stimulating, virtually great, almost sublime. But he had doubts. *Ecce Homo* was filled with extraordinary errors; it was a broken reed. In a review article for the *Westminster Review* appearing in July 1866, Sidgwick subjected the historical portions of the work to a severe and uncompromising analysis. Seeley was careless, uncritical of his sources, unacquainted with German scholarship, curiously casuistic, prone to anachronism. The author had obviously read widely and thought deeply, but his method was wrong and his conclusions only roughly or

[1] *Macmillan's Magazine*, XXXVII (January, 1878), p. 191.
[2] Ibid.

partially correct. He had been unfair to the Jews, he had attributed to first-century Christianity developments which could only have occurred later, he had – it was amusing – virtually made Jesus into a Benthamite; and he had unfortunately contrasted reason and enthusiasm when the two were actually supplementary. There was another fault. So concerned was Seeley with explicating the meaning of the Sermon on the Mount that he had forgotten to mention the thoroughly Christian spirit of the auto-da-fe. *Ecce Homo* clearly would not last. And yet, it was a work of genius. Whatever the errors of the historical portions, the analysis of Christ's teaching was eloquent and inspiring.

Maurice was also impressed by *Ecce Homo*, which he called a very interesting and remarkable book, the author thoroughly in earnest, a layman of much courage. 'All his ways of contemplating the subject are so nearly the direct opposite of mine, that I am less afraid of bearing that testimony.'[1] As already indicated, there were excellent reasons for Maurice to appreciate Seeley's book. Seeley admired Maurice. After leaving Cambridge he sometimes taught classes at Maurice's Working Men's College in London, attracted by the community ideal of christian socialism.[2] This provided him with the sense of purpose which Christ's College, otherwise so stimulating and agreeable, could not give him.[3] Certainly *Ecce Homo* reflected Maurice's influence. The kinship basis of Christianity, requiring self-sacrifice and the 'enthusiasm of humanity' – a phrase Sidgwick much admired in Seeley but which is redolent of Maurice; perfection as a standard necessary but forever unobtainable; the emphasis on the social teaching of Christ and His union of morals and politics, as well as the insistence upon the 'intensely personal character of Christ',[4] were all critical components of Maurice's thinking. Seeley's method, radically different from his own, nevertheless corroborated Maurice's arguments.

Unsurprisingly, the theories of Maurice were more persuasive in the form Seeley gave them than in his own recondite

---

[1] Maurice, *Life*, II, pp. 511–12.

[2] MS draft of an address by Seeley.

[3] Seeley, 'Christ's College Thirty Years Ago,' *Christ's College Magazine* (Easter, 1886), p. 4.

[4] Maurice, *Life*, II, p. 466 n.

writings. 'In *Ecce Homo*,' wrote an admirer, 'we found a presentation of Christ in a form wholly congenial with the larger ideas of the social philosophy that was becoming a part of our religion. It is possible that we might have found this harmony elsewhere: Cambridge men may think that we ought to have been led this way by Maurice: as a matter of personal history, to many of us it was Seeley who effected for us this union between aspects of our mental life that we felt sorely ought to be made mutually illuminative and inspiring.'[1]

Both Maurice and Seeley addressed themselves directly to contemporary problems, but Maurice's idiom and paradoxes derived from theology and were concealed amongst the language of the Bible, the synoptic gospels and the Church fathers. Seeley spoke in 'the language of the open world of politics and legislation'[2] at a time when political questions were uppermost in the minds of students and dons. Maurice's theology solved for a few the dilemma of commitment – the performance of duty was the natural result of being human and had nothing to do with ratiocination – but this statement of duty had to be taken one more step if a larger audience of students were to be reached. If, as Maurice said, our humanity made it natural for us to perform duty, how did we go about it? Seeley answered the question more directly, more straightforwardly, than Maurice.

2.

When he assumed the chair of Latin at University College, London, in 1863, Seeley announced to his class that he would teach only classical linguistics, since this was the subject eminently suited to drill the undeveloped mind into method and accustom it to the satisfaction of certainty.[3] This was a conventional statement of faculty psychology and an appropriate remark for a professor of Latin, except that Seeley's basic interests had little to do with philology. In the same lecture he declared the real purpose of education to be the study of the moral sciences. Classical syntax and grammar, he stated, were simply the means of inculcating the kind of discipline that

---

[1] 'The Late Professor Seeley', *Cambridge Review*, XVI (January 24, 1895), pp. 160, 141–3.
[2] Ibid., p. 160.   [3] *Classical Studies*, p. 9.

could be used to introduce the higher subjects of philosophy and historical method. Having in this way justified classical philology, Seeley quickly passed to his real interest, positivist history, which he defined as a body of data supporting generalizations concerning the nature of man and society. Generalizations were scientific laws, and the purpose of law was prediction. By the 1860's this was a perfectly conventional mid-Victorian statement of history as science.

Seeley's curious London inaugural lecture, explaining what he preferred to teach but would not teach, may have been a rationalization for carrying out the statutory duties of the Latin chair. Another explanation for the cautious, clichéd defence of the teaching of classical languages may lie in the character of Seeley's London audience. Since 1800 the average age of students entering at Cambridge increased about a year or two, but students entering the London university colleges, like undergraduates at Scottish universities, tended to be younger. Frequently the student of a university college regarded his college education as an extension of the sixth form and passed on to the ancient universities to complete his education and also to compete for the numerous awards. If this is a construction that can legitimately be placed on Seeley's inaugural address at London, it will explain his references to faculty psychology and the undeveloped mind requiring method and drill in order to prepare for higher analysis.

In any event, the London inaugural address was not the first time Seeley had upheld the teaching of classical philology nor the first time he had done so reluctantly. It had only been a year since he had defended the linguistic bias of Cambridge classics against Oxford classical philosophy in order to publicize the removal of the mathematics prerequisite from the honours degree in classics, but even then his heart was not in the defence. He was thinking rather of the moral sciences tripos which had been established separately from classics in 1851, a decision which Seeley knew was certain to delay its reception, since few college scholarships, fellowships or university prizes were available to reward the successful moral scientist. If, as at Oxford, moral sciences had been introduced into the classical honours school, the subject would have attracted greater attention. Seeley admitted that Oxford classics gave students an introduction to general philosophy and history which 'we, though endeavouring to promote the same studies by our Moral Sciences Tripos, have hitherto envied without being at all able to rival.'[1]

Whatever the meaning of the London inaugural lecture, once in Cambridge Seeley no longer hesitated to announce his programme for the study of history as philosophy and science. Life he had told his London undergraduates, almost in passing, must not take us by surprise.[2] Cambridge received the same message, only now elaborated and stated in complete form. The finishing school theory of higher education as well as faculty psychology were both discarded. The purpose of education, Seeley announced, was not to apply a polish to the mind or merely to discipline the faculties. The purpose of education was to summarize the human experience, to understand the direction of 'momentous social changes,' to 'furnish a theory of human affairs' which would rescue men and society from the psychological and political delusions which accompanied social change experienced in ignorance: 'The man that has even a glimpse of such a theory, if the theory be itself a hopeful one, cannot but feel tranquillized and reassured; his life, from being a wandering or a drifting, becomes a journey or a voyage to a definite port; the changes that go on around him cease to appear capricious, and he is more often able to refer them to laws; hence his hopes become more measurable, and his plans more reasonable, and it may be that where his own efforts fail he is supported by faith in a law of Good, of which he has traced the workings.'[3]

Picturesque and positivist at one and the same time, this was compatible with the ideas which Seeley derived from Maurice and indeed a characteristic formulation of the mid-Victorian unbeliever in general. To worship or admire the higher principles outside the self, to replace the law of God with the law of Good, was to retain in the face of scepticism a hopeful theory of human affairs and to strengthen the individual against the

[1] *Student's Guide* (1862), p. 23. History was established as an independent honours subject in 1875. It was preceded by the Law and History Tripos, 1870–4.
[2] *Classical Studies*, p. 7.
[3] Seeley, 'The Teaching of Politics', in *Lectures and Essays*, pp. 297–8.

consequences likely to follow the loss of belief. To believe in the possibility of a higher morality unsupported by Christian dogma was to keep from withdrawal, to reserve for oneself a function and a place in society. The crucial point was that the theory of human affairs had to be 'a hopeful one'. Events must never be allowed to triumph over understanding.

Here was another definition of the prophet which Sidgwick could add to his catalogue. Seeley's prophet was a positivist, the medium of his prophecy was the science of history. The superiority of this kind of prophet over Arnold's alienated self was the possibility of vindication within the prophet's own life-time. If the prophet taught that all change was purposeful, that men shaped their goals to a higher necessity, that human behaviour was to some extent predictable, that scientific know-ledge gave control over social movement, that happiness was to be found in adapting oneself to general tendencies, and that, most importantly, perfection was unobtainable although im-provement possible, he would be honoured in his own country.

Sidgwick had found history disagreeable, a mass of insignifi-cant detail, receiving more attention than it deserved and definitely inferior to the study of politics – 'Politik . . . is so infinitely more important just now.'[1] Seeley agreed with Sidg-wick that government and civil society were the most compli-cated of all subjects accessible to the human mind. He differed from Sidgwick only in his belief that positivist history was a superior, even ideal method for establishing high standards of political behaviour. His views on the use of history followed Mill's *Logic* in every particular. History provided the raw material which supported philosophical and scientific generaliza-tions about human behaviour. It was the responsibility of the statesman to transform the generalizations into practical mea-sures which would yield the greatest happiness of the greatest number, to decide – Mill's own words might be quoted – 'What artificial means may be used, and to what extent, to accelerate the natural progress in so far as it is beneficial; to compensate for whatever may be its inherent inconveniences or disadvan-tages; and to guard against the dangers or accidents to which our species is exposed from the necessary incidents of its pro-gression.'[2] In 1869 in the Senate House at Cambridge, Seeley

[1] Sidgwick, *Memoir*, p. 124.   [2] Mill, *Logic* (1843), II, p. 611.

stated that he was ready to translate historical science into a programme of practical education. In one of the most famous of all Cambridge inaugural lectures, Seeley announced that 'our University is, and must be, a great seminary of politicians.'[1] He did not use the word 'seminary' indiscriminately. In *Ecce Homo* Seeley repeatedly compared the Church to a state, the priest to a statesman, qualities of leadership being more important than theology, only the Church was more successful than other states because it was a commonwealth from within, a civil society existing in the unconscious of its adherents. Only if the undergraduate preparing for a civil service or political career—or the undergraduate preparing for a career in the Church—realized that service to society consisted in a religious duty, a devotion to a higher purpose, could he accomplish the missionary tasks Seeley set him. The word 'seminary' applied to university teachers as well as students. They too had to regard the preparation of statesmen as a serious undertaking. Teaching had to be professional, to a certain extent specialized, the teacher displaying method and direction.

It was characteristic of Seeley, whose thinking was eclectic and whose desire it was to reconcile as many contradictory arguments as possible under the most inclusive generalizations— even to the point of gentle evasion—not to include in his celebrated inaugural address any direct mention of Kingsley, his immediate predecessor in the Regius chair. And yet Seeley's programme could be construed as in many respects a refutation of Kingsley's own inaugural lecture of 1860, 'The Limits of Exact Science as Applied to History'. Like other Cambridge anti-utilitarians and anti-positivists of the 1860's, Kingsley greatly feared the influence of Comte on undergraduates and teachers, and he particularly regretted the success positivists appeared to enjoy in underplaying the influence of exceptional individuals on the course of historical events. In the popular Victorian game of attributing historical progress to either religious or intellectual enlightenment (individual conscience or environment in nativist terms) Kingsley naturally opted for conscience. He did not deny the importance of law or pattern in history, nor did he object to the use of scientific method in historical study. His point was simply that the claims for

---

[1] 'The Teaching of Politics', p. 299.

scientific method had been exaggerated, that there were limits to the employment of an exact science of history and that the most important questions of social behaviour were not explained by the application of a number of very general and carelessly-defined physical laws. History for Kingsley was mainly biography. The study of exceptional men, of heroic and even demoniac types, fit well with his own muscular christian notion of character with its undertones of mystery, its awe of great persons—he who would comprehend Luther must be more than Luther–and its fascination with psychic or moral factors that–or so he said–defied all physical laws and upset all calculations.

Kingsley closed his inaugural lecture of 1860 and withdrew from the Senate House on a curious note of humility, as if by drawing attention to the mysterious elements of character and describing them as worthy of study in a university, he had suddenly and painfully realized important deficiencies in his own character, his failure to approach the 'norma' or ideal human character that motivated great men and explained their success. 'If I have . . . too often spoken of myself, and my own opinions,' he said, 'I can only answer that it is a fault which has been forced on me by my position and which will not occur again.'[1]

It was an odd ending but not untypical of Kingsley, and it raises the question of the role of a professor of history at Cambridge in the 1860's, the extent to which Kingsley regarded his chair and his person as influential, the degree to which he would exert himself to convince undergraduates that the method of historical investigation which he advocated was superior to that of positive science. In short, can the Kingsley of the 1860's be included in that category which Sidgwick called the 'new school' of professors, those who regarded themselves 'as much bound to teach and to write as any other salaried functionary is bound to discharge the duties for which he is paid'?

In one respect Kingsley came within Sidgwick's definition. The peculiar self-effacement of the inaugural address did not mean that Kingsley found teaching so embarrassing that he wished to avoid contact with students. On the contrary, he was

[1] Charles Kingsley, *The Limits of Exact Science as Applied to History* (Cambridge and London, 1860), p. 71.

certainly friendly and in fact one of the few professors in Cambridge in the early 1860's to take a personal interest in students,[1] inviting them to his home to discuss reading. In other respects, however, he was not a 'new school' professor. His history was quaint and non-professional. He thought about resigning. Even the fine start with students came to an end when financial problems forced him out of residence in 1862. There was also the factor of his undeniably strange habits and eccentric behaviour. He would go to the rooms of the fashionable set at Magdalene, the college of which he was a member, and in company with undergraduates he would eat anchovy toast and drink port, sherry or coffee; but suddenly he would break away and dash out, much as he had broken off his inaugural lecture, 'and then one would see him out of Magdalene windows sculling with bare arms and with all his might down the river. . . . I do not think any of us quite understood him. He had ways of his own, we thought, extravagant and visionary.'[2]

The entire burden of Seeley's argument was away from the visionary and the mysterious to the practical and the comprehensible. He fully intended to remain in residence and systematically prepare the new generation of students for their roles as future statesmen. He considered his professorial function a decisive departure from the practices of his predecessors in the modern history chair. Palmerston, he observed, had learned nothing from Professor Smyth, Pitt nothing from Professor Symond. 'But history was not then the practical study that it is now, and the kindred subject of political economy was not then taught in this University.'[3] Seeley refused to accept the minimal role of professor implicit in the traditional Cambridge apology that students learnt best about life and society from each other. He rejected the notion that the function of the teacher was simply to correct youthful irregularities. Instead he introduced a new factor into the education of undergraduates that must be considered a revolution in the history of the Cambridge professoriate. That factor was himself. 'It may seem a somewhat exaggerated view of my function,' he announced, 'but I cannot help regarding myself as called to join with the Professor of

[1] Kingsley, *Life*, II, p. 153.
[2] Albert Pell, *Reminiscences* (London, 1908), p. 76.
[3] 'The Teaching of Politics', p. 300.

Political Economy in presiding over this preparation [for political life]. What will at any rate be learnt *at* the University it should be possible, I hold, to learn *from* the University, and I shall consider it to be in great part my own fault if this does not prove to be the case.'[1]

How completely different from Kingsley's odd, public confession of vanity and promise that he would not be forward again!

3.

In one respect Seeley agreed with Kingsley. Character was to be admired. It is true he rejected Kingsley's idea that character was mysterious and if not exactly beyond analysis then certainly independent of environment; but he was no more anxious than other positivists–Mill and the French sociologists, for example –to completely do away with the individual. In one of his essays he nonchalantly suggested the creation of a 'national calendar' of eminent Englishmen and men of other countries past and present who could be admired and worshipped. Admiration could actually begin in the family and then by degrees extend outward and finally backward in history.[2] The point of the calendar was to constantly display great moral examples for emulation. Seeley's calendar was an obvious copy of Comte's well-known secular substitute for saints' days, except that it included great religious personalities as well. Maurice's theory of worship–the religion of humanity–providing national unity under the concept of a higher standard, was a reinforcing ingredient.

The essential difference between Seeley's view of the individual and Kingsley's is that Seeley, like Maurice, always treated the individual as standing for some higher principle, as representing some important generalization. The individual was to be admired for the purpose he represented rather than for his absolutely individual qualities. Kingsley's Luther was above the law–or responsive only to a special moral principle–but Seeley's individuals were all illustrations of the working of the law. The Jesus of *Ecce Homo* was such an illustration, intensely personal as Maurice said, but not intensely personalized. Even the

---

[1] Ibid., pp. 299–300.
[2] 'The Church as a Teacher of Morality', pp. 264–5.

miracles which Jesus performed failed to give him a recogniz-
ably unique personality. As his critics complained, Seeley
described the suspensions of natural law which Christ was
alleged to have accomplished in a thoroughly matter-of-fact
manner, without any special comment except that Jesus's
followers believed in them and without any attempt to establish
them as exceptional or divine in origin. It was *Ecce Homo* rather
than *Ecce Deus*, and the man was important for the principle of
universal brotherhood he taught and not the converse.

Socrates was described by Seeley in the same way, as an
archetype, real and historical, but not in any way individual-
ized, more important for his method of teaching than for his
personal characteristics. In his London inaugural address Seeley
connected Socrates with the origins of social science, calling him,
'the inventor of scientific method, that is of science itself, who
first speculated on morals, who first dreamed that the intellect
might be methodically trained, and thus became the father of
all education properly so called, and indirectly of all universities and colleges in the western world.'[1]

Seeley had a special use for his two famous types. Together
they defined the characteristics of effective teaching and the
qualities of the successful teacher. In *Ecce Homo* he elaborated
the characteristics of socratic teaching. It encouraged disinterested inquiry, exalted logic and scientific method and was therefore naturally disrespectful of authority. This was the reason
socratic teaching did not try to perpetuate itself in a formal
institution, and the fact that this happened was probably accidental. There was another important characteristic of socratic
teaching. Method tended to triumph over individuality, and
consequently the teacher subordinated his own individuality to
the method, letting the dialectic itself guide the student to his
own conclusions. Socratic teaching, Seeley wrote in 'The
Teaching of Politics', was like modern history, 'knowing nothing,
but guiding others to knowledge by suggestive interrogations.'[2]

What might be an asset was also a principal defect of socratic
teaching. Method drilled the intellect but did nothing for the
conscience. Method might produce a highly-trained statesman,
but could it produce a good man? The socratic philosopher who
tried so hard to explain the nature and meaning of good was

[1] *Classical Studies*, p. 12. [2] 'The Teaching of Politics', p. 316.

actually powerless to make men good. Seeley concluded as any follower of Maurice was bound to conclude, that the training of intellect alone could never produce high standards of moral conduct. This was, incidentally, a notable reversal of the well-known positivist hypothesis that moral progress in history was exclusively intellectual in character.[1]

Seeley found in Christianity a more effective way to reform and change character. Christianity depended on the admiration of the central figure of Christ, to a lesser extent on hagiology and the recognition of saintly behaviour. Christianity employed enthusiasm rather than logic, rhetoric rather than science, example and action rather than contemplation. Reason submitted to authority, embodied in the person of the Christian teacher. 'There is no moral influence in the world, excepting that occasionally exerted by great men, comparable to that of a good teacher.'[2] It is by exciting a passion for virtue that the Christian teacher overcomes the 'anarchic and lawless instincts' of passion in every man and makes the Christian a law to him-himself. That is, by internalizing law in all of his followers, Christ did not require a minute code of rules for his commonwealth. Brotherly love, therefore, was more important than science. It was better to be a citizen of the New Jerusalem than of the New Athens.

Actually, it was better to be a citizen of both. Science alone could not improve character, but then brotherly love alone could not guarantee happiness. If a choice had to be made, then Jerusalem over Athens, but Seeley preferred not to make the choice. His special intellectual quality was syncretism. As he explained in *Ecce Homo*, both Christian morality and science were essential to human happiness. Socratic teaching was best for the intellect, Christian teaching was best for morality. Science enabled men to comprehend their environment, morality–the law of philanthropy–made the world a safe place in which to live. Both forms of teaching were necessary in the university, and both forms, he found, could flourish in an English environment.

Apologists for unreformed Cambridge said that an English

[1] For example, as emphasized by Buckle in his *History of Civilization in England*, but Maine too. Burrow, p. 169.
[2] *Ecce Homo*, pp. 237–8, 120.

university could not combine a Germanic devotion to research and learning with a characteristically English concern for the moral welfare of students, but Seeley rejected this position. Cambridge could do both because Cambridge was a collegiate university. Seeley accepted the widely-held idea of a college as a place where conduct was taught. It coincided exactly with his conception of morality grounded in the family, broadening to include friends and the wider community. Communal living forced the individual to subdue his own interests for the sake of college harmony and at the same time subjected the student to the authority of his seniors. 'No doubt the college system makes the great difference between an English and foreign university. Instead of leaving our students to live as they please in the town, we have established large boarding-houses, called colleges, in which the students live under a certain discipline, and with a certain family life.'[1] By drawing a distinction between Christian and socratic teaching, Seeley's intention was actually to purify both the college and university, to keep their educational functions separate and therefore clear, to allow the college to pursue its primary object of moral or character formation and the university to devote itself to the acquisition of knowledge, to become what he called a centre of culture for the improvement of the standards and values of English life. Nearly twenty years after the inaugural lecture, when Seeley once more had public occasion to define the functions of a university, the collegiate ideal was de-emphasized and subordinated to a partly German, partly Scottish, partly missionary conception of a university. In a university, scientific method was to be applied to the acquisition of knowledge and knowledge was to be disseminated to the nation by numerous new universities and by the extension movement, 'a great teaching order which shall have its fixed lecture-rooms in every great town, and shall send out missions to smaller towns,' its purpose to raise the 'dead-level, insipid, barren, abject, shop-keeping life' of England.[2]

[1] Seeley, 'Liberal Education in Universities', *Lectures and Essays*, p. 202, first published in F. W. Farrar's *Essays on a Liberal Education* (London, 1867). Seeley, who bore a great dislike for public boarding schools, stressed the importance of the family in the education of young children in his essay, 'The Chuch as a Teacher of Morality'.

[2] Seeley, *A Midland University: An Address* (Birmingham, 1887), pp. 16, 6.

In the 1860's, however, Seeley accepted the historical, collegiate nature of Cambridge as an accomplished fact; and his remarks and efforts were directed towards correcting the imbalance that he believed resulted from the usurpation by independent colleges of the educational functions of the university.

4.

'The Regius Professor', wrote Maitland in 1903 when he refused the chair of modern history on the death of Lord Acton, 'is expected to speak to the world at large and even if I had anything to say to the W. at L. I don't think that I should like full houses and the limelight.'[1] In the same year he wrote Henry Jackson, one of Cambridge's great classical teachers, that 'The expectation that the R.P. of M.H. must have something to say to the "muchedumbre" seems to me a misfortune.'[2] Maitland's attitude towards the Regius Professorship of History, no doubt personal, may also reflect the opinion of a later generation of scholars. It was certainly not the attitude of the generation of the 1860's. Precisely because the 'new school' of professors worried about the *muchedumbre* and the shifting character and changing nature of moral behaviour, they were anxious to find some means of insuring that the university retain an influential voice in the affairs of the nation. For them it was inconceivable that the Regius Professor would not speak to the world at large.

There can be no doubt that Seeley's appointment to the chair of modern history at Cambridge was made in the full understanding that the Regius Professor of Modern History had a message to convey. Certainly it was not his professional or specialized competence in modern history that recommended him; for as he very candidly admitted, he had only read discursively in modern history and had never studied a single period of modern history critically in the original sources, although he had occupied himself with some of the problems of historical philosophy.[3] At the time of his appointment his most

[1] C. H. S. Fifoot, ed., *The Letters of Frederic William Maitland* (Cambridge, 1965), p. 349.
[2] Ibid., p. 351.
[3] Seeley to Kingsley, March 1869, B.M. Add. MS 41299, f. 142.

ambitious historical project was an edition of the first decade of Livy for the Oxford University Press.

Gladstone, upon who it devolved to select the Regius Professor, a crown appointment, was not to be dissuaded by these defects in Seeley's professional qualifications. For Gladstone, as well as for Kingsley, who may have been asked to name possible successors in the modern history chair, the paramount consideration was not whether Seeley possessed a specialist knowledge of modern history but whether he would address himself to the crucial moral issues of the day, specifically the threat of atheism. Kingsley's task was to ascertain Seeley's opinion of Comte and postive theory; Gladstone himself undertook to learn Seeley's view on Christ and the origins of Christian belief. To both Seeley's replies were cautious and mildly evasive. To Kingsley he replied that he would certainly combat Comte's atheism but that he did not feel equal to the task of refuting Comte's method or philosophy of history. Taking his answer even one step further, anticipating the argument he would use repeatedly in the future when he redefined religion, science or positivism as higher law, Seeley offered one of his typical paradoxes. The proper attitude of the Church, he said, was to recognize the extent to which Comtism might further religion and morality. 'Just at present Comtism seems so irresistibly triumphant, that I have contented myself with pointing out that it is in a sense a Christian movement and with trying to induce the Church to appropriate what is good in it.'[1]

To Gladstone Seeley repeated his theme that Christianity was the brotherhood of man, at the same time relying on *Ecce Homo* to explain his precise meaning. There can be no greater proof of the interest Gladstone had in Seeley than the fact that he completely absorbed himself in the book and indeed was so preoccupied with its contents, that irritated friends and supporters reminded him that problems like franchise reform, Ireland and the unity of the Liberal Party had an equal right to his attention.[2] Undeterred by these reminders of his political responsibilities, Gladstone persisted in his examination of *Ecce Homo* and somehow in 1868 found time to defend the book in

[1] Ibid.
[2] John Morley, *The Life of William Ewart Gladstone* (London, 1903), II, pp. 172–3.

print. He described it as a work eminently suited to the needs of the time and one in which the strength and personality of Jesus were admirably upheld and—this was the decisive point that cleared Seeley for the chair—without denying the theanthropic idea that Jesus was both man and God.[1] At the very least Gladstone was satisfied that if Seeley did not actually affirm the miracles allegedly performed by Christ, he had refrained from recording his disbelief.[2]

Gladstone's invitation to Seeley to undertake the functions of the Professor of Modern History arrived in mid-September 1869, or on the very eve of Michaelmas Term, which suggests the possibility that Gladstone or Kingsley might have had second thoughts after all, suspicions that Seeley's views were not in every respect comforting. But if second thoughts existed they are not to be recovered. The invitation arrived and Seeley accepted: 'nothing could give me greater pleasure,' he said, 'and I believe there is no position in the world in which I could do so much good.'[3]

Seeley did not disappoint the famous prime minister whose odd absorption in a topical book on the life and teaching of Jesus during a crucial period in his own career and in the political life of the nation frustrated friends and advisers. He seized the opportunity afforded by the chair of modern history to speak to the *muchedumbre*; and it was he more than any of his predecessors who established the tradition that Maitland found such a misfortune, if not by any absolutely greater concern for the moral and cultural welfare of society—for Kingsley before him and other professors like Maurice had spent their lives in social and educational reform—then at least by his programmatic statements, sweeping generalizations and frankly publicistic remarks. Seeley's rhetoric and sense of drama, his sensational or epigrammatic sentences, skilfully summarizing and ordering complex historical and sociological information, were perfectly suited to the young audience living in the confusing restless 1860's. His remarks were directly aimed at those students who, absorbing his ideal of service, would one day leave Cambridge and carry the message of the Regius Professor throughout

---

[1] William Ewart Gladstone, *Ecce Homo* (London, 1868), pp. 108–23.
[2] Ibid., p. 7.
[3] Seeley to Gladstone, September 14, 1869, B.M. Add. MS 44422, f. 33.

English society. Seeley's role was to explain the new industrial and democratic society, to establish the principles of leadership in Church and state and to train a new intellectual aristocracy to take over the leadership functions once performed by a territorial aristocracy, or oligarchy as he preferred to call it, in order to recast the meaning of aristocracy.[1] The complexity of modern life, he argued so frequently as to leave no doubt of his prophetic intentions, required more intelligence, more precise knowledge, severer method and firmer character in government than in any other period.[2] The education of the new élite was therefore a serious undertaking and had to be based on a philosophical and historical understanding of the changes occurring in English social and economic life.

Seeley's foremost object was to train men for leadership rather than scholarship; and if he seemed to favour the German ideal of research and the pursuit of knowledge in and for itself, he also believed completely in a teaching university. Universities had the responsibility to disseminate knowledge as well as gather it. Actually the support he sometimes gave to the German belief in the importance of university research was intended more as a means of emphasizing the need for change in higher education and of underscoring the urgency, in a broad sense utility of learning, than it was a definite goal for himself or his students. In practice he preferred not to engage too extensively in original research, and he never approved of erudition for its own sake. Inevitably he found the Cambridge examination system a nuisance and complained that it fastened teaching to a narrow and stilted syllabus. Under his influence the history tripos was changed into its nineteenth-century form, broad periodization and general ideas. The innovations are sometimes attributed to Acton, but they are really Seeley's inspiration, born of his desire to discover those elements of pattern and sequence in history that would prepare the new generation for its future role, to assist each student in locating his duties, or as he explained in the inaugural lecture, 'teaching each man his place in the republic of man, the post at which he is stationed, the function with which he is invested, the work that is required

---

[1] Seeley, *Introduction to Political Science* (London, 1919), pp. 321–2. This work consists of lectures Seeley gave in Cambridge in 1885–6 and in 1891.

[2] Ibid., p. 360.

of him—such a study is History when comprehensively pursued.'[1]

In Seeley the silent teaching revolution accumulating in Cambridge throughout the 1860's explodes in a programme and finds a public voice. Elsewhere in the university through different, even opposing intellectual traditions, dons were arriving at a common destination. That teaching might be a career, that it might in surprising fashion restore to the mid-Victorians a function they despaired of losing, that the individual teacher might be an important influence on the student, a factor in the formation of his attitudes, behaviour and character, had long found expression in the writings of utilitarians and intuitionists and in the work of the Arnoldians in the schools. But Cambridge was slow to absorb the lesson. The institutional structure stood in the way. For the teaching revolution to be ultimately successful, the teaching structure of Cambridge had to be modified. Here again Seeley's activities provide a clue to one aspect of the change. Although in the professorial tradition Seeley gave formal, rhetorical lectures, he did not regard this method of teaching as superior to the informal instruction used in the colleges. He began, in fact, a new practice, inviting advanced students to his home to participate in discussion seminars and informal conversation classes. There the real work of his teaching took place, socratic as he himself defined that word, the man subordinating himself to his method, 'guiding others to knowledge by suggestive interrogations.' Doubtless, however, no one knew better than he the convenience of his distinction between socratic and Christian teaching, for the method no less than the man brought forth admiring students.

'Seeley was witty, charming, sympathetic, entirely void of self importance, never making ignorance an excuse for sarcasm, and under his presidency there was a great deal of serious thought given to politics in the higher sense; though pupils were often too shy to talk in the seminar itself, they did talk afterwards among themselves on the subjects there discussed.'[2]

---

[1] 'The Teaching of Politics', p. 298.
[2] 'King's in 1883', Wedd Papers, K.C.L., Cambridge.

CHAPTER 6

DONNISHNESS

1.

'Cambridge,' complained Seeley in 1867, 'is like a country invaded by the Sphinx. To answer the monster's conundrums has become the one absorbing occupation.'[1] The questions of the sphinx dealt with life, those of the tripos with easily-tested knowledge, but it is perverse to reproach Seeley for a poor simile. The tripos certainly kept honours students extremely busy, for success was generously rewarded. Well before mid-century a high finish in the tripos guaranteed a college fellowship; and until late in the nineteenth century a first class honours degree was still the road to post graduate academic distinction in all the colleges except Trinity. Fellowships were a reward for undergraduate industry rather than a recognition of teaching ability or future scholarship.

The tripos was a written comprehensive examination which originated in the eighteenth century. Originally an examination in mathematics (arithmetic, geometry, algebra, trigonometry, mechanics, optics, astronomy and Newton's *Principia*), it was considered to be the oldest and most famous written competitive examination in England. In 1824 a tripos was established in classics, but mathematics enjoyed a unique prestige for another thirty-three years. Until 1857 no honours candidates except noblemen were permitted to sit the classical tripos without having first taken the mathematical honours examination. But while mathematics dominated university examinations, classics were important in college competitions, especially at King's.

---

[1] Seeley, 'Liberal Education', p. 163.

Until 1851 scholars of King's proceeded directly to a degree without taking university examinations. As a result–and because Eton resisted the introduction of mathematics until 1840–mathematics was virtually unknown in King's.

The tripos examinations stressed method–technique, precision, logic and rigour–and method was transferable: the man who understood the principles of argument and knew how to derive generalizations from a body of factual material could subsequently teach himself any subject. If necessary, the tripos could also be defended as preparation for professional life. Mathematics and classics were of obvious value to the schoolmaster; logic and argument were the tools of the lawyer and politician; generalization enabled the clergyman to read God's will; scientific method was essential to the physician.

The tripos was held to be scientific in ideals, content, and in its method of determining ability. Unlike Oxford, Cambridge ranked its honours men on a strict order of merit, from the senior wrangler or senior classic down. This intensified the competition for honours and made many believe that the tripos system of marking was a scrupulously objective method of selection. As Francis Galton wrote in 1869, 'The fairness and thoroughness of Cambridge examinations have never had a breath of suspicion cast upon them.'[1] The order of merit had faults, however, that did not go unrecognized. Ranking could only be accurate within each year's grouping, making it difficult to compare men of different years who might be competing for the same college fellowship. It also reinforced the character of the tripos as an examination on set knowledge; textbooks were especially compiled to offer the student unimaginative lessons to be gotten up quickly by rote. Nowhere was there a suggestion of original synthesis, analysis or a developing frontier of knowledge.

The nature of the tripos made it a useful device for controlling students. Success in the examinations required considerable advance preparation and cramming, as well as speed and stamina during the long hours of the examination week. The competition was strenuous, and bets were laid in advance as to the probable winners. 'True to their sporting instincts the English had contrived to turn even the university examinations into an

[1] Francis Galton, *Hereditary Genius* (London, 1962), p. 59.

athletic contest.'[1] If a student were conscientious, if he needed the academic recognition and financial reward that the tripos could bestow, if he crammed to the point of injuring his health – particularly in his last year – he would have little time for mischief.

The university of course did not rely solely on the tripos to 'guard the inexperienced against the temptations of youth and the dangers of wasteful extravagance.'[2] The colleges and university had established a number of purely disciplinary measures and institutions: walls, gates and ditches surrounding the colleges were meant to restrict student mobility and prevent townsmen from disturbing the college peace. Compulsory chapel and college lectures, dinners in hall and college examinations were given a disciplinary purpose; and a variety of punishments – admonitions, rustication, expulsion, prohibitions and literary impositions – were customarily meted out for violations. College deans and chaplains, retaining their religious functions, were also made responsible for student conduct, as was the tutor, who ceased to be primarily a teacher.

Responsibility for overseeing the activities of students away from the colleges belonged to the university. Proctors flanked by subordinates called 'bulldogs' policed the streets in order to prevent town and gown conflicts and to enforce regulations regarding academic dress – the latter especially useful in detecting violators. The university also established curfews, licensed boarding and lodging houses, and required prior notification of all dinner and supper parties given in lodgings or in the town. Shopkeepers – particularly wine merchants – were licensed to trade with students; and tutors were given the authority to review student accounts. All bills in fact – college, university and tradesmen's – were first received by college tutors.

Regulations governing student conduct had been framed in a period when undergraduates were of secondary school age; but by 1850 or 1860 entering freshmen were eighteen or nineteen – a year or two older than earlier in the century. Customary restraints no longer applied; but many of the older dons continued to act as if the majority of undergraduates were schoolboys and bravely tried to implement the existing regulations.

---

[1] Annan, *Leslie Stephen*, p. 24.
[2] Graham Commission (1852), Report, p. 16.

Discipline was undermined, however, by jurisdictional disputes between the university and its constituent colleges; college loyalty frequently conflicted with university authority. By mid-century it was still customary for the proctors to report under-graduates suspected of sexual offences to the colleges rather than, as an ancient statute directed, to the Vice-Chancellor's Court; and college justice tended to be more lenient. A statute of 1858 attempted to restore serious offences to the Vice-Chancellor's Court. But even the Vice-Chancellor—himself the head of a college—was reluctant to act against college interests.

University authority was further hampered by disputes with the town corporation. The university's far-reaching regulation of local tradesmen, its assumption of police power within the town, its high-handed treatment of prostitutes and the inquisitorial nature of its examination of prisoners in the university prison—so much at variance with common law—aroused the suspicion and hostility of borough officials. Undergraduates on a spree benefited from the resentment.

Poll or pass men, who comprised the majority of under-graduates in the university, were the principal beneficiaries of relaxed university discipline. They were usually addressed as idle and dissolute, but some of the recrimination was unjust. There were good reasons for avoiding the honours examination, especially before 1851. There were only two honours subjects and both were highly specialized and technical, requiring schoolboy cramming which could impair health. Many of the poll men were secure of the future and saw no reason to abandon three years of leisure and recreation for the rigours of a highly competitive examination. Sons of noblemen and gentry, as well as sons from other wealthy families, frequently adopted this attitude—even those of considerable intellectual ability. The largest proportion of poll men intended to take holy orders and aspired to nothing more than a country rectory. Ambitious students preparing for ecclesiastical careers invariably read for honours. The great bishops and public school headmasters of the nineteenth century took honours degrees.

When the poll degree first came under serious scrutiny in the early 1860's, exhausting argument and discussion resulted in two major reforms. A third or 'special' examination in either theology, philosophy, history, political economy, natural science and engineering (mechanical science) was added as a final degree requirement. In addition, the examination schedule itself was tightened to enable poll men to graduate about six months before honours men, since 'it had long been objected that the Cambridge course for this degree consumed more time than could be spared by young men who were designed for professions, and who would have to spend some further time on education elsewhere to prepare them for their special duties.'[1] This explanation was partly euphemistic, for throughout the century many medical students at Cambridge took the special examination in natural science mainly because they wished to enjoy a period of leisure before commencing a clinical routine in the London hospitals. Scientists and teachers like Michael Foster and Clifford Allbutt, anxious to raise the standards of the Cambridge Medical School, vainly tried to turn all the medical students to the natural sciences tripos. By 1885 students reading for pass degrees deserved much of the criticism directed at them. The establishment of new triposes in philosophy, biological science, theology, law, history and Semitic and Indian languages, the reform of classics and mathematics and the introduction of two-part triposes, enabling a student to read more than one subject, removed many of the traditional objections to the honours degree, a fact generally recognized when for the first time in the history of Cambridge, honours degrees outnumbered pass degrees.[2]

Dons and royal commissioners, despite their occasional discomfort about poll men, were reluctant to abolish the pass degree because they feared that inevitably the standard of the honours degree would be lowered. They did not believe that the

---

[1] *Student's Guide* (1866), p. 277.

[2] After 1885, however, the percentage of honours degrees increased slowly. In 1902 approximately 53 per cent of the degrees given in Cambridge went to honours men, and in 1913–14 about 62 per cent. The number of honours students and degrees varied radically from college to college. From 1851–1906 one-third of all Cambridge students took pass degrees and over one quarter went down without taking any degrees. See *Student's Guide* (1866); Return Relating to the Universities of Oxford and Cambridge, 1866, li, p. 69; Royal Commission on Oxford and Cambridge (1922), Appendices, 154 and 185; and Tillyard, *A History of University Reform*, pp. 299–301.

quality and intellectual distinction of the tripos could be maintained if the poorest students were required to take honours degrees. There were also more positive reasons for retaining the pass degree. Some students did not benefit from early specialization. Their interests and abilities developed late, and the pass degree at least gave them a chance to explore more subjects, to read widely and generally. If they failed to make use of this comparative leisure and latitude, they had only themselves to blame.

In several ways the poll man was an asset and could be used to further some of the important educational reforms of the nineteenth century. Since he often had a family or other guaranteed position awaiting him upon graduation, the colleges were not obliged to assist him in finding employment, and tutors could concentrate on the honours students whom they were anxious to help. Furthermore, since the poll men were invariably pensioners, their tuition fees and miscellaneous college expenditures could be used to subsidize the more expensive education of honours students, especially those who had entered as sizars or possessed limited means. In general the colleges were reluctant to make poor students pay the increased lecture and tuition fees necessitated by the mid-Victorian teaching reforms. The poll man may have been especially useful during the agrarian depression when most college incomes declined and dons were doubly anxious to meet scholarship and exhibition payments. How important a subsidy of scholars and sizars the fees of poll men were is difficult to determine from college accounts, but there are indications the subsidy was valuable. When the cost of educating students rose sharply during the inflationary period following the first world war, a nearly desperate Trinity Hall threatened to revert to a policy of admitting the 'idle rich'.[1]

Despite, however, objections to the tripos as narrow and cramped and despite the fact that the poll men could be used to further some of the reforms begun in the late 1850's, the existence of the poll degree was a continuous embarrassment to the Victorian dons, a standing refutation of their claim that Cambridge was a highly competitive society open to talent from all social classes and groups.

[1] Evidence submitted to Royal Commission of 1919, C.U.L. Box VI, folder 5, p. 18.

DONNISHNESS

Conspicuous among the idle poll men of the first half of the nineteenth century were the young aristocratic bravos who gambled on horses in nearby Newmarket, frequented disorderly houses, gladly returned or provoked the insults of town bargees and turned athletic contests into wild brawls.[1] Their pranks came close to imperilling the lives of dons and other students. An American at Trinity in the 1840's did not believe that young English aristocrats deserved to be called gentlemen. Relating a disgraceful episode in the Union Debating Society in which two undergraduates assaulted one another, he wrote unctuously that 'English young gentlemen at a public meeting are more un-gentlemanly than any *class* of our people (for a meeting of Irish or other foreigners in New York is not to be considered an American meeting), they never look upon the occasion in a serious light, but seem to consider it the most natural one for a lark.'[2] Albert Pell was one of the wealthy aristocratic students of the 1840's who soon saw that he 'might be as idle and un-studious as [he] chose.' He left an instructive account of how he and other privileged and raffish undergraduates passed their time:

'In the year that I entered Trinity one of the proctors . . . rendered himself very unpopular from his diligence and severity. He was feared and disliked. He was attended in his patrols by a wonderfully active little "bulldog", nimble and long-winded as a hare. He chased a little friend of mine twice or three times round Rose Crescent, Market Place, and Trinity Street, when, on the very point of making his capture, he slipped and broke his leg, poor fellow! His master had become so very unpopular and disagreeable that it was decided he must be punished by a dip in the river. Mr. Smith, however, was on his guard, and frustrated the attempt by retreating to his college stronghold, the outer gate of which was promptly closed by the porter. The Trinity men by this time had got together in the street, and using a builder's plank as a battering-ram, smashed the door, only to find a strong chain stretched across the doorway inside,

---

[1] Perhaps the last example of how violent an undergraduate mob could be was the notorious assault on the Newnham gates in 1921, prompted by the vote taken on degrees for women. A photograph of the mob leaving the Senate House is in the Whibley Papers, Pembroke College.

[2] Bristed, I, pp. 180–1.

under which the assaulters would have to stoop in entering. As on the threshold we saw a Caius man with poker uplifted on guard, we all hesitated. Meanwhile the Trinity dons had been sent for—Peacock, Sedgwick, and Whewell. On their coming up, a townsman ventured the attempt of thrusting Whewell aside, whereupon that wondrous example of stature and wisdom took the rapscallion by the coat-collar into an angle of the church opposite and pummelled him unmercifully—a warning to us undergraduates that we had better take ourselves off, which we did. Mr. Smith had so impressed me by the exercise of his University authority, that long afterwards, on meeting him unexpectedly in Regent Street in the evening, I bolted for a moment down a convenient passage.'[1]

In truth the majority of dons had no heart for such disagreeable and dangerous disciplinary assignments and vacillated between permissiveness and a stern paternalism. When wearied by the attempt to enforce a uniform standard of conduct, they turned their attention away to the amusements of a bachelor society. The authority of the university, they said, had not been compromised. Nowhere among the students were there signs of determined insubordination, nowhere indications that students would rise *en masse*, challenge the authorities and force the closing of the university as happened in Russia in the early 1850's. Cambridge undergraduates were not renegade gentry or alienated continental intellectuals. They were pillars of the establishment; two-thirds of them came from clerical and landed families, and the misconduct of a few exuberant poll men could not be regarded as anything more serious than the customary irregularities expected from the youth of the governing classes.

In the late 1850's and early 1860's, however, some tutors took a different view of the polloi. Regarding idleness and wanton behaviour as inappropriate to a university environment, no matter what the social background of students, they made a positive effort to gain the respect and affection of undergraduates who were usually ignored, except when they were deliberately provocative. Leslie Stephen, a tutor of Trinity Hall, and, it has been said, the first of the muscular Christians, led the way by making sports, particularly rowing, activities recognized and supported by the college: 'The undergraduates saw that

[1] Pell, p. 77. For other episodes see EVC, pp. 374, 417–18.

their tutor's heart was in the College and, what was more, in their personal pursuits. It was Stephen who presided at Bump Suppers and wrote the College Boating Song, and they noticed that his enthusiasm was as frenzied as their own when the boat went head of the river. "I shall never forget the joy with which he caught hold of my hand and shook it," said the stroke of the boat on that occasion. "He very nearly upset us all into the river, and, if I had not used some strong language, I believe he would have done so." Undergraduates could forget that he was a parson, for Stephen was ready to take the lead in every new enthusiasm.'[1]

The active participation of college fellows in student sports begins before the return of Maurice and Seeley to Cambridge but is part of the same change of attitude which led those thinkers to stress the importance of teaching. Ultimately the renewed interest in students may be traced to Dr. Arnold; but in Cambridge it may be said to begin with the appointment of the first Graham Commission in 1850. Dons began to respond to the external pressures on the university, to demands that Cambridge broaden its curriculum, remove its civil disabilities and lower its expenses in order to attract more students. Dons were beginning to see the implications of the liberal reforms of the second quarter of the nineteenth century and the rationalist attack on religious orthodoxy. If society was in confusion and values changing, then Cambridge could no longer rely on compulsory chapel, obsolete regulations or the tripos—the sphinx that always asked the same menacing questions—to provide the essential teaching of the university. A more positive and dynamic effort had to be made to reach the mind of the nation through its youth and potential leaders. Students had to be taught to understand themselves, and Cambridge had to give them standards by which to measure the aims of their time.

---

[1] Annan, *Leslie Stephen*, pp. 32, 30–6. Another don who was successful in subduing young bloods was Henry Latham, Senior Tutor of Trinity Hall. 'He was a remarkable figure, unrivalled in the power of controlling full-blooded Undergraduates. No man understood better the need of enforcing order and obedience; no man saw more clearly that petty regulations and frequent interference only serve to make dignity ridiculous and corrupt the moral bonds of discipline. . . . To bring young men together and keep them out of mischief . . . was a function not always performed by College Tutors with success.' Heitland, *After Many Years*, p. 143.

Leslie Stephen resigned his tutorship in 1862 and left for London two years later, well on his way to agnosticism and convinced that Cambridge did not care whether a good man came or went. Signs of a transformation in the university, however, were apparent at the time of his departure. Within the next decade a revolution occurred. Donnishness was in retreat.

2.

In the middle of the nineteenth century there were two undergraduate conceptions of a don which passed under the heading of donnishness. Both emphasized the separation of dons from students. The first conception recalled the amiable neglect and indifference which were the characteristics of an isolated, ageing and idle bachelor community still allied in tastes and values to a hard-drinking and an athletic, county society. Gourmandizing, convivial wine parties and gambling were the typical activities of the amiable don. At best this don possessed a certain gracious demeanour and a talent for witty and pleasant conversation; at worst he was an irresponsible and abandoned man, such as Macaulay described in 1854 when he reminded Whewell of 'two reverend gentlemen who were high in college office when I was an undergraduate. One of them never opened his mouth without an oath, and the other had killed his man.'[1]

The agreeable don remained part of the literature of university stereotypes until at least the First World War. He could be found at undergraduate festivities, sharing their food and their card games; he was noted for his devotion to antiquarian history or eccentric hobbies; he was frequently an expert on college plate and the portraits in Hall; and he kept a close watch on the condition of the lawns and cobbles. Such dons were J. M. Image, a Trinity tutor in the 1880's remembered as 'an agreeable fellow of the old school'; John Cooper, a Trinity tutor in the 1850's—'an amiable right-handed man, of no particular force'—and William Collings Mathison, another mid-century Trinity tutor, an accomplished musician and 'to those whom he liked, generous and kind; but . . . I do not gather that the junior members of Trinity suffered much when he married

---

[1] EVC, pp. 396–7. Macaulay's letter is in the Whewell Papers, T.C.L.

DONNISHNESS

and retired to a college living in Norfolk.'[1] Such too was the Master of Trinity Hall in the 1850's, 'an ancient megatherium, who liked his bottle in the evening and asked only to be left in peace.'[2] Undergraduates soon learned there was little to be gained from the genial topers, accepted the situation and went their own way.

Throughout the nineteenth century donnishness mainly designated the distant and uncompromising don, known to all undergraduates as a vain pedant, a morose scholar, or an arrogant and humourless college authoritarian, old before his time. 'A drawback to the society of the place,' wrote Leslie Stephen, 'was the extraordinary rapidity with which the more permanent residents became superannuated in the eyes of their colleagues. A don of thirty was ten years older than a rising young barrister of forty.'[3] The crabbed and ageing don was expected to show neither friendliness nor sympathy. When instructing small classes his manner was generally formal, antiseptic and unenthusiastic. In his stiff and solemn posture of dignity he attempted to convey a suggestion of moral excellence; his function was not to excite the mind but to correct youthful irregularities and make productive human beings of rebelliously-inclined undergraduates, in which endeavour he was bound to be misunderstood. 'Talk not of an Old Don as an old dry stick who delights in Greek particles and mazy problems and long series,' protested 'Sapere Aude' of St. John's. 'You comprehend us not, our mission, our high and holy purposes,' to make young men 'perform the daily routine of their profession quietly in harness.'[4]

---

[1] John D'Ewes Evelyn Firth, *Rendall of Winchester* (London, 1954), p. 20; A. E. Shipley, '*J.*' *A Memoir of John Willis Clark* (London, 1913), pp. 85–6.
[2] Annan, *Leslie Stephen*, pp. 41 and 41 n.
[3] Leslie Stephen, *Life of Henry Fawcett* (London, 1885), p. 76.
[4] 'The Confessions of an Old Don', *The Eagle*, V (1867), pp. 106–11. References to donnishness may be found in Iris L. Osborne Morgan, *Memoirs of Henry Arthur Morgan* (London, 1927), p. 21; Terrot Reaveley Glover, *Cambridge Retrospect* (Cambridge, 1943), pp. 58–62; Leaf, p. 79; J. P. Whitney, 'Sir George Prothero as a Historian', p. 1, K.C.L. Q.32.33; Headlam Papers, letter dated August 28, 1908, K.C.L. N.21.52; A. W. Verrall, *Collected Literary Essays* (Cambridge, 1913), pp. xxxii et seq. See especially Galton's description of Hopkins in Pearson, *Life*, I, p. 163: 'Hopkins to use a Cantab expression is a regular brick; tells funny stories connected with different problems and is no way Donnish; he rattles us on at a splendid pace and makes mathematics anything but a dry subject by

The stereotypes of the genial don and the pompous, priggish don are undergraduate conceptions of their teachers and as such not altogether reliable estimates of the motives and personalities of the collegiate fellows. There are in the complaints of the 1850's, '60's and '70's recognizable generational elements; and even in the late nineteenth century the epithet 'donnish' was being applied in the sense of the earlier period to dons who were neither stuffy nor wastrels. Certainly appreciations of the intelligence and kindness of many of the older fellows can be found in reminiscences to offset some of the more disparaging remarks about their learning and teaching. Because their scholarship was narrow, in the language of the time 'masculine', does not mean they eschewed intellectual problems or failed to take learning seriously.

Although some of the charges of donnishness were student misconceptions, erroneous interpretations of manner and behaviour, they are not totally unfounded. There were always pockets of serious scholars in Cambridge, but the number varied radically from college to college, and the majority of able and ambitious fellows did not stay long enough to provide any continuity in collegiate teaching or inspire needed reforms. College teaching was not considered a career or a profession, except for tutors; and as there were relatively few official teaching positions within the colleges, there was no reason for successful young fellows to remain. Those who did stay took holy orders, settled into a routine and waited for vacancies to occur in college livings. For every don respected by students, there were many more who rarely saw undergraduates – except perhaps in hall, chapel and in the courts – and gave no attention to their academic or personal problems.

Student complaints about donnishness are in part attributable to unrealized expectations. Earlier generations of undergraduates were certainly aware that Cambridge was not noted for the uniform excellence of its teaching or the inspired learning of the collegiate fellows; but, with some exceptions, undergraduates were content, like Macaulay, to wander at liberty over the college grounds, to rejoice in their freedom from close

---

entering thoroughly into its metaphysics. I never enjoyed anything so much before.' Galton was at Cambridge in the 1840's.

supervision, to study, or not to study, as they chose. This was clearly no longer the case by mid-century. The serious student of 1850 or 1860 needed dons more than his predecessors. One reason was that the pressure for success in the tripos had increased. Macaulay had 'gulfed' the mathematical tripos, failed to place, and yet he had been elected to a fellowship. This was not likely to occur in the 1860's.

But there was another reason why the undergraduate of the 1850's and 1860's needed the dons, and why therefore he expected more of them. The reading man of the mid-Victorian period might have been taught by the Arnoldians in some of the public or older grammar schools; and one effect of Dr. Arnold's influence was to increase the dependence of the serious student on the teacher by enhancing the role of teacher, by investing it with an awesome moral authority, at times even a mystique. For the force and brutality which governed the relations between masters and pupils in the older public schools, making them equals on the battlefield until might prevailed, Dr. Arnold substituted a relationship between teacher and student which depended on admiration and occasional hero-worship. This was why when a great Victorian master was found to have feet of clay, as happened at Harrow with Vaughan, the disclosure could be acutely distressing to the student.[1]

The young man, like Sidgwick, who drank deeply of Rugbeian ideals and values, came to Cambridge fully expecting the same kind of close and dedicated teaching, the same sense of communion between teacher and elect, the same kind of prophetic leadership he had experienced in the sixth form. His earnestness and seriousness sometimes rubbed off on bright undergraduates whose own schooling had not been so principled and who were more inclined to join the fashionable or sporting sets. The reading man of the mid-Victorian period needed a teacher who would take an interest in his studies, in his career and in his personal problems. No longer a schoolboy, and indeed one or two years older than his counterparts earlier in the century, he did not expect to find himself subject to petty and minute regulations or virtually ignored by his teachers. His expectations disappointed, his emotional and psychological needs unsatisfied, he had no alternative but to dismiss his

[1] Grosskurth, pp. 33, 20-41.

seniors, sometimes indiscriminately, with the invidious epithet 'donnish', to fall back on his own resources, or, as happened, to seek inspiration and companionship elsewhere.

The students of the 1850's who accused the fellows of donnishness became the new dons of the 1860's. They criticized their predecessors for confusing manner and knowledge, form and content. They found absurd the argument that Cambridge was a place of moral education because each college had a chapel, less absurd but equally unsatisfying the assertion that it was a place of intellectual education because it had a famous honours examination. They deplored the donnish practice of treating undergraduates as schoolboys, of stressing formal rules and regulations instead of seeking the loyalty of students and trying to capture their minds. In place of the 'old college system' with its antiquated routine and curious combination of formality and leniency, they proposed another idea or ideal of what a collegiate university should be, an ideal which was historical and new at one and the same time. The clearest statement of that ideal was made in 1850 by an Oxford don, Mark Pattison, the Sub-rector and Tutor of Lincoln College; but it exactly captures the discontents within Cambridge and expresses the mind of the new generation. Just before he became sour and cynical, engrossed with thoughts of his possible insanity, embittered by the improbable circumstances that deprived him of the headship of Lincoln and consequently no longer favourably disposed to the college idea—probably because he despaired of its realization—Pattison had a romantic moment in which he told the Royal Commission on Oxford that, 'The perfect idea of the Collegiate system proposed to take up the student from quite tender years, and conduct him through his life till death. A College was not divided into tutors and pupils, but like a Lacaedaemonian regiment . . . all were students alike, only differing in being at different stages of their progress. Hence their life was truly a life in common, with a common direction and occupation, and subject to one law. The seniors were at once the instructors and example of the juniors, who shared the same plain food, simple life, narrow economy, looking forward themselves to no other life. And in that mode then was obtained that which, then as now, constituted the truly invaluable element of the College system—the close action of the teacher on the pupil, of the matured character on the unformed, of the instructed on the learning mind, not indeed without a very beneficial reaction of the young on the aging man, an influence not unknown to the great and experienced men who originated and promoted Colleges. This insensible action of the teacher's character on the pupils' is the most valuable part of any education. . . . But it is contended that this influence is not now exerted by the body of Fellows on the Undergraduates. College life has ceased to be the life in common, even for the Fellows. . . . The relation between the student and the College official is, in general, as distant and technical as that between the officer and the private in our army. The young men associate with, and form one another's character mainly. There remains, however, a very powerful means of influence of the kind above described in the relation of the College tutor to his pupils, felt in some degree at present, and capable of still greater extension. But this is incident to his function as tutor, and is in no way dependent on the circumstance of the Undergraduate being accommodated within the walls. It might be favoured, certainly, by the pupil doing what he does not do now, living with the tutor. But it would exist exactly as it does now, let the pupil be lodged where he would. Indeed little as are the restraints and obligations which College discipline professes to impose on the student, the body of resident Fellows are too often an obstacle in the way of their enforcement. If there be any action of the character of the Corporation of the College on the student, its value must be entirely dependent on the *personnel* of that Corporation. It is to be feared that the moral and religious standard with which a well-disposed youth comes up from a pious home, would not be elevated by close and habitual intercourse with the Senior Common Room.'[1]

Pattison's sentimental, monastic reconstruction of the college idea contrasts markedly with the donnish notion of a college as a building of stone and mortar inhabited by starched clerics playing stock roles and instructing students with the aid of a uniform religious creed. For Pattison, the college was of little use if it survived in form only. The real college was more than

---

[1] Report of the Commissioners appointed to inquire into the State, Discipline, Studies and Revenues of the University and Colleges of Oxford, together with the evidence and Appendix. 1852 (1482), xxii, *Evidence*, pp. 43, 48–9.

walls and gates. It was a life in common, a set of common values, a human relationship, a Porch or Lyceum–exactly what the new generation of dons was saying.

As Pattison suggested, the tutor was especially culpable for the neglect of undergraduates, for as the main adviser to students and principal teaching officer, more was expected of him than of the average fellow. This is precisely what Leslie Stephen realized when taking off his clerical collar and gown–the symbols of established authority–he put on patched flannels to chase the boats along the towpath. In effect he was inviting every college tutor to remember his duties. At the same time, he was trying to determine what those duties were, for by 1860 the exact responsibilities were strangely unclear. Although the office of tutor was of considerable antiquity, originating in the sixteenth century,[1] it had developed informally and the exercise of tutorial functions had become very much an individual matter.

The tutor was appointed by the college head and in smaller colleges generally succeeded the master. The number of tutors varied according to the size of the college. In a small college there might be only one tutor, but in a large college like Trinity there were usually three tutors of equal status–although more was not inconceivable–each with a staff of assistant tutors. The tutor was usually responsible for admissions, for the assignment of rooms and lodgings, for advice on general expenses. He was also in charge of the college teaching programme and was authorized, but not obligated, to use the tuition fund to hire lecturers. Since the tuition fund, composed of student fees, was not part of college revenue or subject to review, and since student caution money was also deposited with the tutors, there was opportunity for peculation. Although caution money was returned when the student graduated, the tutor could invest the money and collect interest in the interim.[2] Instances could be recalled where tutors put off paying tradesmen's bills for which they had received money from their students in order to accrue the interest.[3] Some tutors may have made a personal use of the tuition fund, either investing the money or lending sums at

---

[1] UC, p. 267.   [2] Ewart Committee, Evidence, p. 56.

[3] Ibid. Bristed, I, p. 115, did not think tutors took undue advantage of tradesmen. The fault, he said, lay with students who paid bills late.

DONNISHNESS

interest to students for periods of several years. In 1874 the Cleveland Commission briskly reproved tutors who regarded the disposition of tutorial funds as a private matter.[1]

Where tutorial responsibility was least clear was in the exercise of those functions which related to the moral and physical welfare of students. The tutor was supposed to be a father to the student, and some tutors performed this function remarkably well. Gunson of Christ's was a famous tutor, George Peacock and James Lemprière Hammond of Trinity–a vivacious Channel Islander–were others. J. W. Clark claimed that Hammond 'made me';[2] and both Sidgwick and Henry Jackson, another famous reformer, relied heavily on Hammond's advice in the beginning of the reform period.[3] But although there were conscientious tutors in the first half of the nineteenth century, few undergraduates found the tutorial arrangements satisfactory. 'The Tutor is supposed to stand *in loco parentis*,' wrote Bristed, 'but having sometimes more than a hundred young men under him, he cannot discharge his duties in this respect very thoroughly, nor is it generally expected that he should.'[4] Bristed was referring to Trinity tutors, but there is no reason to believe that tutors in smaller colleges were generally more successful. Leslie Stephen's contention that Cambridge did not care whether a good man came or went was still valid. Sooner or later the best tutors left.

3.

'I am convinced that the Tutor frequently has not sufficient knowledge of the pupil's intellectual habits and progress to guide him on points which might be referred to the Tutor's judgment, or to give to that judgment the influence which it ought to possess. This want of acquaintance with the student's

[1] Report of the Commissioners appointed to inquire into the property and income of the Universities of Oxford and Cambridge (Cleveland Commission), 1873 (*c.* 856) xxxvii, pp. 31–2.
[2] Shipley, p. 86.
[3] Jackson to Maitland, November 13, 1905, C.U.L. Add. 4251 (13) 713, published in John Roach, 'The Victoria County History of Cambridge', *Proceedings of the Cambridge Antiquarian Society*, LIV (1960), p. 123. Hammond was a Trinity tutor from 1854–64.
[4] Bristed, I, p. 15.

progress is due to the fact of that progress being dependent almost entirely on Private Tuition, while the unrecognized existence of that mode of teaching prevents any necessary communication between the College and Private Tutor.'[1]

The tutor performed a teaching function, but at some point in the eighteenth century—it is difficult to know when—this aspect of his office began to decline in importance, becoming virtually a formality by the early Victorian period. Increasingly, and to a much greater extent than at Oxford, the essential teaching at Cambridge passed out of the colleges and into the hands of private teachers or tutors called coaches.

The private tutor or coach had been an integral part of English education for over a century. Locke approved of home tutors, and tutors were to be found outside the great public schools coaching boys in subjects not provided in the foundation. In addition private tuition was provided in many grammar schools.

In Cambridge private tuition survived mainly because the tripos was used to award fellowships; and fellowships were essential to any intelligent and ambitious graduate of moderate means anxious to launch himself into the Church, the public schools, politics or a learned profession. In 1781, 1807, 1815 and 1824 the university attempted to limit the amount of time students might spend in preparation with coaches; but since the colleges did not provide adequate substitutes, coaching naturally continued and even accelerated after the creation of a classical tripos in the 1820's. In 1854 William Hopkins, the most famous of the early Victorian mathematical coaches, declared that the teaching of mathematics had never before been so completely and systematically in the hands of private tutors.[2] It was certainly apparent that coaches were not simply providing supplementary or remedial instruction. They were the most important teachers in the university: and all undergraduates were forced to use them.

Private tutors were mainly college fellows, college lecturers or B.A.'s kept from a fellowship by marriage. Nearly all resident fellows were coaches for at least one period in their career.

---

[1] William Hopkins, *Remarks on the Mathematical Teaching of the University of Cambridge* (1854), p. 23.

[2] Ibid., p. 7.

Because coaching was a full-time activity, the college lecturer who coached was not inclined to stimulate his classes at the expense of his pocket;[1] and college lectures were therefore neglected. No reading man regarded them with sufficient confidence to forego private tuition. College lectures did not even cover the full examination syllabus; honours students in classics received instruction only in composition and not translation. Moreover, few undergraduates found the repetitious, dull and routine classes they were frequently compelled to attend little more than formal, schoolboy lessons.

Little teaching assistance could be expected from the professors, whose lectures were expected to embody the results of original work. A few lectures, such as those given by the Regius Professor of Greek in the 1840's, were valuable to the classical reading man; but most bore no direct relation to the triposes. Even when professorial lectures were related to the ordinary degree most pass students preferred the coaches. And whenever a new pass examination was introduced or alterations made in an existing one, attendance at professorial lectures decreased even more.[2]

The reputation of a coach was measured by his ability to cram an undergraduate, to drill him intensively for a high place in the examination lists. He was hired to do a job, and his performance could be strictly measured by the number of first class honours or poll men he coached. His labours were given a market price and evaluated in commercial terms. A well-paid coach had to be competitive, sure of his technique, well-organized and willing to work at least six hard tutorial hours every day, as well as grade written exercises and problem sets. The best private tutors in fact developed a system of drill and exercises that was later used as a model for examination papers set by lecturers in history, philosophy and some branches of mathematics.[3]

Coaching was an intercollegiate activity. The coach drew his pupils from all colleges by virtue of reputation. The student was

---

[1] Isaac Todhunter is a good example of a college teacher who neglected lecturing because of coaching. See Edward Miller, *Portrait of a College* (Cambridge, 1961), pp. 87–8.

[2] EVC, pp. 177–81.

[3] *Student's Guide* (1893), pp. 71–2.

not a captive bound over to the lecturer as he was in the college, but a voluntary attendant, willing to work, open to suggestion. And since the student came willingly, he was under no obligation to remain; if he felt at any time that the coaching sessions had become unprofitable, no statute could detain him. The coach was a hired teacher, a sophist in search of clients. He had to take the initiative in all relations with the student, win his confidence, convince him that no better coach existed. This entailed a knowledge of the student equal to a knowledge of the subject taught; and the student soon realized that he could expect from the coach the warm and personal interest which college officers failed to provide. Whewell himself, a sworn enemy of coaching, frankly admitted in 1852 that 'the pupil values more what he has to himself, what he pays for himself, or what is given to him in a familiar and companionable tone.'[1] And thirty years later, when classics but not mathematics coaching had almost ceased, a writer to *The Cambridge Review* asserted that an undergraduate went to a private tutor not because his college lecturer was incompetent, but because he was recognized as an individual.[2]

Virtually every graduate living in Cambridge, whether a fellow or not, tried coaching because the remuneration was exceptionally good. If not occupied with other duties an ordinary private tutor could teach perhaps a dozen students every term, seeing each student several times a week for approximately one hour per visit. At £7 a student for a term's coaching an ordinary private tutor could make £252 per academic year, or about £50 less than the customary value of a fellowship in the mid-nineteenth century. If the services of an ordinary coach were required daily, 'whole tuition' as it was called and very common in the second quarter of the nineteenth century, he could double his fees and add appreciably to his basic income. Ordinary coaches not greatly in demand of course earned less. The best classics coach who handled on the average more

---

[1] Graham Commission (1852), Evidence, p. 417.

[2] *Cambridge Review* (May 12, 1880), p. 66. Heitland also complained that college lecturers 'did not study their pupils personally so as to diagnose individual cases. Even the set lectures to full classrooms were apt to be a blend of what men either knew or did not want to know at all'. *After Many Years*, p. 128.

students than an ordinary coach and worked a longer, fatiguing schedule, or the crack mathematics coach who taught even more students, naturally received higher annual incomes. Frequently too their fees were greater. As Hopkins remarked, it was possible for an outstanding coach to make £700–800 per academic year,[1] and even more if he coached in the Long Vacation when he could expect to make 10 guineas per student. This was an extraordinary amount, almost within the definition of an upper middle class income.[2] If coaching were combined with a fellowship or college lectureship, the total emoluments available to the successful private tutor might equal the income of the Lady Margaret's Professor of Divinity, the most highly endowed chair in Cambridge.[3] Few coaches earned the maximum amount, but the range of possible remuneration was nevertheless tempting.

Money alone, however, did not make a resident fellow take private pupils. Many fellows became coaches in lieu of any other satisfactory alternative. There were simply not enough official teaching positions within either the university or the colleges; and research was not an attractive choice because only professors were expected to write. Reformers like Seeley and Sidgwick, who proposed that all teachers unite German scholarship and English teaching, encountered formidable opposition. There was not much sympathy for a class of *gelehrten*, regarded as isolated and politically unimportant. It was feared they would 'distract the energies of the nation from the broad highways of civic life and lead them into the by-paths of abstract study, so that, while thought and speculation might be busy and free, political action might be inert and shackled.'[4] As Seeley noted,

---

[1] For coaching fees see Chapter 2.

[2] Banks, *Prosperity and Parenthood*, considers £900 to be an upper class income about 1851. Other historians use £1,000 as the lower limit of an upper middle class income. See F. Musgrove, 'Middle-Class Education and Employment in the Nineteenth Century', *Economic History Review*, 2nd series, XII (August, 1959), pp. 99–111.

[3] The Lady Margaret's Professorship of Divinity was worth £1,085 per annum in 1885 and possibly more earlier. See the returns compiled by Thorold Rogers and published in the *Pall Mall Gazette* (November 5, 1886), p. 2, and Graham Commission (1861), p. 6.

[4] Lord Houghton, 'On the Present Social Results of Classical Education', in *Essays on a Liberal Education*, p. 368.

Cambridge was considered a place of moral edification from which obedient and observing men returned to society; and this view of university education discouraged scholarship, denounced in some quarters as a continental apology for anarchic free-thinking.

Dons who did not hold a college office had to make a difficult choice. If they remained in Cambridge, they had either to coach or fill their time with some kind of routine. Time was on their hands—hence the lengthy meals, parties and hard drinking —and coaching was therefore important not only because it paid well, but because it was so time-consuming. But it was also an endless and wearisome routine, competitive yet arid. It required repeating the simple rules of Euclid and grammar term after term and in the Long Vacation. Tripos teaching was a feverish activity in which a man stood absolutely still; and sensitive men inevitably became profoundly dissatisfied with themselves.

William Hopkins was one of the few coaches to have surmounted the deficiencies of the tripos syllabus. By refusing to be donnish and by encouraging his students to take a speculative and philosophical view of mathematics, he conveyed a genuine love of learning. Marriage had kept him from a college career, and he turned to coaching as the only satisfactory alternative. Among the undergraduates whom he coached were George Gabriel Stokes, William Thomson (Lord Kelvin), James Clerk Maxwell and Isaac Todhunter, some of the most important names in English science and mathematics. Next to his pupil, Edward John Routh, he produced more senior wranglers than any other coach. He is reported to have said in 1849 that he had nearly two hundred wranglers to his credit, of whom seventeen were senior and forty-four were in one of the first three places.[1]

Routh succeeded Hopkins as a 'wrangler maker', coaching more than six hundred students in the period 1855–88, and producing from this group no less than twenty-seven senior wranglers, twenty-four of whom were consecutive. He himself had been senior wrangler in 1854, the year that Clerk Maxwell was second, and like Hopkins he managed to make original contributions to mathematics. There is no doubt, however, that his work as a coach detracted from his reputation as a mathe-

[1] DNB.

matics scholar, for he was by-passed for the Sadlerian Professorship of Mathematics in 1863 after announcing his intention to stand.[1] Like Hopkins, Routh had married and was forced to vacate his fellowship in 1864. Not until 1883 was he made an honorary fellow of Peterhouse, a distinction which provided neither the privileges nor satisfaction of a regular fellowship.

Although he was employed as a lecturer by Peterhouse and Pembroke, Routh's college teaching suffered for the sake of his coaching. He was firmly committed to the challenge of the tripos and accepted its limitations. His methods were both a reflection of the demands of the tripos and his sober, taciturn, efficient manner. His organization and clarity were considered exemplary. He taught in classes of six to ten, set weekly problem papers, gave moot tripos exams and rated his students according to merit. He devoted himself single-mindedly to the formula which produced success: set problems, set books, set solutions: 'Independence on the part of a student was not encouraged; for independence would rarely, if ever, be justified by the event. Foreign books were seldom mentioned: Routh himself had summarized from them all that could be deemed useful for the examination. ... Regularity and steady diligence were two demands which he always made from his pupils.'[2] Routh knew how to raise the level of individual performance, but not the level of individuality. As a manufacturer he was unsurpassed: he used the best materials and turned out finished, machined products. It may perhaps be suggested that had William Hopkins not been so prone to the distractions of meta-mathematics, he might have produced a coaching record more equal to that of his famous successor.

Although hired teachers, Hopkins and Routh retained their self-respect. It is difficult, however, not to concur with Heitland that Richard Shilleto, the most famous Victorian classics coach, was a pathetic figure. A Salopian trained under Butler, he was widely known as a Thucydides scholar and occasionally lectured in King's and Trinity; but he spent most of his time coaching students in Shrewsbury alcaics and elegaics. Early

[1] C.U.L. Add. 6580 (55). Arthur Cayley was elected instead.
[2] A. R. Forsyth, 'Edward John Routh', *Proceedings of the London Mathematical Society*, ser. 2, V (July 5, 1907), xvi. Also Thomson, *Recollections*, pp. 35–42.

marriage ruled out a Trinity fellowship; and heavy drinking, according to Heitland, kept him from the Regius Professorship of Greek, to which an Ely canonry was attached. Shilleto had taken holy orders but could not live down his reputation as an alcoholic and eccentric acquired after years on the fringes of university and college life. The bitterness of his situation, the exclusion and dependence which characterized his life, is obvious from the alternately sarcastic and suppliant letters to undergraduates in which he alluded to his position as an outsider. 'Will you come on Thursday evening, and, if you have such strange tastes, take a cup of tea?' he once wrote an undergraduate. 'It will undoubtedly be followed by a Tankard if not of Audit at least of Guinness.'[1] His teaching technique was derived from the schools: it was narrow, exact and formal. He exhausted himself by applying it in his prime to about a dozen students every day, six days a week. This gruelling life of disappointment was only partially redeemed by an amended Peterhouse statute of 1867 which allowed him to become the first married scholar to assume a fellowship in the college.[2]

By the end of the 1850's, Macaulay's ideal of the independent scholar, he who 'read Plato with his feet on the fender,' was almost out of fashion among even the best reading men. Ironically, his own nephew rushed into the arms of Shilleto the moment the uncle's influence was removed.[3] Progressively coaching had become *de rigeur* in Cambridge.

4.

In the second quarter of the nineteenth century lecturers and fellows left the colleges to serve as coaches, and college teaching declined. In the 1850's and 1860's members of royal commis-

[1] G. M. Trevelyan, *Sir George Otto Trevelyan, A Memoir* (London, 1932), pp. 40–1. 'Audit' is a reference to the ale served in colleges.

[2] For Shilleto see Heitland, p. 131, EVC, p. 412, and Reginald St. John Parry, *Henry Jackson* (Cambridge, 1926), p. 15. Jackson wrote to his sister in 1860 that 'Shilleto nearly poisoned himself on Monday: just before going to bed he drank a glass of furniture varnish by mistake for his ale, and was so frightened that he telegraphed to his sister that he should not be surprised if he were dead tomorrow. He seems all right again today.'

[3] Trevelyan, *G. O. Trevelyan*, pp. 42, 38–9. Macaulay died in December 1859.

sions and select committees suggested that the colleges adopt coaching methods and compete with private tutors, but many dons resisted this solution. Whewell, especially depressed by the increase in private teaching, considered coaching exclusively a university matter. He idealized the college, regarding it as an inviolate society, and refused to commit Trinity to any course which might corrupt its purpose. If lecturers took over the functions of coaches, he argued, the worst abuses of coaching would be transferred to the colleges. Lectures would be tied directly to the examinations, and lecturers would give students only such technicalities as they could master with little effort.[1]

Whewell's reluctance to commit Trinity to an attack on private tuition convinced many critics that the colleges could not easily be persuaded to take the initiative in the reform of Cambridge teaching. Their doubts increased when they reflected that the small colleges relied on private tuition to provide teaching they were unable to afford and that few lecturers and fellows cared to deprive themselves of an excellent source of revenue. By mid-century there was considerable support for the opinion that only university teaching or an intercollegiate arrangement could solve the problems arising from coaching.

Hopkins and the Graham Commission advocated a programme of teaching that was actually a prototype of the university lecture system established by statute in 1882. Sub-professors or public lecturers drawn from outstanding coaches or college lecturers were to be added to the university teaching staff. Most professors were to continue to devote themselves to scholarship and research, although some could participate in the new scheme. In the 1860's Seeley suggested a compromise measure that would inspire life into college teaching but at the same time would make the colleges more competitive and university-minded. He proposed an intercollegiate scheme of teaching with lecturers occupying a position midway between the professoriate and the teachers of the old college system. The colleges would retain their teaching staffs; all college lectures would be open to students from other colleges; small colleges would specialize instead of attempting to offer a full programme of studies. Seeley also advocated abolition of the order of merit; and he agreed with other reformers that coaching could not be

---

[1] Graham Commission (1852), Evidence, p. 417.

superseded unless the new university lecturers were given every advantage enjoyed by coaches. Celibacy and the requirement of ordination would have to be eliminated.

The problem of remuneration still remained. Unless lecturers were adequately paid, no coach would consent to lecture. Hopkins and the Graham Commission decided that salary guarantees would have to be made if a university teaching staff was to be recruited; but both also agreed that the standard of teaching improved when lecturers were forced to compete for students, as coaching was successful precisely because students voluntarily sought out the better teachers. They therefore suggested that lecturers be paid partly by fees and partly by salary. Hopkins set the minimum salary for lecturers at £300, the customary value of a fellowship, and suggested that lecturers could earn an additional £150 more in fees. He proposed to raise the lecture-ship endowment by diverting bequests no longer providing educational benefits or by the remission of university taxes imposed on degrees, and by adding to the sums thus released annual contributions from the colleges that could consist of fees collected from undergraduates for obsolete services.[1] The Graham Commission also suggested that the colleges contribute to the support of the university lecturers; and in order to forestall collegiate hostility added that lecturers might be induced to exchange a high salary for a guarantee of permanent employment.[2] This was still another attempt to tempt teachers away from private tuition, for coaching was a precarious occupation, particularly for the non-fellow who had no other source of income or the inept teacher who failed to attract students. It was the economic insecurity of coaching as well as demand that inflated its fees.

The Graham Commission found little enthusiasm in the colleges for its proposals to strengthen university teaching in order to diminish the importance of coaching. Only Trinity, Peterhouse and Christ's were willing to accept a 5 per cent tax on distributable income for university purposes; and only Christ's was willing to open its fellowship competition to the entire university—an essential step if the small colleges were to acquire sufficient teaching talent to forgo their dependence on

[1] Hopkins, pp. 36–7.
[2] Graham Commission (1852), Report, pp. 81–3.

private tuition.[1] Furthermore, another alternative to coaching, intercollegiate lectures supported exclusively by the colleges, had not been started. As Seeley remarked in 1867, 'Trinity refuses to let the men of other colleges attend its good lectures, and the small college refuses to excuse its own students from attending its own inferior lectures.'[2] In addition, new honours courses raised problems of staffing even more serious than for classics and mathematics. The colleges were reluctant to detach endowments in order to establish fellowships and provide scholarships in new, untried tripos subjects like philosophy, introduced in 1851 but even a decade later cautiously advertized and unsatisfactorily rewarded.[3] All in all, coaching was still the rough remedy.

5.

The significance of the system of private tuition that developed in Cambridge at the end of the eighteenth century and expanded in the second quarter of the nineteenth century has been completely overlooked by historians of university education. Coaching was not simply a substitute for the teaching which the colleges neglected and which the university was unable to perform. It was the only practical school of education in Cambridge, the only place where a prospective university teacher could prove his worth in a competitive situation. Coaching provided jobs for married men and supplementary income for the young resident don with no college duties; it supported the B.A. who had failed to receive a fellowship and was awaiting another chance; it enabled young dons like Sidgwick, unsure of their religious belief, to divorce themselves from college life while deciding whether to assume holy orders. Coaching was also the means by which many impecunious sizars and sons of poor parsons earned enough money to repay tutors and creditors for an expensive university education;[4] it enabled Henry Knights

[1] Ibid., (1861), pp. 7–8, 16.
[2] Seeley, 'Liberal Education', p. 167.
[3] *Student's Guide* (1863), pp. 150 and 152.
[4] 'When the student takes his degree, he obtains by pupilizing enough to render further assistance unnecessary, and soon begins to pay off his debt, and when he gets his Fellowship, he clears himself very speedily. It is in fact

to become bishops. Despite its obvious educational limitations, coaching was a major contribution to the reform of teaching in the second half of the nineteenth century; for in the coaching relationship mutual respect developed between teacher and student, donnishness could not survive. Nevertheless, no reform was possible in Cambridge as long as coaching remained unchallenged.

---

pledging his labour and time two or three years ahead, and though such a mortgage may in some cases prove an awkward incumbrance, the general result is good: it enables many first-rate men to get a first-rate education, which they could not otherwise have obtained.' Bristed, I, pp. 114, 214.

CHAPTER 7

THE IDEA OF A COLLEGE

I.

The relationship between the private tutor and his students embodied several of the essential requirements of a college: friendliness, mutual respect and a sense of common effort. But the reformers agreed that these were gained at the expense of higher educational ideals. Whewell may have confused a donnish manner with dignity and intellectual achievement, but he was not incorrect in believing that the coach had to demean himself in order to attract students. The coach won the confidence of students by, as it were, publishing his list of tripos successes. He was a sophist-utilitarian hired to produce results, a remarkably skilful crammer. The coaching relationship favoured the student and did little to raise the self-esteem of the teacher. The college lecturer at least was supported by all the conventional means of enforcing discipline, but the coach was completely dependent on his customers. The student paid for what he received, came and went at his pleasure, and was not under the guidance of his elders and superiors. In part the coach was penalized for living in an aristocratic age. The well-born expected toadying, and their example could be infectious.

While the system of coaching, therefore, contained several of the fundamental principles upon which the idea of a collegiate university was based, it did not contain others, notably, the idea of education as character formation, teaching as a dynamic process leading to individual growth and self-cultivation on the part of both teacher and student. Coaching was not concerned with moral education, with socratic inquiry, with Christian admiration. The defects of coaching could be traced to its unofficial and spontaneous growth. It had arisen outside the university to supply a practical need. It was an extra-collegiate activity, although with intercollegiate implications, lacking any sense of community, of the college as a Christian family, the tutor as a surrogate father. Teachers like Hopkins surmounted some of the limitations of private tuition, but technicians like Routh only perfected the system. To borrow the Victorian distinction, coaching trained but did not educate.

By the late 1860's coaching was so firmly established in Cambridge that many critics no longer regarded the individual college as the best teaching unit. They turned instead to schemes that would improve university instruction, hoping that this would also reduce the demand for coaches. At the same time, however, another development occurred. A group of new dons, sometimes with the encouragement of older dons, began to take measures of their own to end the supremacy of coaching, bring students back under the authority of the colleges and restore the moral influence of the teacher. The colleges, they concluded, had to be awakened to a positive teaching effort. They agreed that on the whole past generations of dons had failed to make a lasting impression on undergraduates. It was necessary, then, to emulate the example of the best coaches and win the respect, loyalty and even affection of undergraduates.

The first step was to recognize the changing character of students. Because of the emphasis the Arnoldians had placed on gentlemanly behaviour, manners had softened, traditional discipline had become largely unnecessary. Also because of the Arnoldians greater attention had been given to the sixth forms. Students stayed in school longer and came to the university later, but the colleges had failed to notice that the sixth forms had encroached upon college instruction. No wonder undergraduates complained of boredom and *déja vu*. They were treated as schoolboys, and they were young men, requiring instruction and discipline appropriate to their age level and educational experience. The Graham Commission recognized the changes when they stated that late adolescence was a transitional stage. Students 'are at an age, when they cannot be subjected to the minute surveillance and rigid constraint exercised in a school, and when, on the other hand they are not fit to be intrusted with absolute liberty and independence in acting for themselves.'[1] They had to be handled with a mixture of constraint and liberty, 'so much constraint as may guard the inexperienced against the temptations of youth and the dangers of wasteful extravagance; so much liberty, as may serve to develop the qualities of their moral character, and prepare them gradually for the weightier responsibilities and fuller freedom of after life.'[2]

Acknowledging this advice, the new dons set about replacing the older Cambridge mixture of formality and licence with the newer formula of constraint and liberty.

The decision to overturn coaching was made and led by the reform parties in three colleges, Christ's, Trinity and King's, but there were stirrings in other colleges as well, especially St. John's. The reformers were known to each other in various ways, through the Apostles, the Grote Club, reading parties, or school. Peile and Seeley had been undergraduates together at Christ's, and Peile had followed Seeley as senior classic and chancellor's medallist. When Seeley's critique of the university appeared in 1867, Peile was tutor of the college and impressing students with his warmth, sympathy, knowledge and teaching ability. However, he was also known to be a stern disciplinarian when circumstances called for firmness.[3] Sidgwick and Peile met as undergraduates and went on a summer reading party to Oban in Argyll in 1858.[4] Both men were instrumental in the establishment of Newnham College for women in Cambridge in the late 1860's and early 1870's. Seeley and Sidgwick had also known each other as undergraduates, and Sidgwick was disappointed that Seeley was not elected a member of the Apostles, since he thought *Ecce Homo* the most exciting book he had read.[5] Similar contacts existed between the reformers at Trinity and King's, partially through the Etonian connection. Henry Jackson recalled that in the 1860's he had many friends in King's and admired the 'friendly domesticity' of the college.[6]

This 'friendly domesticity' was lacking in Trinity. Reformers

[1] Graham Commission (1852), Report, p. 16.
[2] Ibid. Adam Sedgwick's influence is apparent here. He was a member of the Graham Commission. See *Discourses*, cccli.
[3] *Christ's College Magazine*, XXV (Michaelmas, 1910), pp. 143–57.
[4] Sidgwick, *Memoir*, pp. 20–5.   [5] Ibid., pp. 63, 140–50.
[6] William Austen Leigh, *Augustus Austen Leigh* (London, 1906), pp. 258–9.

agreed that Whewell was especially culpable. A man of formidable intellect, high integrity and generosity, he was also 'arbitrary, unconciliatory and sometimes excessively rude.'[1] He was portrayed in comic literature as the archetype college don and university snob. His work as college tutor had not been successful, coinciding as it did with other and more scholarly concerns, to which undergraduates were sacrificed.[2] In 1848 Maurice complained to Julius Hare that Whewell was so insolent and arrogant that 'I do mourn for the sake of the Universities, where the young men are daily feeling themselves more utterly estranged from those who might be their guides. For them thus utterly cast off I care far more than for the working classes.'[3] As master Whewell set himself entirely apart from students and the college fellowship, withdrawing into the Lodge from where he issued occasional bulls calling for the vigorous suppression of private tuition.

Whewell died early in 1866. On the thirteenth of March Jackson was writing, 'Our hopes and fears about the Mastership have been set at rest. [William Hepworth] Thompson has been appointed and we are most of us very well satisfied, except those of course who have found him an awkward antagonist in argument.'[4] Two months later Henry Sidgwick wrote home that 'We are in a considerable state of agitation here, as all sorts of projects of reform are coming to the surface, partly in consequence of having a new master–people begin to stretch themselves and feel a certain freedom and independence.'[5] The enthusiasm of Jackson and Sidgwick was not misplaced. The young reformers knew that since the master of Trinity was a crown appointment, they had the support of the Government. They also knew that Thompson was an intellectual descendant of George Peacock, Julius Hare and Connop Thirlwall, the Cambridge liberal reformers of the 1820's and 1830's. It was not surprising that as the Regius Professor of Greek and therefore an

[1] LVC, p. 240.

[2] J. W. Clark, 'Half a Century of Cambridge Life', *Church Quarterly Review*, XIV (April, 1882), pp. 162–3.

[3] Maurice, *Life*, I, p. 477.   [4] Parry, *Jackson*, p. 27.

[5] Sidgwick, *Memoir*, p. 145. Of Thompson's appointment Sidgwick wrote, 'Thompson will make a very good sort of master, though not perhaps the best. He is a little too lazy or dyspeptic (perhaps the first results from the second) for that.' (p. 144).

THE IDEA OF A COLLEGE

elector of the Knightbridge Professorship he remembered the ideals of his youth and welcomed Maurice's return to Cambridge.

Relations between Whewell and Thompson had not always been easy; they had crossed in 1851 on a major point of university government.[1] Yet Whewell, one of the electors to the chair of Greek, had favoured Thompson's election in 1853 and had not used this as a means of depriving Thompson of his Trinity fellowship in the litigation that followed.[2] Thompson became a titular fellow and lost his place in the Trinity Seniority by a chancery ruling that the chair of Greek, only recently attached to an Ely canonry, could not be held concurrently with a fellowship. Hence from 1853 until his election as master Thompson lived on the fringe of the college. Possibly because of this, possibly also because of the long illness that accompanied his tenure as master,[3] Thompson's earlier reform interests were forgotten, and he was generally acknowledged to be a university conservative. Jackson corrected the record many years later. In a commemoration sermon given in 1913 he pointed out how essential Thompson's encouragement had been to the reformers of the 1870's.[4] Long before he became master Thompson had favoured the creation of additional professorships and had desired an increase in the proportion of lay to clerical fellows. His attitude towards coaching was mixed. He regarded the existence of poll coaches as a complete evil, likening them to the *Répétiteurs* around the University of Paris, but he also believed that the half dozen distinguished mathematics and classics coaches made positive contributions to Cambridge teaching. In a learned paper on Plato's *Sophists* he repeated Plato's distinction between the hack and the genuine teacher. According to Thompson, the purpose of Plato's dialogue was to distinguish the sophist from the philosopher, 'the trader in knowledge from its disinterested seeker: surely no unimportant distinction, nor one without its counterpart in reality, either in Plato's day or in our own.'[5]

[1] EVC, pp. 239–40. [2] Ibid., pp. 289–313.
[3] James Ramsay Montagu Butler, *Henry Montagu Butler: A Memoir* (London, 1925), p. 17.
[4] Parry, pp. 294–6.
[5] W. H. Thompson, 'On the Genuineness of the Sophista of Plato', *Transactions of the Cambridge Philosophical Society*, X (1858), p. 163. See also Graham Commission (1852), Evidence, pp. 198–9.

Thompson impressed his contemporaries in various ways. Those who knew him well considered him kind, genial and warm-hearted, as well as a meticulous and reflective scholar more interested in matter than manner. Those who did not know him, especially undergraduates, were put off by his tart epigrams and the impression he gave of being a typical don, 'a grim classical veteran, I had almost said Gorgon, with his sea-green complexion and wave of glaucous hair looking incredibly far removed from youth and gaiety.'[1] This unflattering description by an undergraduate was written in the years before Thompson's death and during the period of his illness. Little has been written of his youth; but in the 1850's, when he was a Trinity tutor, he did not strike J. W. Clark as uncordial:[2] 'In days when undergraduates were kept at a distance by their seniors, he made his pupils feel that he really stood to them *in loco parentis*. He could be severe when discipline required it, but he was always inflexibly just and untrammelled by pedantic adherence to tradition.'[3]

On October 5, 1886, Sidgwick entered in his journal a final appraisal of Thompson: 'I shall miss him, though not deeply. He was not a great man: and his work, though good in quality, was too meagre to make a mark, or really justify his academic position. But he was a striking personality: nor will his place be filled: and, to me uniformly kind and genial.'[4]

Just three days earlier the *Pall Mall Gazette* had called Thompson 'one of the finest specimens of the don of the old school'. By this they meant he was neither a convivial dissolute nor an olympian or Mosaic don, but rather a don who lived the life of dignified retirement and scholarly refinement, a life which the *Gazette* significantly concluded, 'contrasts so strongly with the restless activity of a newer school.'[5]

Henry Jackson embodied just such restlessness. Although his manner and disposition contrasted sharply with Thompson's, he was in a sense the man Thompson had chosen to do the work

---

[1] Firth, *Rendall of Winchester*, p. 22.   [2] Shipley, '*J*', p. 32.

[3] DNB (Thompson). The article is by J. W. Clark. Thompson had praised his own tutor, George Peacock, whose widow he married, as 'the best and wisest of tutors.' (DNB)

[4] Sidgwick, *Memoir*, pp. 458–9.

[5] *Pall Mall Gazette* (October 2, 1886), p. 3.

his own temperament and health had prevented. Thompson had, for example, passed on to Jackson his theory that the platonic dialogues, when their correct order of composition was determined, advanced a comprehensive and specific doctrine which developed progressively.[1] Jackson was particularly interested in epistemology and psychology and their relationship to teaching. His interest in nineteenth-century literary anthropology may in some degree have influenced the early work of his student, James Gordon Frazer.[2]

It was as a Socrates that Jackson made his late nineteenth-century Cambridge reputation, and the analogy did not displease him. '[I]t is to me a pleasure,' he concluded a Senate House Praelection in 1889, 'to read or teach about Socrates, "Whoso hears him," says the intoxicated Alcibiades in Plato's dialogue, "nay, whoso hears a feeble report of what he has said, is struck with awe and possessed with admiration. Were I not afraid that you would think me more drunk than I am, I would make oath to you how his words have moved me, aye and how they move me still. When I listen to him my heart beats with a more than Corybantic excitement; he has only to speak and my tears flow. Orators such as Pericles never stirred me in this way, rousing my soul to the sense of my servile condition, and making me think that life is not worth living so long as I am what I am." Something of this fascination I feel and I am not ashamed to confess it.'[3]

Allowing for the rhetoric of a praelection and Jackson's desire to fill a vacant chair, it is fair to see Jackson as a socratic figure. His interest in Greek philosophy and history: his enthusiasm, passion and driving energy; but above all his ability to involve the student in his processes of thought, fired students into believing that he was the greatest teacher they had ever seen.

Jackson was well prepared for his new role. For two years after election to a Trinity fellowship he took private pupils, learned how to attract students and developed his teaching

---

[1] Jackson to J. W. Clark, October 2, 1886, Cam. a. 500.6.194. Jackson explained that Thompson in turn followed the lead of Thirlwall, who based his platonic theories on Schleiermacher.

[2] See Frazer's 1879 fellowship thesis, *The Growth of Plato's Ideal Theory* (London, 1930).

[3] Parry, pp. 270–1.

abilities. He was made assistant tutor in 1866 when Thompson became master and was joined in that position by William Edmund Currey, an Harrovian whom he had met six years earlier. Currey, who became a fellow one year later than Jackson, was a sporting and a reading man: he ran, rowed, joined the rifle corps, played football, acted in amateur theatricals, probably rode the hounds, but kept up his scholarship as well.[1] His energy and *brio* were joined to Jackson's iconoclasm, and the two young turks set about shocking traditional proprieties in a dozen small ways. Their appointments as assistant tutors gave them a position on the classical lecturing staff, at which time they appear to have made the crucial decision to alter the methods of college teaching. Whereas earlier colleges usually provided class instruction only in classical composition, leaving translation completely to private coaches, Currey and Jackson now added translation papers to their teaching; and their classes of three and four rose to thirty-eight students within a year. 'In a word we superseded classical coaching.'[2] The job was not undertaken lightly: 'During the next four years, 1867–1870, Currey and I constantly discussed together the details of our work. If one wrote a composition or a translation, the other criticized it: and we frequently compared notes about difficulties which met us in our oral lectures and in our reading.'[3]

Nor was it regarded without suspicion: 'A College Tutor once told me that he never sent his pupils to Currey's lectures because he had been told of a saying of his, "I know nothing of Cicero's letters, but I suppose that, with a good stout crib and a fortnight's start, I can teach the men something." The pupils were the losers: for Currey was an excellent teacher, he made a careful preparation for his lectures, and he had a start which was not to be measured by weeks or months.'[4]

The decision to challenge private tuition was bold but precarious. In order to attract students, Jackson and Currey had to

---

[1] Information on Currey is to be found in Jackson's manuscript notice of June 16, 1911, T.C.L. Add. c.27, 87–119, and in Jackson's obituary notice in *Cambridge Review* (January 21, 1909), pp. 187–8. See also W. W. Rouse Ball and J. A. Venn, *Trinity College Admissions, 1851–1900* (London, 1913).

[2] Parry, p. 19.   [3] *Cambridge Review* (January 21, 1909), p. 187.

[4] T.C.L. Add. c.27, 87–119.

prove they could do as well as the private coaches. If they failed, they might set back the course of college reform and jeopardize their reputations as coaches. They had to risk antagonizing those members of the college who remained private tutors, and they had to forgo the lucrative income that coaching brought. Furthermore, unless the college formally recognized their activity by revising the teaching programme, they could not be certain that their efforts would have a permanent impact on the university. Thompson's encouragement was heartening, but even Currey soon lost interest and left Trinity in 1870 to become a school inspector. Jackson felt that Currey had become too restless for the life of a don; but the statutory restrictions which governed the tenure of fellowships discouraged an ambitious man from assuming a university career. Jackson himself had not been immediately attracted to college teaching. It was virtually his last alternative: 'I have to confess that I myself drifted. I had no definite choice. When I was an undergraduate, I assumed that, like others, I should become a schoolmaster, and presumably take orders. Early in 1863 I had temporary work at Rugby, and decided that I did not care for it. At this time . . . I said that I would *not* be a resident don. . . . But I began to incline to the don's life. Then in 1864 I quarrelled with Mathison. I applied for an inspectorship of schools, but had no hope. I debated whether to ask D. N. Barker to take me into the lead works, but did nothing. I applied to Barry for the Vice-Principalship of Cheltenham College, but he was taking an Oxford man. Meanwhile I was taking pupils hard, and in this way I much improved my scholarship. I learnt to teach, and gained in confidence. By the way, I debated whether I would try Australia.'[1] He also considered reading for the bar but 'decided that for want of money I must not think of it.'[2]

The same indecision confronted Sidgwick. He became a fellow and assistant tutor of Trinity in 1859, but he does not appear to have thrown himself into classical lecturing with any enthusiasm. According to Jackson, Sidgwick prepared his lecture at breakfast and gave the rest of the day to Arabic.[3] Like

[1] Parry, p. 18. Jackson's father was a Sheffield surgeon.
[2] Ibid., p. 19. The expenses of reading for the bar came to about £200 a year in 1870. See Banks, p. 174.   [3] Parry, p. 18.

everyone else he took private pupils as a means of increasing his income,[1] since career and income were then foremost in his mind. About 1861 he ceased private teaching and thought of entering for the bar or becoming a schoolmaster. 'After all, I am getting to believe in you schoolmasters: not that I feel any more disposed to become one. But I fall back on my old idea that the only valuable education of the human soul is the moral one: and schoolmastering is at least as favourable to that as anything else.'[2] Sidgwick had already begun to question the orthodox Christianity in which he had been raised, and he was determined to study the problem philosophically, using the historical method of Mill and Renan. He therefore began to study Arabic and Hebrew as the proper introduction to the investigation of monotheistic religion. But philosophy as a Cambridge career appeared doubtful, since the establishment of the moral sciences tripos in 1851 had not raised any general interest. J. B. Mayor of St. John's was the only college moral science lecturer in Cambridge in 1865.

Sidgwick's increasing religious scepticism made the prospect of a university career still more bleak. The chair of moral science to which he might aspire included moral theology, and Sidgwick was certain that an unorthodox layman would never be appointed. He also knew he would soon have to relinquish his fellowship unless he agreed to take holy orders; but since he had come to believe that religious tests were out of place in Cambridge, he could not accept ordination merely to extend the tenure of his fellowship. As a consequence of these deliberations which consumed him throughout the 1860's, Sidgwick recommenced private teaching as a mode of employment that rendered him independent of his college position and involved relationships that did not weigh on his conscience. Meanwhile he continued to teach in the college as a lecturer and acted as a university examiner in moral sciences. Thus if he resigned his fellowship, he would still have an adequate income while he decided on his future.

For most of the 1860's Sidgwick's private concerns occupied him to the detriment rather than the improvement of college teaching. He characteristically vacillated from one subject to

---

[1] Sidgwick, *Memoir*, p. 36. [2] Ibid., p. 63.

another and from one activity to another, sometimes taking on a heavy load of private pupils when weary with semitic philology and philosophy; sometimes reducing his teaching obligations in order to investigate his personal problems. The appearance of *Ecce Homo*, however, made him feel that a Cambridge career was not altogether impossible. He realized that some practical reconciliation could be made between historical criticism and a loose membership in the Church of England, and that there was even some possibility of retaining his fellowship—he almost resolved to challenge the right of the college to deprive him of it.[1] By mid-December 1866 he had at least made one decision: 'I do not feel your polite irony about philosophers touch me at all,' he answered one of Oscar Browning's jibes. '[My] view is that we ought to be more, not less, strictly educational than we are. If ever I become a power in my College a considerable increase in work (at least of teachers) will take place.'[2] Years later a splenetic Alfred Marshall would perversely remind him of his decision, taunt him for failing to be a prophet and contrast him unfavourably with his great Oxford rival, T. H. Green;[3] but in the 1860's his resolve to be a good teacher had not yet been tested. He eagerly joined Jackson and Currey.

Richard Claverhouse Jebb, the son of an Irish barrister-gentleman, senior classic, first chancellor's medallist in 1862 and fellow of Trinity in 1863, was the fourth member of the quartet. Although considered the finest pure classical scholar in Cambridge, he was in many ways an unlikely recruit. He had none of Jackson's fire and none of Sidgwick's modest, engaging charm and idealism.[4] While an undergraduate he was considered to be a Charterhouse swell.[5] Throughout his life friends and relatives considered him a punctilious, overly reserved if not unkindly man, with a conventional regard for social proprieties. Maitland found him distinctly unattractive. 'I never knew anyone with

---

[1] Ibid., p. 146: 'if they wanted to turn me out, I do not feel at all sure that I should not take the legal view and defy them.'

[2] Ibid., pp. 158-9. [3] Ibid., pp. 394-6.

[4] In a beautiful tribute Maitland called Sidgwick the most truthful man that ever lived and a supremely great teacher. Herbert Albert Laurens Fisher, *Frederic William Maitland* (Cambridge, 1910), pp. 7-8.

[5] Parry, p. 13.

whom I found it more difficult to talk–my own fault I suppose; but so it was.'[1] His wife, the exciting American Caroline Slemmer, found in him an appealing helplessness. She also discerned that 'Like most Irishmen, he has keen wit, but he has no humour, and often is a great help to me in the way of amusement when he does not know it. He has enough strong points to afford to be laughed at sometimes, though not if he knows it.'[2] In scholarship he mastered the traditional Cambridge approach to Greek studies, producing tightly-reasoned textual criticism in a strict Addisonian style. He had no patience with the anthropological interpretation of Greek myths, the approach of the 'unwritten assumption' which was already emerging in Cambridge in the early 1870's. The Odyssey cycle interpreted as a solar myth struck him as 'a mass of that half-crazy ingenuity in which comparative mythologists almost rival the expounders of scriptural types.'[3]

Jebb could have been accused of donnishness. Precise and vain, socially correct, formal in manner and scholarship, he seemed a sharp contrast to Jackson and Sidgwick. But Jebb was nonetheless a man of serious purpose, recognized as such by the Apostles who elected him a member in his first year at Trinity. An heir to the tradition of Bentley and Porson, not inclined to wander too far from the evidence, Jebb was dissatisfied with the state of classical studies and the methods of classical teaching in Cambridge and England. Like Peile, he felt that the study of classics had to be made more scientific and exact before it could become the means to a new humanism, the proper end of philology; and he praised the Scots for studying Greek as an integral part of a general liberal education rather than as an end in itself. Quoting Sir William Hamilton, he told an audience of Glasgow students in 1875 that language was both an exercise of applied logic and the key to the study of literature, 'the entering into the mind of men eminent in thought and in power of expression. That is why it is called *humanising*. It makes you a

---

[1] Maitland, *Letters*, p. 462.

[2] Mary Reed Bobbitt, *Dearest Love to All: Life and Letters of Lady Jebb* (London, 1960), pp. 118–19. See also Gwen Raverat, *Period Piece* (London, 1960), and Carolyn Jebb, *Life and Letters of Sir Richard Claverhouse Jebb* (Cambridge, 1907), with the appended memoir by A. W. Verrall.

[3] Carolyn Jebb, p. 150.

more representative human being, because it gives you a share in the best things that have been thought and said by the best ones of our race.'[1]

For Jebb, the proper end of knowledge and the proper end of teaching was conduct. Education was the means to a better self. Jebb insisted all his life that the quality which made men influential in society was not wealth, or rank, or intellect, but 'force of character'.[2] He appreciated the message of *Ecce Homo* from the date of its first appearance.[3] 'Crises in the expansion of our ideas, like crises in the formation of our characters, are more often determined by personal than by logical influences.'[4] An enthusiastic personal attachment, not reason, made men pure, generous and humane. It was not theology or dogma or ritual but the imitation of Christ that was responsible for the moral influence of Christianity. This was not a donnish sentiment; and the Apostles knew it.

While Jebb, Currey, Sidgwick and Jackson led the reform movement in Trinity, King's College was emerging from a long and peculiar sleep. King's was almost exclusively composed of Eton collegers who matriculated as scholars on the foundation and proceeded to fellowships as a matter of course. Before 1851 the undergraduates of King's retained their ancient right to a university degree without having to sit university examinations, yet Kingsmen entering for university prizes inevitably did well. Because King's did not fall under the domination of the mathematical tripos, Kingsmen simply continued to study classics, their subject at Eton. There was some coaching in classics; but because no mathematics was taught in the college, King's acquired the reputation of being the only Cambridge college devoted to a genuine intellectual ideal, the only one whose

[1] Ibid., p. 186.

[2] Ibid., pp. 287, 388–92. Jebb, *The Work of the Universities for the Nation, Past and Present* (Cambridge, 1893).

[3] Carolyn Jebb, pp. 136, 84–5. Jebb appreciated Seeley's reluctance to deny the divinity of Christ—'I am satisfied that the man is not a Unitarian' –and was delighted to learn that scientific agnostics like Huxley denounced *Ecce Homo* as feeble. Jebb was certain that Seeley believed in the divinity of Christ, but Sidgwick realized that Seeley had avoided the problem. Some years later Seeley surprised Jebb by telling him that *Ecce Deus*, the supposed sequel to *Ecce Homo*, was really his *Life of Stein*.

[4] Ibid.

students did not look upon examinations as the sole road to success.

King's prided itself on still another tradition. Since both fellows and scholars were Eton collegers, teacher-student relations seemed to be closer than in other colleges in Cambridge. But there were defects in the tradition that admirers might overlook. Most fellows entered the professions or returned to Eton as teachers and housemasters; those who remained in residence frequently found themselves separated from the scholars by differences in age and generation. The close relation between teacher and student at King's was in fact really a development of the 1860's and owed much to the very important work of William Cory, an Eton master from 1845–72 and a fellow of King's. Cory admired Dr. Arnold, but he borrowed little from Rugby. Instead of establishing a system of prefects, he revived the Eton tutorial office neglected in the brutal reign of Keate. He was joined in this endeavour by his student, the incorrigible Oscar Browning, an Eton housemaster for fifteen years. A thorough platonist, full of mid-Victorian emotion and affection, Cory, like Browning, totally involved himself in winning the affection and respect of his students; but again like Browning, his motives were misunderstood, and he was ejected from the school. His work at Eton was noted in King's, however, especially when the college decided to reform itself under pressure from Westminster in the 1860's.

The reputation of King's as an intimate college was therefore of recent origin but strong enough to convince Henry Jackson that it was a model college. Jackson, in fact, imported the spirit of King's into Trinity. For more than 30 years he made himself accessible to all members of the college at virtually all hours. His famous card and smoking parties in Neville's Court, full of talk and song and piano music, were part of his calculated programme to bring the junior and senior members of the college into close association; and his friendliness and talent for putting others at ease earned him the title, upheld by successive generations of undergraduates, as the 'least donnish of dons'.[1] Jackson's social activities, in fact, must be included among the techniques he used to end the hegemony of private coaching.

It was widely appreciated that the intimacy of King's was

[1] Parry, pp. 32–4.

based on the common educational background of dons and students; that is, the success of King's was due to its sense of exclusiveness. But if King's were to take its place among the leading Cambridge colleges and participate in the mid-Victorian expansion in higher education, it could no longer afford to waste its considerable endowments by maintaining only a few scholars on the foundation. Sensitive minds realized that the college would have to risk its reputation for friendliness by admitting an unprecedented number of pensioners from all schools; but in order to minimize the shock and also guarantee an amicable welcome to the non-Etonians, even the Eton oppidans, the college decided to revive the office of tutor.[1]

Until 1865 the Provost performed the college's tutorial functions, supervising the dozen or two dozen scholars in residence. The man chosen to revive the tutorial office in 1867 was Augustus Austen Leigh, who had gone down from King's in 1863.[2] Leigh came from a clerical family and had taken deacon's orders in 1865; but two years' parochial work in Henley convinced him that he could never be a parish priest. His work in King's began in 1867 when he joined those who were altering the relationship between Cambridge and the Church of England.

Leigh was a far more moderate reformer than Jackson or Sidgwick but equally conscientious and no longer willing to accept the traditional concept of the college as an ecclesiastical institution. Still firm in matters of college discipline – convinced that public worship was an edifying experience – he was willing to excuse an undergraduate from chapel only if the student proved he was not simply wasting his time. Leigh believed that undergraduates should be brought into close relationship with dons and began to break down student defences in a manner typified by the new dons. He acquired a piano, asked after rowing results and cricket scores, made his rooms a meeting place for undergraduates and proved that he could take a broader view

[1] Certainly no adjustments were necessary for the first two pensioners admitted in 1865, for both of them, Alfred Arthur Bodkin, King's College School, London, and Thomas Holmes Blakesley, were brothers of Etonian scholars of 1863. See J. J. Withers, *A Register of Admissions to King's College, Cambridge, 1850–1900* (London, 1903), p. 24.

[2] The principal sources for Leigh's work in King's are the biography by his brother, the Wedd Memoirs and the Wedd Correspondence.

of classics by instructing his scholars in classical philosophy when this subject was introduced into the classical tripos in the 1870's.

Like the other colleges, King's provided college instruction only in classical composition; and Leigh was expected to teach classics and exercise his tutorial duties at the same time. For some years he carried out this dual function, but his primary aim was the recruitment of a teaching staff which would be resident within the college and able to influence students out of lecture hours. He found it difficult, however, to offer any pecuniary inducement. The tutorship itself was only worth £100, and the income from the tuition fund was limited because the number of pensioners was still small and because Leigh was not always willing to exact full tuition fees if he felt his pupils had nothing to gain from college lectures. In 1872 the governing body of the college created a classical lectureship with a stipend of £150; and shortly thereafter J. E. Nixon, a fellow since 1862, returned into residence and assumed the deanship and the new lectureship. By 1882 Leigh had secured the services of several more fellows; and when a gap in the college teaching occurred, he called in Heitland of St. John's to provide interim instruction. The process of establishing adequate college instruction took more than ten years. But when the new college and university statutes came into effect in 1882, King's was prepared to face the future.

Leigh was given financial and moral support by Henry Bradshaw, the University Librarian, who had been the mainstay of the college while Leigh was an undergraduate and whom many regarded as its natural leader.[1] Bradshaw was the leading bibliographer of his day, a specialist in Irish literature and Celtic and ecclesiastical antiquities. He was also a famous Chaucerian scholar at a time when Chaucer was scarcely known. Mommsen, on a visit to Cambridge in 1885, declared himself more impressed by Bradshaw than by any other Englishman he had met.[2]

Bradshaw's experience with the Eton collegers points up the magnitude of the problems confronting Leigh. As King's was small, Bradshaw was naturally acquainted with all the under-

---

[1] Leigh, pp. 217–18.

[2] George W. Prothero, *Henry Bradshaw* (London, 1888), p. 314.

graduates. He was anxious to prevent the formation of factions and cliques within the college, and tried to use his influence to persuade fellows and collegers to accept graciously the admission of non-Etonian pensioners and students from nonconformist families. He believed that the college could retain its intellectual interests and unique friendliness even when its Etonian connexion was no longer paramount.

In his quiet way Bradshaw sought to make his rooms in King's a college centre where boys from all educational and religious backgrounds would meet, and where the Etonians would unite with the 'outsiders'. He tried to protect the nonconformist pensioners and scholars, as well as college radicals like Karl Pearson, from slander and insult; and one of his notable successes was his brusque reproval of J. E. C. Welldon, fellow of King's from 1878–89 and later headmaster of Harrow and Bishop of Calcutta, who had impugned the morals of Cambridge undergraduates before a Church Congress in 1880.[1]

Despite his continual efforts, Bradshaw was a fallen god. A kindly, tactful and informal man, extremely shy and prone to periodic depression, sensitive to controversy, and too much involved personally and emotionally with the scholars and their families, he was unable to act as the college arbiter. The 'out siders' saw him as a man surrounded by Etonians and stayed away. Even Nathaniel Wedd, a fixture in King's in the thirty years before the First World War, failed to respond to one of Bradshaw's invitations.[2]

[1] 'How sharply the whip could crack was shown on a famous occasion when Welldon, who had recently taken holy orders, and become headmaster of Harrow, became famous by an address at the Church Congress in which he deplored the alleged atheism of Cambridge, and asserted that in his own personal experience loss of faith on the part of his fellow undergraduates had always been followed by loss of morality. This pleased a wide public and Welldon was at once a great man in newspaper headlines. Flushed with triumph, with the laurels still green about his brow, he came to show himself in King's and naturally went straight to Bradshaw's room. There was a great crowd in the room, but Bradshaw saw him as he entered and called out "Well Welldon, you lied, and you know it".' Wedd, 'King's in 1883'. Wedd, who matriculated in 1883, is repeating a story he heard only by report.

[2] Wedd, 'The University', p. 103. Wedd had been a day boy at the City of London School and found himself a member of the excluded at King's.

Bradshaw's worst fears were realized when dons and undergraduates divided into two hostile camps in the 1880's. The famous Arthur Benson, a fashionable snob and son of the future Archbishop of Canterbury, led the 'best set' which viewed the outsiders as common clay. Benson was supported by A. H. Cooke, a charming Eton scholar and fellow of the college. The outsiders were led by the oppidan J. J. Withers, son of a solicitor and himself a future solicitor for the college and Conservative M.P. The feud continued even after the departure of Benson and Withers and ended in violence in 1889, at which time Cooke, then Dean, reconciled the factions.[1] Leigh was alarmed by the situation and in his first sermon as Provost preached unity: 'It is only family love which makes men to be of one mind in a house; it is only Christian love which can knit hearts together in a College.'[2]

Bradshaw died in 1886 a disappointed man, unable to hasten the transition of King's into the modern period. There were too many petty obstacles; too much insolence, cavil and misunderstanding in the college; too much 'weakly picking holes in their neighbour's work', as he told one correspondent. King's needed more Darwin-like men, 'who go at truth because they can't help it. . . . There are several here as it is, and the more we have the more we shall get on. . . . Cambridge is becoming every year more and more such a hive of workers, that I do long to see King's possessed of some good share of these workers in different fields. Only none of these changes for good will ever

---

[1] Wedd, 'King's in 1883', 'The University'. Sidgwick's opinion of Benson, his nephew, coincides with Wedd's account. Commenting on a fictitious biography Benson had written, Sidgwick wrote in 1886 that 'it ought . . . to interest a certain portion of the "company of well-dressed men and women out in search of a religion", as Emerson calls modern society. One point in it that struck me was the complete absence of the *socialistic* enthusiasm which I have always regarded as the main current of new feeling among thoughtful young men during the last few years here–the years that my nephew was here as undergraduate. It might have been written in the last century, so far as the relations of rich and poor are concerned.' Sidgwick, *Memoir*, p. 440.

[2] Leigh, p. 231. There is no specific mention of the episode between the collegers and the oppidans in Leigh, only an allusion to 'difficulties in the undergraduate society of King's, which have never reappeared in anything like the same shape.' Bradshaw was close to the Benson family, a circumstance which no doubt contributed to his sense of helplessness and confusion.

come of themselves, or without strong individual effort on the part of each one of us–that is certain.'[1]

2.

A new group of dons emerged in Cambridge in the twenty years preceding the statutory reforms of 1882. They were distinguished by their professional interest in scholarship, by their intention to make university teaching a career and by their desire to revive the unique feature of a collegiate university, the close relation between fellows and students. They regarded the college as a family and themselves *in loco parentis*, as in fact did their predecessors, but underlying their conception of the family was an altered meaning of authority. They did not require obedience for its own sake. They preferred admiration to fear, loyalty to regulations. No less than the old dons they believed in the necessity for moral education; but regarding the task of character regeneration as critical and urgent, they attached a new importance to the teaching experience and to themselves as teachers.

It would be misleading to claim that the personalities of the new generation of dons differed profoundly from the old. A full range of types were represented by the new dons. Some were shy or humble,[2] others vain or arrogant, still others elegant or ebullient. It was their *attitude* towards students and teaching which set them apart from the previous generation and made them so remarkably different. They identified with a spirit of reform, they spoke freely of socratic and Christian behaviour, they talked about the necessity to help students; and they let it be publicly known, keeping their doubts for the most part to themselves, that they were first and foremost interested in academic careers in Cambridge.

The new dons graduated to positions of responsibility within

[1] Prothero, pp. 293–5. Bradshaw was specifically referring to the constant bickering between Oscar Browning and Prothero, for which Browning was mainly responsible. See Wedd, 'King's in 1883'.

[2] The famous scholar and Bishop of Durham, Joseph Barber Lightfoot, described by Sidgwick as a member of the 'new school' of professors, was quite shy as a tutor in 1860. He was more at ease in company than with individual students. But he was also one of those tutors who could be found racing along the towing-path. George R. Eden and F. C. MacDonald, *Lightfoot of Durham* (Cambridge, 1933), p. 6. Sidgwick, *Memoir*, p. 153.

the colleges and in every instance improved the quality of collegiate instruction. The methods they used to attract students were singularly uniform and were frequently borrowed from private tutors. The new dons gave parties, teas and dinners to introduce junior and senior members of the college to one another. They opened their rooms to students at all hours of the day and night and made themselves available for serious or informal conversation. They took an interest in student activities, frequently in student sports and athletics, and they treated students kindly without jeopardizing collegiate and university discipline. They did not, for example, forgo the right to require compulsory chapel of undergraduates who were members of the Church of England; but in general they preferred a new kind of discipline and authority—internal rather than external—instead of formal restraints. They made the student believe he was important, respecting him as an individual and encouraging him to share his personal thoughts and problems with them. In short, they did not 'come don over the student'.

The new dons favoured the honours men. These were ambitious students for whom success was important, and they were the least likely to resist authority. The new dons did not entirely neglect the poll men; they tried in fact to encourage special interests in all students. No doubt they were anxious to keep the student busy and therefore out of mischief, but they had other reasons as well. They wanted to continue the 'masculine' or 'manly' tradition of aristocratic Cambridge; they wanted a vital, alert and energetic student body, one not prone to degeneration, the vice of the age. They also wanted every student to have some activity—intellectual, social or sporting—which they could share or pretend to share in order to gain his attention and confidence. 'It was the man who read hard, the man who rowed hard, and let me add, the man who did both, whom I and my contemporaries respected and admired,' wrote Jackson after fifty years.[1] Even in 1866, when the revolution of the dons was just getting under way, their methods were surprisingly successful. Cheered by the good-will between teachers and students, Maurice remarked to Kingsley that 'In my day there would have been nothing like it.'[2]

[1] Henry Jackson, 'Cambridge Fifty Years Ago', pp. 449–51.
[2] Maurice, *Life*, II, p. 547.

Dons had usually ignored most student activities; but in the late 1850's they began to interest themselves in student clubs and sets, either by forming new clubs to rival existing organizations or by promoting new kinds of activities. This too was part of their programme to acquire influence over students and guide undergraduate behaviour. One of the first important instances of co-operation between fellows and students came in 1858 with the founding of the most famous and long-lived of all Cambridge magazines, *The Eagle* of St. John's. Joseph Bickersteth Mayor, the son of a Cheshire clergyman, one of the first of the new generation of moral scientists and an original member of the Grote Club, helped a number of Johnians from the college Shakespeare Society found *The Eagle*. He was an important member 'of a band of young Fellows who really cared for the undergraduates'.[1] At first the magazine attempted to broaden undergraduate interests by drawing attention away from mathematics. When this proved altogether too successful and sets, activities and studies multiplied, the college seemed threatened with division and *The Eagle* changed its goal. It now sought to make itself a centre of unity, ' "a rallying point and a watchword" to all members of the College ... [to] bind men still to it when they went away.'[2]

In the next decade, in his inaugural address, Seeley deliberately set himself up as a rival to the university debating society, the Cambridge Union. Students valued the Union as a training ground for statesmen, but it was an unimaginative imitation of the House of Commons. Its debates were amateurish and ill-informed, needlessly hysterical about the democratic future of England. Seeley's object was to reduce the Union to its proper size as a social club by making his lectures on scientific politics the real seminary of statesmen.[3] Other dons established societies with themselves as presidents. Oscar Browning, echoing Seeley's manifesto that Cambridge should be a great school of politicians, founded a Political Society in King's, to which he invited other students as well; he also started a Dante Society to introduce undergraduates to a wider area of culture as well as to impress them with his cosmopolitanism. He arranged concerts and Sunday afternoon 'at homes' to which he invited

[1] *The Eagle*, XV (1889), p. 327.   [2] Ibid., pp. 315; 309–27.
[3] Seeley, 'The Teaching of Politics', p. 299.

leading European personalities, frequently without success. He took Kingsmen to the London theatres and on trips to Italy in the hope of winning their admiration. The leading principle upon which he based his actions was virtually the same as that of the other new dons; but mixed with his higher ideals was a napoleonic ambition, an egregious vanity, which led him to exceed the limits of tact and common sense and made him a caricature of the new don.[1]

3.

The attack on coaching proceeded along several fronts. Around 1868 the colleges began to grope towards an intercollegiate system of instruction. Although in the past students from one college had sometimes received special permission to attend the lectures in another, college rivalry generally prevented co-operation. Sometimes the rivalry was not collegiate but intra-collegiate. Each of the two mathematical sides at St. John's, for example, was responsible for its own scheme of lectures. Participation in intercollegiate mathematical teaching by St. John's therefore had to be preceded by an amalgamation of the tutorial sides, accomplished about 1859 or 1860.[2]

Partly because the colleges awaited the decision of the statutory commissioners on a university lecture system, inter-collegiate teaching developed unsystematically. Groups of colleges arranged lectures for their own students in a particular tripos; and additional combinations—not necessarily composed of the same colleges—were formed for other triposes. Thus Christ's, St. John's, Corpus, Jesus and Trinity agreed to divide the subjects of the classical tripos between them, each college to lecture on a different subject.[3] Sidgwick and Jackson were influential in this innovation, which was not fully developed until after 1875.[4]

[1] For Browning see Wedd, 'Memoirs', H. E. Wortham, *Victorian Eton and Cambridge* (London, 1927) and Oscar Browning, *Memories of Sixty Years* (London, 1910).

[2] *The Eagle*, XV (1889), p. 315.

[3] T.C.L., Rec. 16.1, meeting of tutors and lecturers, June 3, 1868. Participating in the scheme were Gunson and Peile.

[4] T.C.L., Rec. 5.1, October 12, 1874, December 12, 1874 and March 16, 1875.

One major factor in the growth of the intercollegiate system of lectures was the Trinity praelectorship. The praelector was a fellow whose lectures were open to members of other colleges. Retention of his fellowship was not bound by the conditions of celibacy and holy orders, thus allowing the college a certain latitude of choice not usually possible in the appointment of tutors and assistant tutors. In 1870 Trinity created a praelectorship in natural science for the famous physiologist Michael Foster, who was brought to Cambridge in order to improve the quality of Cambridge medicine. In 1875 the college created a praelectorship in moral and political philosophy for Sidgwick, who had earlier resigned his fellowship in protest against the tests requirement. In the same year Jackson was appointed praelector in ancient philosophy, allowing him to remain a fellow after his marriage.[1]

At approximately the same time that the colleges joined together for intercollegiate teaching, the new dons turned their attention to college lecture classes, and the attack on coaching took a form that was to produce a striking and historic change. Traditionally college teaching was supposed to be catechetical—question and answer like the Scottish 'examination-cum-tutorial hour system'[2]—rather than rhetorical like the professorial lecture; but most college lectures had deteriorated into formal school lessons. The new dons revived catechetical college teaching by borrowing from the methods of the best coaches, who excelled in the teaching of small groups. Routh had perfected the teaching of mathematics to groups of six or ten, but the classics coaches found that Cambridge classics did not lend itself to production techniques to quite the same extent as mathematics. They preferred to teach students in groups of two or three, or they took students singly. It was this latter practice that most influenced the new classical dons. They began to supplement group instruction with individual assistance; and borrowing again from the coaches, they added written exercises in translation to college composition classes, an excellent method for working closely with students. In 1875 the Board of Classical Studies announced that college honours classes in composition and translation had proven to be of the greatest use

[1] Parry, p. 25.
[2] George Elder Davie, *The Democratic Intellect* (Edinburgh, 1961), p. 16.

in securing individual communication between teachers and students.[1]

By 1883 an embryonic system of supervisorial instruction existed in Trinity. Classical dons continued to supplement catechetical class teaching with personal assistance, providing approximately one hour a week of individual instruction to honours students.[2] Similiar assistance was provided students reading mathematics. In 1887, however, Trinity mathematical lecturers declared themselves in favour of more casual arrangements, preferring formal lectures during classtime with additional help for students as required in individual cases.[3] Two years later a Tutorial System Committee was appointed to extend supervision to all members of the college and to place the inchoate system on a regular basis. Responsible for reforming the office of tutor and improving the quality of Trinity teaching, the Tutorial System Committee was equally concerned with establishing close relations between undergraduates and the teaching staff. The committee declared that 'There are some classes of undergraduates who are inadequately provided by the present system with opportunities of coming into close relationship with members of the staff capable of guiding their studies, and chiefly in consequence of this, the tutorial relation is in a considerable number of cases unreal and insignificant.'[4]

Matriculations at Trinity had continued to increase despite the agrarian depression, but the committee did not follow the usual practice of suggesting a proportionate increase in the number of senior tutors. Instead it proposed to create 'studies tutors,' or in the form finally adopted by the committee and still used today, 'directors of studies'. These were dons who would exercise a general supervision over students reading a particular subject, who would dispense advice, be readily available and keep themselves informed of the progress of students attending Trinity classes or intercollegiate lectures. It appears that the

[1] Report of the Cambridge Studies Syndicate, March 27, 1876, reprinted in Parliamentary Papers, 1876. lix, p. 9.

[2] T.C.L., Rec. 5.2., May 1883.

[3] Ibid., Permanent Classes Committee, March 12, 1887 and May 30, 1887.

[4] Minutes and Reports of the Tutorial System Committee, inserts opposite pages 27 and 28, 1889. (Records of the Junior Bursar, Trinity College, no class mark.)

'director of studies' proposed by the committee was in part a continuation of the office of assistant tutor, as developed by Jackson, Currey, Sidgwick and Jebb.

One member of the Trinity College Tutorial System Committee, V. H. Stanton, Ely and later Regius Professor of Divinity and a friend and admirer of Jackson,[1] recommended that tutors engage in some teaching and encourage the best students in 'general intellectual interests' in order to counteract modern overspecialization.[2] He also hoped to bring the college lecturers into closer association with students. He suggested that all composition and translation lecturers be prepared to dispense general advice, sometimes dropping all academic work simply to have a good talk with students.[3]

Members of the Tutorial System Committee drafting the new schemes seemed to regard the union of academic and moral instruction as the ideal educational work of the college. The supervisorial system proposed in 1889 and 1890 was a deliberate effort to consolidate the victory won over private tuition by an extraordinary generation of mid-Victorians. It was a conscious attempt to institutionalize the relationship between teacher and student which was one of the great legacies of the new dons, and which, in its broader features, has lasted to the present. By overlapping the functions of tutors, directors of studies and lecturers, by blurring the distinction between Christian and socratic teaching, the committee tried to re-establish the authority of the college on a new basis. By making every college teaching officer stand *in loco parentis* to the student, Trinity hoped to acquire maximum corporate influence over its undergraduates without

---

[1] Stanton was appointed Ely Professor in 1889 and wrote Jackson apologetically that 'I feel ashamed of the success which, through belonging to a well endowed faculty, has fallen to me, when you are still left without full University recognition, whose work deserves it so much more. I hope the founding of a Chair of Ancient Philosophy may come, in time for you to enjoy a good tenure of it; but at all events we all pay you honour in our hearts.' (T.C.L. Add. c. 43^{91}.) When Jackson was appointed Regius Professor of Greek in 1906 Stanton wrote him, 'It would not be easy for me to say, & you would not like me to try, how very large I feel the debt to be which the College & the University owe to you, & in which I have my own personal share from undergraduate days onwards.' (T.C.L. Add. c. 43^{92})

[2] Minutes and Reports of the Tutorial System Committee, flysheet insert by V. H. Stanton on 'Duties of Tutors', page 5 of insert.

[3] Minutes and Reports of the Tutorial System Committee, insert page 11.

having to rely exclusively on the personal qualities of any one don.[1]

Coaching continued throughout the late Victorian period partly because college or intercollegiate instruction was not provided for every paper in the honours and poll examinations and partly because some students were either too ill-prepared or too unintelligent to get through the examinations without additional assistance. The existence of the order of merit in mathematics also kept coaching alive as unusually ambitious (and fearful) honours men reading mathematics were afraid to forgo special preparation. Increasingly, however, coaching was becoming remedial rather than essential. Except perhaps in the Long Vacation, coaching for honours classics men in St. John's and Trinity ceased about 1880,[2] and for poll men in classics a decade later.[3] In 1902 the *Student's Handbook* announced that there was no need for most students to seek private tuition, as college, intercollegiate and professorial teaching were quite sufficient.[4] One other important development in coaching appears to have taken place in the later nineteenth century. Probably in the late 1870's coaches began to send their bills for services rendered to the colleges for collection. This had the advantage of freeing coach and student from the embarrassing financial arrangements that existed earlier when the student virtually hid the money somewhere in the coach's rooms, and the coach was allowed to bury his pride by pretending an exchange of money had not taken place.[5] This change in practice also allowed the college tutor to exercise closer control over out-of-college tuition arrangements and enabled him to keep better informed of a student's general educational progress.

[1] The origins of the Cambridge supervisorial system is a totally neglected subject. A brief narrative sketch, based mainly on the fragments in Parry's memoir of Jackson, appears as Appendix G to the Bridges Report on the relationship between the university and colleges of Cambridge, *University Reporter* (March 13, 1962). None of the larger historical questions are touched.

[2] *Cambridge Review* (October 15, 1879), p. 12, and (November 30, 1881), p. 99.

[3] *Student's Guide* (1893), pp. 71–2.   [4] *Student's Handbook*, p. 60.

[5] Sometimes, however, the student paid directly into the coach's bank account. Henry Sidgwick to Arthur Balfour, 1 November [? 1878], B.M. Add. MS 49832.

The symbolic death of coaching occurred in 1907 when the order of merit in mathematics was abolished. A remarkable episode in the history of Cambridge came to an end.

4.

Many conceptions of a college emerged in nineteenth-century England. Some colleges were actually miniature universities organized on a professorial basis like University College, London, or King's College, London, the latter being a denominational college which tried to preserve the union of Anglicanism and learning. Other colleges were really schools devoted to a particular subject or group of subjects, such as religious seminaries, teacher-training colleges or polytechnical and vocational institutions. Within Cambridge several colleges still retained a residue of the professional intentions of their founders. Trinity Hall kept its connexion with canon law, while Downing College, pitifully underendowed, struggled to keep alive its obligation to educate lawyers and doctors. The idea of a specialist college without specified vocational functions was advanced in the 1860's when the colleges appeared unable to provide teachers for the numerous papers of the honours and pass examinations. Seeley suggested that small colleges specialize in order to find a means of overcoming their resistance to the introduction of new university subjects.

Within Cambridge, and also outside, there was a popular belief that genuine collegiate diversity existed within the university, but such differences that did exist were not usually deep or lasting. It is true that most wealthy or aristocratic students tended to congregate in Trinity; but in general, except where a racial policy was in force—more a feature of the late nineteenth century—the colleges were socially homogenous. Most college diversity was simply a matter of emphasis or tone, and at any time a new master or tutor could transform a sporting college into a serious college or otherwise alter its reputation. Still, many students undoubtedly sought private advice on which college best suited their interests before applying for admission. Certain students might be advised to attend a small, less competitive college: in the mid-Victorian period Trinity Hall had a reputation for accepting students in delicate health. Some colleges were noted for athletics, some for aesthetics, still others for their friendliness or attachment to Low or High Church. Students reading science would prefer Trinity, those reading history perhaps King's–at least after 1870; but a large college was generally strong in all subjects and activities. In Trinity a man could be a rowing blue or an intellectual *sans-culotte* without fear of interference. A very small college was apt to be paralysed by any disagreement among its dons, as the pathetic history of St. Catharine's shows;[1] and as a small college King's had experienced the shock of a divisive conflict.

The principal idea of a Cambridge college, that which really distinguished it from the other kinds of colleges known to the nineteenth century and continues to distinguish the collegiate university today, derived from its characteristics as a residential institution. The student was away from home, he was separated from the influences of the family and the environment which had conditioned his behaviour. He was not as completely receptive to new influences as younger boys in boarding schools, but his greater maturity meant that he could be entrusted with more responsibility. Discipline was not likely to be as onerous and unrewarding a task as it was in the schools. The student was at an age when he could appreciate advanced learning and higher ideals; and being close to the time when he would take his place in society, he was particularly anxious to benefit from the advice and assistance of his superiors. In these respects he was very responsive to collegiate influence. In the college, with its communal life and surrounded by the symbols of a long and distinguished tradition, the student began to identify with what were represented as the tone and atmosphere of the place. The antiquity and beauty of the college lent it an air of historical purpose and serenity and appeared to require of the student a sense of humility and self-denial. He became desirous of living up to the ideals of the society and learned to forgo some of his own pleasures in the interests of the larger college community. At the same time, because the college was not so large that he felt lost within it, he retained a sense of his own individuality.

After a number of years the student unconsciously absorbed

[1] W. H. S. Jones, *A History of St. Catharine's College* (Cambridge, 1936). In the 1870's King's and St. Catharine's discussed the possibility of a merger, but no agreement was reached.

the ideals of the college society so that a distinct change in his character could be produced. This is why dons claimed throughout the later nineteenth century that in Cambridge a man's social background did not count for much. They did not mean that money and family were totally unimportant; for quite obviously money could buy better Cambridge accommodations and amenities, and a man's family background might guarantee him admission to the college of his choice. What dons meant when they said that Cambridge did not inquire about a man's background was that in the final analysis, distinction was related to intellectual merit, to personal integrity, to a sense of duty, to character, to use that vague and important word. No amount of money or family connexions could produce a first class in the tripos, or a college friendship, nor could it buy the genuine respect of the reading man. In this narrow and limited sense Cambridge was classless.[1]

Just before the revolution of the dons, the communal idea of a college appeared to have lost some of its appeal. It was said that the morality taught in college chapels was irrelevant to the changing conditions of English social life. Only lip-service was paid to the ideal of character formation, and then mainly as an argument against dissenters, whose admission, it was claimed by academic tories, would overturn the existing bases of authority. One former tutor of Trinity, Joseph William Blakesley, an actor's son educated at St. Paul's, an original member of the Apostles and a future Dean of Lincoln, criticized the communal ideal by recommending a 'salutary supplement'. He suggested that families resident in the town of Cambridge with sons at the university might well keep their sons at home instead of in colleges and take in as boarders other students of limited means or diligent habits, with 'more advantage to their religious habits likely to follow from family prayers, than from the daily service in the College chapel.'[2] Such families, he thought, could become the nucleus of a revived university hostel system and a means for restoring the importance of the university.

[1] For an analysis of the influence of the collegiate form of residence on the values and class identity of students today in three universities in north Britain, see Joan Abbott, 'Students' Social Class in Three Northern Universities', *The British Journal of Sociology*, XVI (September, 1965), pp. 206–20.

[2] Graham Commission (1852), Evidence, p. 151.

It could not even be maintained that the tutor exercised an important influence over undergraduates, since no one disputed the fact that the coaching relationship was far more important than the tutorial relationship; and it could certainly not be claimed that discipline was successful, since college rules had never dissuaded wealthier students from intemperance. The decline in extravagant student behaviour, noted by Sedgwick in 1849,[1] had really nothing to do with the colleges but reflected the waning of aristocratic influence generally and important changes in the public schools. Critics could even argue that discipline in approved lodging houses, where in 1867 over one-third of all Cambridge undergraduates lived,[2] was, in some respects, superior to college discipline. Even though there were more lodging houses than proctors, deans or tutors could effectively supervise, it was easier to impose curfew regulations or ban late parties in a lodging house with only two or three students than in a college with many more, especially since some of the lodging houses were run by college servants anxious to avoid displeasing their employers.

In the late 1850's and throughout the 1860's reformers and parliamentary commissions of inquiry became increasingly interested in non-collegiate forms of residence. The college was criticized as too expensive and snobbish. It was thought that if the college had no distinct contribution to make to education – if it could not even house all of its students or teach its own undergraduates – other forms of residence would be just as satisfactory and certainly cheaper. Both the Graham Commission and the Ewart Committee influenced the passage of legislation which allowed students to matriculate directly in the university without having to associate with a college. In 1859 or 1860 the Deputy-Professor of Anatomy opened a hostel for five medical students,[3] and a decade later Fitzwilliam House was founded.

Despite, however, the considerable interest in non-collegiate residential plans and university teaching expressed in the middle decades of the nineteenth century, the communal ideal of a college did not perish. At precisely the moment when the uni-

[1] Sedgwick, *Discourses*, cccxlviii–cccxlix.
[2] Ewart Committee, Evidence, p. 105.
[3] Graham Commission (1861), p. 5.

versity emerged as a rival to the college and both the university and the colleges became interested in the advancement of professional study, the communal ideal was revived and the college was once more put forth as a place of moral education and character formation.

What was a college? Certainly what a lodging house, hostel or non-collegiate body could never be, a human relationship, 'the close action of the teacher on the pupil, of the matured character on the unformed, of the instructed on the learning mind, not indeed without a very beneficial reaction of the young on the aging man.'

Previously the teacher had not been a conspicuous part of the college. The friendships that sprang up between undergraduates and tutors were incidental to the education of Cambridge and in the main restricted to a handful of superior students and young dons who soon left when they found no satisfactory career before them. It is significant that Macaulay's biography does not include the name of a single Cambridge teacher who made a lasting impression upon him during his undergraduate years in the early 1820's. Macaulay did not think of Trinity as an institution in which a dynamic and consistent attempt was made to influence his mind and character. He was indeed devoted to the name and memory of Trinity, regarding it, we are told, as an ancient Greek regarded his native city. But Macaulay also found Trinity a place where he was left alone and could read at his pleasure, a liberation from an evangelical home and father, an arcadian sanctuary. 'The only dignity that in his later days he was known to covet was an honourary fellowship, which would have allowed him again to look through his window upon the college grass-plots, and to sleep within the sound of the splashing of the fountain; again to breakfast on commons, and dine beneath the portraits of Newton and Bacon on the dais of the hall; again to ramble by moonlight round Neville's cloister, discoursing the picturesque but somewhat exoteric philosophy which it pleased him to call by the name of metaphysics.'[1]

After the 1860's the college was no longer mainly a romantic retreat, but a place where the teacher influenced the student by

[1] George Otto Trevelyan, *The Life and Letters of Thomas Babington Macaulay* (London, 1932), I, pp. 69–70.

example, knowledge or sympathy; and where, in the imagination of the student, the teacher and the college merged as one. Compare Macaulay's dream of Trinity with the recollections of an undergraduate who was at King's three-quarters of a century later: 'When I describe King's and the Kingsmen of those days nobody believes me but . . . there was such a golden age. To me Wedd, Lowes Dickinson, O.B., [William Herrick] Macaulay and the rest are still a wind dream. Will any College ever contain such characters, such Dons or such undergraduates again? . . . King's–King's! . . . Those were happy but exhausting days and what vistas of the mind and even of the Soul were opened to us.'[1]

What was a college? What Seeley and Austen Leigh said it should be, a Christian family, with the tutor as a very undonnish father. A college was in fact what all the dons had always said it was, an educational institution deeply influenced by religious precepts and dedicated to the preservation of high moral standards. But–college chapels, more meaningful religious services and fellows in holy orders notwithstanding–there no longer was a Church of England to influence the tone of the colleges, define correct behaviour and act as a final court of appeal in matters of taste and discipline. The authority previously derived from the maintenance of religious uniformity, itself made possible by a special connexion with the state, now depended primarily on the relations between teacher and student.

Both the older conception of a communal college and the birth of the new are dramatically illustrated in the foundation of Selwyn College in 1882. Selwyn adopted as its distinguishing feature the traditional conception of a college as a residential educational institution governed by a uniform religious doctrine –a recognizable authority–without which neither proper discipline nor moral education was possible. To achieve this goal the college proposed to restrict admission to members of the Church of England–or those willing to attend Anglican, in this case high church, services–and to elect into fellowships only loyal churchmen, lay or clerical. As the master-elect explained, 'The first object, the definite Church purpose and tone of the College, would of course not have been a "distinctive feature" a

[1] Sir Shane Leslie to C. R. Fay, February 28, 1951, K.C.L. Misc. 17[9].

few years ago. But the course of events had made it impossible for any of the old Colleges to maintain a general and uniform system of religious teaching and discipline. The admission within their walls of students of any creed and denomination cannot but tend to hinder these older foundations from giving definite Church character to the education they provide.'[1]

Following the examples of Selwyn himself, Bishop of New Zealand before his death, and of the master-elect's father, Lord Lyttelton, one of the earliest founders of the Canterbury Mission in New Zealand, the founders of the college planned to make special provision for the training of missionaries. They also hoped to attract the poorer sons of clergy–perhaps too as one enthusiast cried, 'the sons of poor professional men and shop-keepers, whom no scholarships corrupt, nor wits endow'[2]–who were finding it difficult to enter older colleges because of the greater competition for scholarships and prizes resulting from the rapid increase in enrolments. In order to attract sons of clergy, however, the necessary expenses of a collegiate education had to be reduced–impossible unless Selwyn could convince undergraduates that coaching was unnecessary. Accordingly discussions about the purpose and future of Selwyn emphasized the desirability and the necessity of reforming the tutorial system in order to promote close ties between college officers and undergraduates. But this was not the only reason for wishing to change the customary relations between clerical dons and students. If the supporters of Selwyn truly believed that occasional acts of rowdyism and the competition of ethical views argued the collapse of college discipline in Cambridge and provided fresh evidence of the need for moral education, for 'a manly self-restraint'[3] and simple, inexpensive habits 'in days of luxury and self-indulgence,'[4] they could not rely exclusively on the older, indulgent and indifferent implementation of the idea of a college. They would have to adopt a means by which the college fellows could directly influence the young men in their charge; they would have to join the revolution of the dons.[5]

[1] Undated flysheet but probably 1880 or 1881 by A. T. Lyttelton, master-elect, C.U.L. Cam a. 500.6[113]; also flysheet June 1, 1881, Cam.a.500.6[116].

[2] 'Selwyn College', *Cambridge Review* (February 15, 1882), p. 163.

[3] Ibid.   [4] Flysheet (Lyttelton).

[5] Ibid. A Trinity M.A. at Cuddesdon, the High Church Training College in Oxford, urged the clerical fellows of Cambridge to cast off their reserve

5.

In 1882 celibacy restrictions on the tenure of fellowships were removed, and a rash of marriages followed. Within the year all but one of the resident fellows of Jesus College married, and the news soon spread, with probably some exaggeration, that throughout the university forty marriages had taken place.[1]

Tutors were among the first to marry because their income was more suitable than the average fellow's for supporting a family at the standard required of Victorian professional men.[2] Some of the colleges were concerned lest marriage interfere with tutorial work, and various arrangements were made to keep tutors in or near the colleges. In 1885 Jesus built two houses for married fellows within the college close, so that there would always be at least two fellows resident in the college.[3] At Gonville and Caius the senior tutor actually requested that his family be housed in college, and some undergraduate rooms were converted into a makeshift residence where the tutor and his wife lived inconveniently for seventeen years.[4] In 1886 the Trinity Governing Council appointed a married tutor but resolved 6–3 not to make the appointment an absolute precedent.[5] Three years later, while the tutorial system was under-

---

and shyness and mix more freely with undergraduates. A supporter of Selwyn College, he believed that more friendliness on the part of the clerical dons of other colleges was required to overcome undergraduate doubts and perplexities caused by the mixing of nonconformists and Anglicans and to keep students from immoral and idle behaviour. *Cambridge Review* (February 22, 1882), pp. 182–3. Another letter in the same issue, page 183, doubted that Selwyn would be able to reduce educational costs below the level obtaining in other colleges where students practiced economy and concluded that 'it seems to me that the true claim for Selwyn lies in the fact of its trying a new system as to discipline, which most will allow is much wanted.'

[1] Gray and Brittain, p. 169. W. F. Reddaway, *Cambridge in 1891* (1943), p. 5.

[2] A tutorship in combination with a fellowship yielded £700–2,000 per annum, about £1,000 on the average. H. A. Morgan, *The Tenure of Fellowships* (London, Oxford and Cambridge, 1871), p. 8.

[3] Gray and Brittain, p. 169.

[4] Mrs. Ernest Stewart Roberts, *Sherborne, Oxford, and Cambridge* (London, 1934), pp. 123–4.

[5] Minutes of the Trinity College Council, 1886 volume, pp. 135, 243, 245 (Records of the Senior Bursar).

going reform, it was proposed that the tutor sleep in college at least three nights per week.[1]

It has been suggested that the removal of celibacy restrictions weakened college life, that marriage made fellows even more aloof from undergraduates,[2] but there is no evidence that this was actually the case. Certainly in the past celibacy had been neither an essential ingredient of the communal idea nor a precondition of good teaching. College concern in the 1880's for the maintenance of a strong bond between tutors and students is a sign of the regeneration of the tutorial system rather than a symptom of its further decay.

In the late Victorian period the tension between marital and college life was far from critical. No doubt there were wives less understanding than McTaggart's bride, who told the young philosopher before their marriage that he was to keep to his college routine – that 'she likes being left alone;'[3] but in general the demands of the home did not press heavily on the average don's professional life. The large, ugly but impressive houses that inhabit the Madingley Road and Storey's Way indicate a high degree of modest comfort. Domestics were used to perform menial household tasks, 'nannies', governesses and boarding schools took over the responsibility of child-raising. The pace of academic life was still relatively leisurely, and dons were mainly occupied with undergraduate teaching. The revival of the idea of a college, extended through the supervisorial system, eliminated the need for a celibate fellowship, and the late Victorian period is perhaps the greatest period in the history of Cambridge undergraduate teaching.

In the long run, in another century, perhaps the home was a factor in the weakening of college life. Domestics disappeared, ideas of child-rearing and family obligations changed, draining some of the attention of dons away from undergraduates. More potent causes, however, were changes in the structure of academic professional life and in patterns of student leisure and behaviour. Scholars and scientists became more mobile and

---

[1] Minutes and Reports of the Tutorial System Committee, insert in page 10.

[2] Bury, *History of Corpus*, p. 92.

[3] J. M. E. McTaggart to Wedd, January 24, 1899, Wedd Papers, Box III, K.C.L.

more research-minded. Large numbers of graduate students working for advanced degrees appeared in Cambridge, and students in general became more independent and self-reliant, as well as more experienced socially and culturally. These changes indicated that the association of dons and students established in the mid-Victorian period and caught in the idea of a communal college, was due for a decisive readjustment.[1]

6.

When the foundations are cast down, what shall the righteous do? The England and Cambridge of the aristocracy and an established Church behind them, dons remembered that they were university intellectuals, professional men, who had to aid society in the difficult but imperative transition from one set of values to another. They examined every available intellectual theory in the hope of finding a guide for their actions. Every new or old idea that came to hand, scientific, historical, theological, logical or aesthetic was anxiously inspected for possible prophetic content. Religion, which had played such a vital role in the history of Cambridge, was investigated from every conceivable point of view. Dogmatic Christianity was rejected but not Christian morality. Dons remained in several important respects products of clerical Cambridge. They believed that an ideal of conduct was possible and that the university, no less than the Church, had to find that ideal. They believed that no matter what occupation a man assumed in society, the first requirement was that he be a good man.

Dons sometimes spoke earnestly of the benefits of material civilization and of the contributions of the machine to the welfare and progress of society; but they never displayed much

---

[1] See for example Jasper Rose and John Ziman, *Camford Observed* (London, 1964), Chapter V, and the Report of the Hale Committee of the University Grants Committee on University Teaching Methods (London, 1964), especially pp. 31–2. The Hale Committee asked a sample of Oxbridge students whether there was a person to whom they had been told to go at regular intervals and from whom they could seek advice, and 47 per cent of the students answered 'no'. In view of the tutorial arrangements at both universities, the Hale Committee believes its question was misunderstood. It is possible, however, that the answers of the students indicate that the content if not the structure of the Oxbridge tutorial system is changing.

enthusiasm for a business career. And when pushed they would concede, implicitly if not explicitly, that professional life met the requirements of morality better than business life. Usually, however, they were reluctant to make an open declaration of the superiority of one occupation over another. Instead they preferred to repeat the teachings of Christianity that the unrelieved pursuit of wealth corrupted moral natures. At least in Cambridge, they would say in a mood of self-congratulation, no one inquired into the length of another's purse.[1] 'For me it is one of the great happinesses of the happy life here,' wrote Jebb, 'that one can live with such men, not with men who are starving their minds or making their moral natures hopelessly ugly in order to be millionaires or, as the crown of their career, expectant baronets. Here, at all events, there is a true and refined republicanism; for there is no rank except what culture gives; and the society is composed of people who have forgone the pursuit of wealth or rank because they preferred prizes of another kind. I have never been in a place where the men seemed to me, on the whole, so honest or so manly or so true to each other; for they are bound to each other by the ties of interests which can never become slack, and which no self-interest can ever dissolve.'[2]

Whether or not they agreed with Matthew Arnold, the new dons recalled his strictures against philistines, and they remembered that Mill had turned with relief to Coleridge. Seeley told his students to read Cobden rather than Macaulay, but he urged them to enter politics and not business, as Cobden himself eventually did. Sidgwick quoted Tennyson for the benefit of Matthew Arnold,

> The heavens fill with commerce, argosies of
>   magic sails,
> Pilots of the purple twilight, dropping down
>   with costly bails—

but in his review of *Ecce Homo* he could write that 'Jesus with his intense apprehension of what constitutes true human worth,

[1] Stephen, *Fawcett*, p. 96.

[2] Bobbitt, *Dearest Love to All*, p. 82. This letter was written in 1871. A year earlier Carolyn Slemmer wrote home from Cambridge that 'All these people here seem to me to lack something, backbone perhaps, which a business life gives (they despise business, and money, apparently).' (page 63.)

would feel a peculiar horror at the hard insolent selfishness that often accompanies wealth.'[1]

The new dons sought a place for themselves in Victorian society. They contemplated one form of employment after another, casting about for the appropriate place to begin a career. They went from the parish to the lead works, from the university to the bar. They gave a thoughtful hearing to schoolmastering not simply because it was the logical place for a classic or mathematician to go, and certainly not, as is frequently said, merely because of the high income of a form master or housemaster. If dons had merely wished to make money, they could have continued in the slavish, dreary routine of coaching urged on by the prospect of high returns for their labour. Instead they looked to the public schools because Thomas Arnold had given teaching a redeeming ethic, purpose and status. Expecting no immediate pecuniary reward, guaranteed no satisfactory income and willing to make do on impromptu arrangements, the new dons elected to remain in the colleges. They translated the example of the schools into Cambridge and found that in forming the character of students, by which they meant restoring the influence of the teacher, they regained their self-respect.

High churchmen, muscular Christians, followers of Maurice's doctrine of sacrifice, humanists, intuitionists and positivists agreed on secondary ends. In thought syncretic, intrigued by paradox, they united in the search for a new central idea from which Cambridge could derive its values. Afraid that the confusion of political and social change would result in weak, unmanly and ineffectual human beings, they seized upon the necessity for a regeneration of the self. Preferring action to submission, they believed that enthusiasm—reading hard or rowing hard—was required to arrest the effeminacy which threatened to overcome the English character.

Regeneration of the self was one of the important reasons for the teaching revolution. It explains why Leslie Stephen, regarded as sick and weakly by his father, felt that he had triumphed over his nature—made himself a better man—when he excelled at athletics and sports in Trinity Hall. Having restored his inner harmony and recovered his true self, he believed he

[1] *Westminster Review*, LXXXVI (July, 1866), p. 76.

could effect the same change in the poll men of the college. Regeneration of the self explains why Mark Pattison said that 'the truly invaluable element of the College system – the close action of the teacher on the pupil' resulted in a 'beneficial reaction of the young on the aging man'. It explains what Seeley meant in his essay on 'The Church as a Teacher of Morality' when he said that by educating his son a man left the counting house to educate himself. It explains why Oscar Browning, a wasted talent and a bitterly disappointed man, died with the saving thought that in Curzon, his pupil at Eton, he had created a great statesman. And it explains why, confronted by a social, religious and psychic crisis, the new dons instantly turned to their students. Through socratic and Christian teaching they sought to change society before it changed them. By creating men who would influence the direction of social change, they hoped to affirm their own importance and authority and regain their independence. By producing men who would stand up to public opinion, they tried once and for all to escape the bewildering paradoxes of the environmental theory of behaviour.[1]

[1] Years later Jackson would write to a correspondent, 'If you have not read in to-day's [July 11, 1910] *Times* or *Morning Post* Lord Selborne's speech *ad portas* at Winchester on Saturday, read it. The concluding words are – "of the three, muscles, brain, and character – the greatest is character." By "character", Selborne means "moral courage – the courage which enables a man to defy public opinion and to take his own line." Is this what you meant? If so, I most heartily agree with you. I have sometimes doubted whether the school and the University did what they ought to do. but I am glad to say as I grow older, I answer emphatically that they do. What we learn is to recognize our limitations, and, although we cannot do this or that, which our neighbours do, to find something which we can do, and to do it with all our might.' Parry, p. 145.

EPILOGUE

'The proper function of an University in national education is tolerably well understood,' Mill stated in his inaugural address at St. Andrews in 1867. 'At least,' he corrected himself, 'there is a tolerably general agreement about what an University is not. It is not a place of professional education. Universities are not intended to teach the knowledge required to fit men for some special mode of gaining their livelihood. Their object is not to make skilful lawyers, or physicians, or engineers, but capable and cultivated human beings. . . . Men are men before they are lawyers, or physicians, or merchants, or manufacturers; and if you make them capable and sensible men, they will make themselves capable and sensible lawyers or physicians.'[1]

In Mill's definition of a liberal education, general qualities of mind and character came first, occupational skills second. It is not inconceivable that Mill's objective of a liberal education might have emerged as the primary goal of Victorian Cambridge had there been no university, only colleges. But Cambridge was and remained a collegiate university with a dual teaching structure. Education in Cambridge was both university and collegiate, the former professional in its objectives, the latter concerned with character formation. The same dons were engaged in both forms of teaching. In the 1860's there had been a certain overlap in the two kinds of education. A similar ideal, duty and service to society, had been urged in both. The crisis between Cambridge and society had brought collegiate and university education together in an agreement on secondary ends, but as the century progressed, the air of urgency dispersed.

---

[1] John Stuart Mill, 'Inaugural Address at St. Andrews', in *James and John Stuart Mill on Education*, ed. F. A. Cavenagh (Cambridge, 1931), pp. 133–4.

The two forms of education separated and contrasted, the ideals which they represented criss-crossing in complicated and uncertain patterns. The dual functions of Cambridge were difficult to keep straight, and no less difficult for individual dons. There was, for example, the Oscar Browning who was a professional historian and hoped to astonish the world with a masterpiece of historical learning conceived in the grand manner, the Oscar Browning who wished to make the education of teachers unmistakably professional, the would-be Regius Professor who wanted, like Seeley, to use political science to educate an élite for positions of government. There was also the Oscar Browning of the Sunday afternoons in King's College, the comic impressario whose brilliant promotions never came off, the Etonian O.B. who valued charm and style more than academic knowledge and one day complained bitterly to John Neville Keynes, University Registrary, that a favourite student had been needlessly failed in the India Civil Service Examination. 'The University should not for the sake of these students surrender what is the corner stone of all University teaching [,] that it is in its higher aspects non professional,'[1] he protested. To which Keynes replied, suitably piquant, that 'If it is the corner stone of all University teaching that it is in its higher aspects non-professional, then it must also be admitted that our University teaching in its higher aspects constitutes but a small part of all the teaching that is going on here.'[2]

Cambridge had a long history of preparing men for professional positions in society. It is true that before 1850 Cambridge had effectively lost contact with lawyers and doctors, whose professional education took place elsewhere; but Cambridge never ceased to believe in the principle that the university and the liberal professions should be united and that students must be assisted in finding professional occupations. Only a different means had been adopted of effecting the same end. Mathematics and classical philology provided the intellectual discipline, prize fellowships and college livings the resources for a professional career. After 1850 there was greater emphasis on the need to prepare students for the professions, and professional education was a continual topic of discussion, even if the precise content

[1] Browning to Keynes, December 7, 1888, C.U.L. Add. 7562.
[2] Keynes to Browning, December 7, 1888 (copy), C.U.L. Add. 7562.

could never be agreed upon and the word professional still retained its peculiar ambiguity. At the very least the idea of professional education, the idea of a professional career for university students, was regarded as a solution to the alternative of withdrawal, and the motive of service provided an effective deterrent to possible alienation, a means of bridging the crisis between Victorian Cambridge and society. In order to further the professional interests of dons, professors and students, the university changed almost beyond recognition. Laboratories and museums appeared, medical and engineering schools were founded. The amount of research activity increased, new chairs were established, and the university as distinct from the colleges acquired a large teaching staff of lecturers. All these changes were undertaken in the hope that professional standards could be raised and Cambridge's connection with the principal professions made more secure. As the educational role of the university expanded, it was apparent that character formation and the ideal of a liberal education could only be one of several functions of a university in national education.

2.

There were in Edwardian Cambridge a number of educational controversies at times extraordinarily virulent. It would be convenient to find in them an echo of sweetness and light, to see them as essentially a conflict between the supporters of the college idea of general cultivation of mind and character and the university idea of education as a preparation for a professional career. It would be easy to contrast humanism and practical efficiency, culture and science, as did T. R. Glover after the First World War when he complained that 'the ideal seemed to be the transformation of Cambridge into a copy of the huge American "State University".'[1] Such distinctions were in fact made; the disputes contained arguments against narrow and limited forms of education. But for the most part it appears unlikely that the controversies over the content of Cambridge teaching and the disputes about emphasis and method originated in clear and distinct loyalty to either the ideals of a liberal or professional education. Rather the search was for an educa-

[1] Glover, *Cambridge Retrospect*, p. 110.

tional programme that could in some measure provide for both.

Theological studies in Cambridge are a case in point. The traditional emphasis had been exegetical and philological on the Cambridge classical linguistic model. In the second half of the nineteenth century Cambridge's great triumvirate of theologians–Hort, Lightfoot and Westcott–added history to the tripos on the grounds that the primary concern of religious studies should be the origins of Christian belief and the authenticity of the biblical statement. Theological study as represented in the tripos had a very practical aim: the truth of the Christian historical record; and Cambridge-educated theologians had to be disciplined, professional historians and critics. This is not to say that Cambridge theologians did not believe in theology as general cultivation of the mind, but simply that they thought the purposes of a liberal education would better be accomplished by institutional means–college life, student friendships, chapel– than directly through subjects lectured on by Cambridge professors. What the great Cambridge theologians did not advocate was purely pastoral training; and when reluctantly Westcott started Westcott House, his Cambridge Clergy Training School, it was only because he feared that unless some form of practical training for service in the Church was provided near Cambridge ordinands would prefer the burgeoning seminaries to the university, the liberalizing influence of Cambridge institutions would be denied them and the historic connexion between Cambridge and the Church of England would end.[1]

When in 1896 the theological tripos came up for discussion, critics argued that reform was imperative on both professional and intellectual grounds. Essentially they maintained that biblical scholarship was no longer as important as the systematic, philosophical teaching of Christian doctrine in its later, post-biblical phases and that this emphasis on the social meaning of religion was far more relevant to the work of parsons than

[1] For the increasing reluctance of Church authorities to recognize the scholastic and academic clergy as an important section of the priesthood see a letter of Hort in Butler, *Henry Montagu Butler*, p. 20. For Westcott see Owen Chadwick, *Westcott and the University* (Cambridge, 1962), and for the theological tripos see the *University Reporter* (November 3, 1896), p. 190, and the flysheets in C.U.L. Cam. b.896.3.

determining the accuracy and truth of specific historical documents. The theological tripos, they concluded, taught a dead rather than a living religion and was nearly useless, except in the most preliminary way, for men intending to take holy orders.

On both sides of the dispute over the composition of the theological tripos changes were urged that would improve the practical importance of Cambridge theology, only one side was thinking mainly of theologians and scholars and the other of parish priests. Within the limits of their discussion there was no apparent antagonism between liberal and professional forms of education. Both parties agreed that it was undesirable to make the tripos merely professional or merely concerned with seminary-type instruction, and both equally agreed that the tripos could not be exclusively liberal in character.

If any discussion of educational reform in Cambridge were to raise the question of liberal education it would have to be the disputes in 1900 over the mathematical tripos, for in the past mathematics more than any other Cambridge subject had been least liable to the charge of careerism. Yet interestingly enough even here the issue could not be reduced to that of a conflict between professional and liberal ideals, no matter how hard defenders of the traditional tripos tried. It is true that the reformers indicated that their changes would improve a student's preparation for professional work; but just as equally and convincingly they argued that the two principal reforms, abolition of the order of merit and a new division of the tripos, would redeem Cambridge mathematical teaching by removing the one factor which more than any other had turned the tripos into a race for success, and was most responsible for the narrow spirit and manner in which Cambridge students pursued mathematical studies.[1]

There is no better example of the confusion among dons concerning the precise definition of liberal, professional or utilitarian education, nor of the social context into which any discussion of educational ideals must be placed, than the strident, impassioned exchanges over compulsory Greek in the Previous Examination that took place in 1904 and 1905 and directly involved over 2000 Cambridge M.A.'s. The quarrel received wide publicity and for several months became practically a

[1] See the flysheets in C.U.L. Cam. b.899.6.

national issue. Newspapers and periodicals rehearsed the arguments, and resolutions were drafted in all the associations of teachers in secondary education. The issue of compulsory Greek, however, was never decided on its own merits. From the outset it was apparent that one party to the debate was convinced the proposal to make Greek optional was actually a blind, and their strategy was to rest their case mainly on a philippic, a warning that the abolition of compulsory Greek represented not only an ominous threat to liberal values but to the very independence of Cambridge. Nor was this strategy unjustified when the chairman of the syndicate responsible for recommending optional Greek to the Senate led off the debate with the unfortunate words 'that the truly conservative course was to recognize in time the working of educational forces, which they might perhaps be allowed to regret, but which it did not lie within their power to control, and to maintain and to forward a policy of sober and moderate reform.'[1] Once the syndicate itself presented its reforms as a response to outside pressure, there was no alternative but for the opposition to cry that the philistines had descended on Cambridge.

The supporters of optional Greek heartened and rallied their opponents. Rumours circulated of a royal commission to effect the end desired by the syndicate. From the industrial cities of Birmingham and Wolverhampton came letters warning of the threats to higher education which could come from technology and the neglect of classical teaching.[2] From the famous grammar schools and from country rectories came Greek masters and clergymen to repeat their experiences with parents who thought only of useful education and to remind Cambridge of the meaning of independence and academic freedom. The syndicate was assailed with cries that it had shown itself only too willing to welcome chairs of brewing and commerce, only too eager to make concessions to outside pressures.

It may have been a false issue, for the resident dons had not united as they did in the 1860's. On the final vote they divided almost equally, two hundred and eighty-eight in favour of optional Greek and two hundred and forty against.[3] But it was

---

[1] *University Reporter* (December 17, 1904), p. 354.
[2] C.U.L. Add. 5958 (25), letters 14 and 20.
[3] *The Times* (November 4, 1905), p. 6.

at least the issue which the syndicate itself had done nothing to prevent and a good deal to encourage. By constantly repeating that there were important influences within society which the university ought to recognize, the supporters of optional Greek united the opposition and enabled them to make common cause against such distinct, separate and complicated problems as science or the vulgarization of the scientific ideal, state-aided secondary education, government-supported schools of technology, the new civic universities and mass culture. Optional Greek was defeated by a margin of approximately five hundred votes. Victory was carried by the clergy, over 87 per cent of whom voted to retain compulsory Greek.[1] They at least had not forgotten the 1860's.

The proponents of compulsory Greek were able to defeat the grace not because they put up a persuasive case for the liberal value of classics, but because they convinced the majority of M.A.'s that the syndicate was prepared to compromise the integrity of the university by a sordid bargain. It was well known that Cambridge was in dire need of financial assistance. During the last decades of the nineteenth century university revenues, meagre to begin with, had drastically fallen because of the agrarian depression. The percentage of distributable college income declined, and college contributions to the university chest as required by the statutes of 1882 were reduced. University income from capitation tax and degree fees also diminished owing to the decline that occurred in total matriculations, the first fall in over forty years. Had there been no attempt to expand the teaching and research functions of the university, however, neither the reductions nor the decline would have been disastrous; but it was precisely at this time that an ambitious building and staffing policy was decided upon, and money was desperately needed for laboratories, museums, lecture halls, new chairs, new subjects, additional lecturers and laboratory assistants.

The university could seek emergency assistance mainly from two sources. The first was the Treasury; but there was still an orthodox liberal fear in the university that state assistance to education meant state control over curricula. The fear was not totally unwarranted. Examples could be cited where state and

[1] Ibid.

local authorities used their influence to encourage unpopular school or university subjects–industrial design, engineering, agriculture and modern languages. In 1889 a University Grants Committee of the Treasury had been formed to assist Victorian university colleges, regarded by many Cambridge dons as poly-technical schools in the control of industrialists and entre-preneurs. Government support to university colleges, agricul-tural schools and technical colleges divided the Cambridge academic community and reinforced the suspicions of a number of dons, including science dons, that a humanistic or liberal education could only be had in the ancient universities. In their opinion the state had to be prevented from interfering with the teaching of Cambridge, no matter what penalty might follow.

It was the second source of possible financial assistance, how-ever, that was mainly responsible for the anger and suspicion displayed in the debate over compulsory Greek. At the end of the nineteenth century prominent dons began to court philan-thropists. In 1897 T. Clifford Allbutt–sometimes said to be the original of Lydgate in *Middlemarch*[1]–complained to *The Times* that Cambridge was continually neglected by the millionaire.[2] *The Times* repeated the cry that the Victorian Renaissance had involved Cambridge in unprecedented expense and asked for a, 'millionaire who will win himself an everlasting name by en-abling an ancient and famous but now straitened University to hold its own in an age in which the coarser and more material influences of mere wealth need more than ever to be refined by learning, culture, and the disinterested pursuit of knowledge.'[3] The number of appeals from Cambridge to the public increased, especially with the formation in 1898 of The Cambridge Uni-versity Association, a private organization consisting of mem-bers and friends of the university. The Association was formed to publicize the financial condition of Cambridge, and one of its principal objects was 'To enlist by means of its corporate in-fluence and the personal influence of its members the active sympathy of persons of wealth and position who may be dis-posed to become benefactors of the University.'[4] In 1899 the

[1] Sir Walter Langdon-Brown, *Some Chapters in Cambridge Medical History* (Cambridge, 1946), pp. 105–6.
[2] *The Times* (April 15, 1897), p. 10. [3] Ibid. (April 21, 1897), p. 9.
[4] John Willis Clark, *Endowments of the University of Cambridge*, p. 597.

Association issued a *Statement of the Needs of the University* which was a catalogue of university needs by faculties in language meant to impress men of humanitarian impulses with the practical benefits of university teaching and research. The great economist Alfred Marshall, for example, emphasized the usefulness of economics in the training of officials of large public and semi-public enterprises.[1] In 1904 John Willis Clark issued a volume entitled the *Endowments of the University of Cambridge* in still another attempt to dramatize, by a detailed statement of university income from all non-collegiate sources (endowments, gifts, subscriptions, books and equipment), the desperate poverty of Cambridge. But few men of wealth, it seemed, were willing to aid Cambridge with princely contributions. By 1906 only £100,000 had been raised, an insignificant sum when compared to the amounts reportedly given by great philanthropists to North American universities and by Andrew Carnegie to the Scottish universities.[2] Frequently Cambridge had found its most generous benefactors within its own walls. Rayleigh had donated his 1904 Nobel prize to Cambridge, and a number of fellows of private means had returned their fellowship dividends.[3] 'A great benefactor who would free the University of Cambridge from a sordid struggle,' concluded still another appeal, this time by A. E. Shipley of Christ's, a member of the Cambridge University Association, and H. A. Roberts of Caius, 'would earn enduring fame in the annals of British education.'[4]

3.

The disputes over Greek and mathematics indicate the continuing distrust within Cambridge of the business community. So deeply rooted was the disdain for commerce and industry, for the values which they were supposed to represent, that

[1] *Statement of the Needs of the University* (Cambridge, 1899), pp. 26–8.

[2] [A. E. Shipley and H. A. Roberts], 'A Plea for Cambridge', *Quarterly Review*, CCIV (April, 1906), pp. 516, 525.

[3] Ibid., pp. 515–16, 521.

[4] Ibid., p. 525. Curzon also complained in 1909 about 'the large financial contributions which the merchant princes are in the habit of making to the younger Universities as compared with Oxford and Cambridge.' *Principles*, p. 118. During Curzon's nine years as Chancellor of Oxford public subscriptions amounted to £150,000, the greater part of which went to science with the approval of arts men. H.L. Deb., xxii (July 19, 1916), col. 798.

numerous dons and non-resident M.A.'s decided the worth of an academic subject by its usefulness to commerce and industry. In their view almost no subject which could be turned to the benefit of business deserved university recognition. Even French and German could not be instruments of humane learning like Greek and Latin, because they were useful in international trade. Karl Breul, the first Professor of German in Cambridge, spent considerable energy trying to convince classical dons that no subject possessed intrinsic value, that the criterion of a 'higher subject' was how it was taught. But classical dons remained sceptical, especially as they could so easily associate some of the demands for the teaching of modern languages with the acute economic and imperial rivalry between England and Germany. Whenever it was suspected that the impetus for curricular reform came from commercial or political sources, Cambridge dons arose to denounce the proposed changes as technical, illiberal, utilitarian and soft options.

The academic controversies of the Edwardian period also indicate that dons were especially sensitive to the possibility that either the business community or the state would upset the balance between university and college which had been established in the great period of reform. Even ardent supporters of optional Greek like Jackson and Maitland distrusted the activities of the Cambridge University Association.[1] In the last decades of the nineteenth century, relations between the university and the colleges had generally been cordial, character formation and professional training, it seemed, nicely harmonized. Most dons believed that the ideal education was a combination of the two, that expert knowledge and general qualities of character best characterized the professional man. The leaders that Cambridge hoped to produce, whether civil servants, engineers or physicians, had to be doubly educated. Their university education enabled them to be supreme practitioners of their profession, and their collegiate education enabled

---

[1] Jackson wrote Maitland in March 1904 that 'Shipley is running a private association which aims at taking over all the College teaching and controlling the payments.' Maitland wrote back that Shipley had requested his signature on a manifesto. 'I am much too far from Cambridge to sign such things and am wondering what is the inner meaning of it all, for of course there is some inner meaning.' Maitland, *Letters*, pp. 383 and 383n.

them to acquire the broad culture and social graces, the wider understanding of men and behaviour without which leadership was impossible.

Cambridge had always been proud of the important leaders and influential men it had educated. Dons did not want their students to avoid active participation in the affairs of society, nor did they themselves wish to be solely *gelehrten*, isolated from political life and powerless to effect change. Their ideal was never learning for its own sake or self-cultivation for its own sake, for these signified alienation. Seeley repeatedly insisted that the ends of education were practical and that erudition for its own sake was undesirable. Even intuitionists insisted on the useful purposes of education. John Grote could speak about the intrinsic value of high ideals, about the necessity to love justice for its own sake and not for the special rewards that might follow from just behaviour; but he could also speak about the value of a classical education in utilitarian categories. The importance of a classical education, he wrote in 1856, lay in its use as a common denominator, a means of communication among educated men and therefore a source of social harmony. 'The destruction or disuse of it will destroy one bond of intellectual communion among civilized men, and will be, in this respect, a step not of improvement.'[1]

Dons insisted on the values of duty and service; and at times, when the collegiate ideal seemed especially appealing, they professed not to care what occupation a man entered, provided he was, in Mill's words, capable and cultivated. Dons had, however, so closely tied being capable and cultivated to the ideal qualities of the professional man, that it was obvious a man of character could not remain a man of character unless he avoided business and the pursuit of wealth.

Business could be avoided, however, only if there were sufficient jobs for professional men. Fortunately, an unprecedented expansion in the numbers and prosperity of professional men occurred in the period 1850–70. Places in the home civil services increased in the wake of administrative problems arising from the reforms of the early Victorian period. Civil service positions were appearing overseas with the extension of imperial influ-

[1] John Grote, 'Old Studies and New', in *Cambridge Essays, 1856* (Cambridge, 1856), p. 114.

ence. Solicitors and graduate engineers were taken into the ranks of professional men. Positions in the public and grammar schools multiplied as a consequence of the work of the Arnoldians and the royal commissions of the 1860's. Medical education was reformed, the Cambridge medical school revived. Dons could promote professionalism and professional occupations confident in the knowledge that sufficient positions existed. They could allow increases in the numbers of students matriculating at Cambridge without undue fear that they were about to produce a superfluous intelligentsia, such as they could point to in Russia and France.

The optimism of the Victorian dons did not last. Towards the end of the 1870's a sense of disquiet and uneasiness over the future of graduates settled in Cambridge. Complaints were heard that the professions were drying up and customary employment opportunities closing. The prize fellowship system, regarded in earlier decades as a connecting link between Cambridge and the professions, was now regarded as a liability. Prize fellowships had long been under attack for diverting teaching talent away from the university, but the argument against prize fellowships took another turn. When Sidgwick in 1876 complained that prize fellowships discouraged learning and research, he also meant they encouraged overcrowding in professions like the bar.[1] To what extent the fears of Sidgwick and other dons that professional opportunities were decreasing can be justified is difficult to determine. Professional men have always feared overcrowding, and one of the principal objectives of professional organizations has been to limit entry into the professional market. Many of the controls designed to define professional status and raise standards – professional societies, examinations, registration fees, periods of apprenticeship or similar types of well-defined junior status – have also been useful in limiting numbers.

Historians have yet to present conclusive evidence that the professions in the nineteenth century were actually overcrowded,[2] but there is reason to believe that Cambridge under-

---

[1] Sidgwick, 'Idle Fellowships', in *Miscellaneous Essays and Addresses* (London, 1904), p. 330.

[2] The current debate on unemployment in the nineteenth-century professions is misleading, for it fails to take account of imperial and colonial

graduates sometimes thought that the supply of professional positions lagged behind demand. There is even the possibility that dons at both ancient universities may have occasionally made employment opportunities a factor in admissions, although this is difficult to prove. There were occasional statements in the 1890's that genuinely poor boys without family or social connexions should be admitted to the ancient universities only if they were intellectually outstanding; for otherwise little could be done for them after graduation, and the universities would be accused of contributing to the formation of a discontented 'academical proletariate'.[1] Certainly the poll man was sometimes defended on the grounds that he had a secure position awaiting him upon graduation.

One of the reasons for rumours within Cambridge that professional positions were diminishing was the lack of any source of accurate information on employment opportunities. Advice on careers was considered a minor tutorial function, but tutors were busy enough with teaching and the new educational reforms and had little time, if even the desire, to systematically collect information on available jobs. Tutors were perhaps most useful in placing graduates in teaching, for contacts between Cambridge and the public and leading grammar schools were frequent and close. Students were normally expected to find their own positions, to rely on the contacts made in school or college, to use family connexions, to sit civil service examinations, to use commercial employment agencies or rely on their own ingenuity.

Among Cambridge graduates civil service positions were popular because, unlike medicine, law, insurance or engineering, no capital outlay was required, no premiums were demanded, and because Cambridge provided special instruction in the subjects of the civil service examinations. The competition

---

demands for lawyers, physicians, teachers, engineers and civil servants. See R. Musgrove, 'Middle-Class Education and Employment in the Nineteenth Century', *Economic History Review*, XII (August, 1959), pp. 99–111, and 'Middle-Class Education and Employment in the Nineteenth Century: a Rejoinder', *Economic History Review*, XIV (December, 1961), pp. 320–9; H. J. Perkin, 'Middle-Class Education and Employment in the Nineteenth Century: A Critical Note', *Economic History Review*, XIV (August, 1961), pp. 122–30.

[1] Bryce Commission, xliii, 218–19; xlvii, 156–7.

EPILOGUE

was very keen, however, especially as the Foreign Office and Diplomatic Corps were closed preserves. Pressure was greatest on the Treasury, where promotion opportunities were said to be best, and on the Home Office and India Civil Service. Cambridge graduates could also consider the possibilities of overseas colonization – a relief 'to to the present dead-lock among candidates for a livelihood'[1] – and with all its disadvantages perhaps a less dreary prospect than the position found by a classics graduate in 1900, inspecting hotels for the lower middle-class salary of £120 a year.[2]

In 1881 and 1882 the *Cambridge Review* ran a series of articles on possible careers in public school teaching, the civil service, City of London firms; but none of these appeared to offer unlimited opportunities. Frequently there were letters from Cambridge graduates who were in the professions. The letters were usually pessimistic or discouraging. Of men called to the bar, wrote one new barrister, not one-third earns enough to live by; and there is very little chance of a man becoming a successful barrister, wrote another, without social or family connexions, especially in the law. Still another graduate advised students to become solicitors, as barristers were born but solicitors made.[3] An articled clerk in a solicitors' office in a provincial town wrote that the profession of solicitor was becoming overcrowded 'and it will be a case of the survival of the fittest in a few years.'[4] It was rumoured that opportunities in the City were decreasing,[5] but one Cambridge graduate wrote that the work was tedious anyway and did not add to one's social connexions as much as the bar. There were, however, the partial compensations of money and the fact that at least 'nowadays no one loses caste by the mere fact of "being in the City".'[6] Even public school teaching, a Cambridge standby, was said to be overcrowded.[7]

[1] *Cambridge Review* (February 4, 1880), pp. 4–5; (May 17, 1882), pp. 307–8.
[2] H. A. Roberts, *Careers for University Men* (Cambridge, 1914), p. 9.
[3] *Cambridge Review* (May 24, 1882), pp. 322–3; (November 16, 1881), p. 77; (May 10, 1882), pp. 291–2.   [4] Ibid. (May 17, 1882), p. 308.
[5] Partly to counteract these rumours the City of London issued a report citing increased employment opportunities. See W. J. Richmond Cotton, 'The City of London: Its Population and Position', *The Contemporary Review*, XLI (January, 1882), pp. 72–87.
[6] *Cambridge Review* (June 7, 1882), p. 354.
[7] *Cambridge University Magazine* (December 7, 1886), p. 174.

EPILOGUE

All of this information on employment, whether based on hearsay, rumour or limited knowledge sent back by graduates, was effective and gave rise to fears that Cambridge might produce an alienated educated class. A danger successfully avoided by the generation of the 1860's reappeared in the 1890's. A group of worried dons was therefore relieved when a number of businessmen – several with university education – invited them to join in a plan to open a channel between the university and the business community.[1] It was decided in 1899 to form an unofficial university employment agency, a Cambridge Appointments Association, in order to advertise the merits and versatility of Cambridge graduates and end the mutual distrust existing between the university and men of business. An employment agency had actually existed in Cambridge since 1884 when William James Lewis, Professor of Mineralogy, started an unofficial Cambridge University Scholastic Agency to help students find teaching positions without recourse to commercial employment agencies.[2] The Cambridge Appointments Association differed from its predecessor in having a much broader scope and a more ambitious objective. As the Vice-Chancellor explained to a distinguished group of business leaders that included Nathaniel Louis Cohen of the London Chamber of Commerce; Baron (Nathan Meyer) Rothschild; George Stegmann Gibb, general manager of the North Eastern Railway; Sir Andrew Noble, a pioneer in ballistics, vice-chairman and later chairman of Armstrong, Whitworth and Co. Ltd., one of the largest industrial enterprises in Britain in the period before the war, 'The larger the number of occupations for which a University training could be made a preparation, the more they would strengthen the numbers and the energy and the influence of the University.'[3]

The reactions of the business leaders to the prospects for success for a university employment agency varied but were generally favourable. Gibb, a graduate of Aberdeen University,

---

[1] Third Report of the Royal Commission on the Civil Service, Minutes of Evidence, 1913. xviii, p. 250.

[2] Flysheet, February 21, 1902 (William James Lewis), Whibley Papers, 29.9.3.

[3] The Cambridge Appointments Association, Report of a Meeting held November 4, 1899, in the Senate House, p. 1. C.U.L. Cam. b.899.11.

EPILOGUE

and Noble, a former artillery captain, were both enthusiastic about business opportunities for Cambridge graduates. Cohen, who had publicized the Association in the London Chamber of Commerce, shared their hopes but could not conceal one unsettling note; among businessmen, financiers and manufacturers he had found a deeply-rooted belief that graduates were unsuited for business careers: 'Might that prejudice be very soon dispelled by those men whose names would be put forward by this Association! For his own part he believed that the traditions of University life, its comradeship, its many-sidedness, and the goodfellowship which characterized its sports and pastimes formed an essential factor in the thorough training of young men.'[1]

In 1902 a university syndicate recommended that the Appointments Association be given full university status as a Board. Interestingly enough, in view of the controversies that were soon to break out over Greek, there was little opposition to the syndicate's recommendation, even when supporters alluded to the factors behind the drive for a University Appointments Association: the likely competition of 'richly-endowed' new colleges and universities threatening the popularity of Cambridge and necessitating new allies; and the disheartening fact that leaders of industry seemed to take little notice of Cambridge, neither responding to the appeal for money nor sending their sons to be taught. The recommendation that an Appointments Board be established easily passed the Senate, despite the fact that over half the signatories to the report of the syndicate were members of the managing committee of the Association and could be accused of special pleading.[2]

From 1899 to the outbreak of war in 1914 the Appointments Association and its successor, the Appointments Board, obtained two thousand five hundred and fifty-three jobs for Cambridge graduates, or for approximately 20 per cent of those actually taking degrees in the same period. Measured in another way, the success of the Board was greater, for more than 20 per cent of all Cambridge undergraduates, not merely those taking

[1] Ibid., p. 8.
[2] For the discussion of the grace to establish an Appointments Board see the *University Reporter* (February 4, 1902), pp. 518–25.

degrees, registered for employment in the period up to 1911.[1] Acceptance of the Board within Cambridge is attested by the fact that whereas in 1902 only eight or nine colleges showed a willingness to contribute money to the Board on a regular basis, the number had grown to twelve in 1903. By 1908 all Cambridge colleges and the Non-collegiate Students Board as well were regular contributors.[2]

In 1912 H. A. Roberts, son of a physician, scholar of Caius in 1883, sometime mathematics master at Bath College and the co-author of an appeal for benefactions which appeared in 1906, summarized the work of the Appointments Board for which he had been secretary since 1902. Roberts recalled that undergraduates in the later nineteenth century hardly knew of possible careers outside the liberal professions. Those who did enter business were usually sons of businessmen.[3] Late Victorian students in general, he claimed, even knew little of the home and civil services. 'This want of knowledge was a serious drawback to graduates, and I often heard parents disparage the value of a University career; nothing seemed to be known about possible openings for a man with a degree.'[4] Roberts went on to list the best employment opportunities which, he said, were all overseas. Good careers were available in teaching and in administration in the India Civil Service, Ceylon Civil Service, Egyptian and Sudanese Civil Services, and in crown colonies and protectorates. Men trained in scientific agriculture were wanted throughout the Empire. Domestic opportunities were also best in government, especially positions in the patent office, factory inspectorships, Board of Education examinerships and inspectorships which were filled without examination.Roberts also mentioned administrative and teaching vacancies in local government or in imperial universities and colleges. Other job possibilities included positions in charitable organizations, Board

---

[1] The total number of appointments has been computed from the annual returns of the Board published in the *University Reporter*. The proportion of those registering for employment is based on a statement by the Board that it had been able to meet 50 per cent of student demand for jobs. *University Reporter* (November 14, 1911), p. 244.

[2] Ibid. (February 23, 1904), p. 534; (March 9, 1909), p. 642.

[3] Third Report of Royal Commission on Civil Service, p. 252.

[4] Roberts, *Careers*, p. 4.

of Trade labour exchanges, scientific surveys and governmental scientific departments.

When he came to careers in commerce and industry for the man of liberal education, Roberts spoke optimistically yet cautiously. A few years ago, he observed, 'A course at the University would . . . have been regarded as perhaps the least promising avenue to a career in business which it was possible to adopt.'[1] He noted that there 'existed in many business circles a strong prejudice against the graduate,' and concluded that 'every man who adopts a career of this kind must expect to do something, perhaps even a good deal, to win the fight.'[2] The majority of Cambridge graduates entering business had gone into their family firms;[3] but since 1907 more positions had opened, especially in large overseas trading firms where the first major breakthrough for Cambridge graduates occurred. There were also good opportunities in overseas banking firms, occasional openings in domestic financial houses, a few in insurance and valuable managerial positions in large limited liability companies and partnerships.

If prospects in business for the man of liberal education were better than before, what about the graduate with technical training? Roberts' discussion of employment opportunities for Cambridge-educated engineers and scientists was curiously ambiguous. He referred to a 1910 return on the employment of one hundred and seventy-six Cambridge engineers. Only a little over half the engineers had actually taken positions in engineering firms, and a number of these were really in businesses of their own. The largest single group were employed in subordinate positions in manufacturing firms and were drawing rather low salaries of about £200 per annum on the average,[4] although raises could be expected in time. Salaries in teaching could be higher, at least initially, and pay seemed better in government engineering services abroad. Careers in railroads, Roberts noted, were still limited by large, prohibitive premiums paid to chief engineers, 'and it is moreover suggested in some cases that the better posts in the service are a close preserve.'[5] There appeared to be a need for industrial chemists, and scientific training could help graduates obtain junior executive posts. In

---

[1] Ibid., p. 8.   [2] Ibid.   [3] Ibid.
[4] Ibid., p. 21, see Appendix III.   [5] Ibid., p. 22.

general he thought the 'outlook for the industrial chemist trained at the University is nowadays a much improved one,' but only the best men, graduates who managed a first or second class in Part II of the natural sciences tripos, should try to enter the field.[1]

Throughout his discussion of career opportunities, Roberts had been alternately hopeful and hesitant, as if he wished to minimize unpleasant realities yet not raise the expectations of graduates too high. In his estimation at least, the domestic market was restricted, not only because of an absolute shortage of positions, but because many employers practiced favouritism and nepotism or demanded high premiums—sometimes defended as the cost required to train an engineer. There was the additional factor of a prejudice against the university man, whether he had been in the arts or sciences, a belief that he was unsuited for business either because his education had not been sufficiently practical, or because he was too set in his ways and his attitude or style made him an unattractive prospect. Roberts could not avoid concluding on a pessimistic note. 'Work in an old country is naturally scarce, and, further, so much civil work is dependent on borrowed capital that a general rise in the rate of interest tends to prevent the execution of all but the barely necessary. I seriously doubt whether the services of corporations, municipalities, etc., are recruited in a really satisfactory way.'[2]

International trade, but especially imperial and colonial government, fortunately rescued the university graduate, mitigating the effects of a limited home market by carrying off potentially unhappy and distraught graduates to overseas positions. Britain's imperial possessions, it appeared, may have helped prevent the formation of an intellectual proletariat, a functionless and therefore alienated group with forced leisure in which to scheme against the social order. At least Roberts was probably thinking of an imperial safety valve when in 1912 he addressed a meeting of the Congress of Universities of the British Empire. Dwelling at length on the importance of a university employment agency, particularly one which did not have the advantage of a location in an important commercial and industrial centre, Roberts described the general qualities of a

[1] Ibid., p. 18.   [2] Ibid., p. 22.

university man – his broad preparation for life – that business should learn to respect. The 'university man' was too often regarded as a special type, as a member of a class with definite qualities or defects, when in actuality his university experiences made him suitable for any kind of employment. He was prepared for all jobs by being specially prepared for none. Roberts indicated, both in his address to Cambridge students and in his remarks to the Congress, that it was necessary for graduates and businessmen alike to take the broadest possible view of one another, to seek the mutual advantages that would result from a union. Failure to do so could produce distressing consequences, as it had in France, where a surplus of graduates existed. 'The University of France has been, since the Revolution, organized on a thoroughly democratic basis. Is the result, so far as the product of the education is concerned, satisfactory? I am told that there is one very disquieting feature – the number of *déclassés* – of graduates who do not prove good enough to attain to such positions as their education aimed at, and who yet are lifted out of their class and unfitted for other work they might have done well. . . . If the great majority of its graduates – those who are not destined for higher teaching or research – are not ready to take a reasonable and useful place in the community, and are driven to merely parasitic occupations, the public welfare will be affected, and the reaction on the university itself must be ultimately disastrous.'[1]

Roberts echoed a fear which had lingered in Cambridge since the last decades of the nineteenth century. The fear was renewed, no doubt exaggerated, when dons became concerned that newer universities—backed by the money they professed to despise – would push Cambridge graduates out of professional positions. The Balfour Act and even the meagre assistance local authorities were giving to students who had qualified for the universities added to the worry that there would be more graduates leaving without the aid of money or family influence than Cambridge could arrange positions for. Still, many dons continued to resent business values, remaining faithful to the Victorian tradition of regarding professional activity superior

[1] H. A. Roberts, 'Action of Universities in Relation to the After-Careers of Their Students', in *Proceedings of the Congress of the Universities of the Empire* (London, 1912), p. 228.

to commerce and industry. Politics and administration, the bar, medicine, public school and university teaching were the higher activities. According to one estimate only about 7 per cent of all Cambridge undergraduates entered business, to include banking, in the period 1800 to 1899, or less than half the percentage of students coming from business backgrounds. Owners of family firms who sent their sons to Cambridge obviously lost replacements.[1]

Leaders of commerce and industry returned the resentment. Not only were they reluctant to employ arts graduates, they saw little use for science and engineering graduates as well. For at least sixty years prominent intellectuals, parliamentary spokesmen, heads of scientific associations and institutes, government committees and royal commissions had urged the schools and the universities to produce scientists and technologists to staff industry and increase the importance of British manufacturing. University colleges, which grew into universities, and colleges of technology had been founded to help produce men of science and technology. Government had been used to establish adequate science teaching in schools. Voices demanding the union of science and industry had become more strident and occasionally hysterical with the rise of industrial Germany and America, but industrialists had not responded. The overwhelming majority of trained science and engineering graduates from all universities, chemists as well as physicists, were employed in teaching rather than in industry. Manufacturers continued to favour industrial chemists or engineers who had received their training essentially in the works itself.[2] The attitude that college life ruins a man for a business career was still prevalent.

In 1912, at the same Congress to which Roberts presented his paper, Sir George Gibb, one of the distinguished businessmen

[1] See Jenkins and Jones, p. 99, and Charles Wilson, 'Economy and Society in Late Victorian Britain', *Economic History Review*, XVIII (August, 1965), pp. 197–8. H. A. Roberts, without giving the source of his figures, speculated that about 3 per cent of Cambridge undergraduates entered business before 1870, about 6 per cent in the '70's and 11 per cent in the '90's, reaching 20 per cent in 1900. His estimate for 1900 appears generous. Third Report of Royal Commission on the Civil Service, p. 252.

[2] D. S. L. Cardwell, *The Organisation of Science in England* (London, 1957), pp. 144, 157–73.

who had been present at the formation of the Cambridge University Appointments Association thirteen years earlier, criticized old-fashioned rule of thumb procedures still used by industry. The structure of modern enterprise, utilizing complicated machinery, vast quantities of capital and large staff, required minds trained in scientific method and principle. This was by now a common, if not universally-accepted observation. More novel were Gibb's concluding remarks on labour relations: 'Problems connected with the relations of capital and labour grow more urgent and more difficult every day. When facing these problems we must patiently remember that our present conditions are largely due to causes for which the origins must be sought in the past. How much of the present labour unrest is due to the action of employers within the last fifty years? Is it not an accumulated debt? Employers of labour have been on the whole a very miscellaneous lot – good, bad, and indifferent. Would we be far wrong in thinking that if a higher standard of education had prevailed amongst the business men of the last half century, many of the troubles from which we are now suffering would not have arisen?'[1]

Gibb placed the argument for the employment of university graduates in business in a new form and in a new context. Perhaps, after all, dons were right. There was something special in the 'university man', a social quality which the non-university man lacked, a particular character, general qualities of mind, an ability to get along with others, a knowledge of human behaviour. England had experienced six years of unprecedented labour difficulties, syndicalist agitation, demands for collective bargaining. Industrialists had failed to anticipate labour unrest and only belatedly were they establishing management-instituted welfare programmes,[2] inadequate measures in the face of the magnitude of the labour disturbance. In order to arrest the erosion of management-labour relations, corporations had to take an entirely new attitude to personnel problems; perhaps only the university man could show the way.

At least Frank H. Taylor, Director and General Manager of Linotype and Machinery Ltd., of London, thought the university

[1] *Congress*, p. 254.
[2] E. H. Phelps Brown, *The Growth of British Industrial Relations* (London, 1960), p. 293.

could be especially useful in the area of labour relations. In a lecture he gave at Cambridge in 1911, an undisguised recruitment effort, he mentioned the novelty of having the director of an engineering firm address a body of Cambridge undergraduates on a business subject. 'Only a few years ago,' he reflected, 'it would probably have been considered out of place for an address of this kind to be delivered here, upon the theory that business matters occupied too low a plane in the world to accord with the strictly academic aims of the University.'[1]

Taylor emphasized that both the university and business had entered a new age. Practical preparation and even special training for a business career were no longer absolutely necessary. Business, like the professions, required men of general education and strength of character, able to take a broad and detached view of circumstances and people, but also, if necessary, to accept and return hard and effective blows. Taylor contrasted the qualities of the new business executive to those of the old and alluded to the varied and responsible functions of the business leader. The head of an old-fashioned family firm, he noted, had been especially backward in labour relations. Little effort had been made to understand the personal problems of employees or instruct them in their duties. Workers were treated with indifference or caprice, bullied, exploited and prodded by a system of crude incentives and deterrents. It was not surprising that they failed to develop a sense of identity with the firm. The new business leader could not rely on archaic methods. The labour problems of the future were to be dealt with 'by bigger men in a bigger way'. The new kind of manager had to be more intimately concerned with the life and problems of workers. He had to act as their counsellor and teacher, obtain their loyalty and co-operation without resort to arbitrary and obvious authority.

Here, one year before Gibb's remarks before a gathering of university and business representatives, was a similar vindication of the collegiate ideal, a surprising application of the qualities that were supposed to spring from communal life. Was it possible that the arguments for a Cambridge education were receiving unprecedented attention from leaders of the business

[1] Frank H. Taylor, *The Need of Educated Men in Industrial Affairs* (May 15, 1911), p. 3. Cam. c.911.6.

community? Not unless, of course, Taylor was willing to make another concession, reduce the importance of the profit motive and give business activity a higher purpose and aim. Taylor obliged. The monetary rewards of a business career were ample, he said, similar to those of the professions and varying according to the independent means of the graduate. In any case, the real measure of a business career was not financial at all but 'service-ableness'. Satisfaction in business derived from the service the businessman performed. The remuneration, Taylor added, was simply a useful detail.[1]

The underlying strategy of Taylor's recruitment talk in Cambridge is apparent. Not only had he attempted to correct the unfavourable picture of a business career which he knew to be prevalent in the university, but he had also tried to correct the tendency for Cambridge graduates to follow the career of their fathers by obliterating the classic distinctions between the professional man and the businessman. The businessman whom he described was no less than the professional man whom Cambridge idealized. The qualities required of both were the same and consequently both deserved similar social recognition: 'A student who is from necessity or otherwise training for business in your University should stand among his mates with his head just as high as if he were working toward the Law or the Ministry, and should not be pitied and patronized. . . . Equal reward should be given by society in both fields of effort.'[2]

4.

A victory for the dons? Because of industrial management changes, unprecedented labour difficulties and a sixty-year denigration of business values, is it possible to find in the remarks of Gibb and Taylor a symbolic shift in the attitude of the business community towards the value of a Cambridge education? Is it one of the ironies of history that the generation of the 1860's, employing a subtle donnish chemistry of ancient origin, had abolished the businessman by transforming him into a professional man and had at last triumphed over the philistines and the spirit of money-making? A study of the employment of Cambridge graduates in business in the late 1930's would

[1] Ibid., p. 8.   [2] Ibid., p. 15.

EPILOGUE

almost make it appear that the revolution of the dons had been uniquely successful. A committee appointed by the Cambridge University Appointments Board reported that employers were not particularly interested in specialized university training for graduates in business, apart from a desire to have Cambridge men more familiar with the general features of industrial organization and problems of management. Even where scientific skills were required employers preferred a theoretical, broad and less practical education. Their emphasis was on vaguely humanistic qualities, or on logic, clarity of thought, intellectual independence and general mental discipline.[1] Both employers and graduates in business gave character as the most important ingredient for success in business; and it was emphasized that Cambridge, as a collegiate university, was singularly able to provide for character formation. Character was defined as initiative, as an ability to promote group loyalty and secure the co-operation of all types of men, in all occupations and from all social backgrounds.[2] The man of character was equipped with an ethic of social service and did not regard himself as a capitalist or businessman engaged in profit-seeking. His role was to broaden the experience and knowledge of businessmen, to serve business, in fact, much as the Cambridge-educated civil servant served the state and politicians.[3]

If just before the Second World War the Cambridge service ideal was regarded so favourably by businessmen, it was also apparently still a deterrent to a business career, for the study of the employment of Cambridge graduates noted some disquieting tendencies. In the 1930's perhaps 46 per cent of all Cambridge graduates came from business families;[4] and yet in 1937–8, the period covered by the committee's report, only one-third of all graduates whose after careers were known, returned to business.[5] Of all the major careers entered by Cambridge graduates, commerce was virtually the only one to show an occupational loss. Furthermore, fewer sons from business fami-

---

[1] *University Education and Business*, Report by a Committee appointed by the Cambridge University Appointments Board (Cambridge, 1946), pp. 20–1, 41, 45.

[2] Ibid., pp. 33, 39, 40, 47.   [3] Ibid., pp. 47, 49.

[4] Jenkins and Jones, p. 99.

[5] *University Education and Business*, p. 26.

lies were inclined to follow their fathers' occupations than were sons from other families.[1]

The committee reported other, even more, disturbing factors. The very best graduates were not attracted to careers in business; and many who did enter frequently decided only at the last minute or regarded business as their second choice.[2] Science graduates employed in business had better academic records – although not as good as graduates in government science – but they entered industry mainly because they followed their fathers and had perhaps developed a professional attitude toward industrial science. Certainly no other positive inducements were offered them, for scientists in industry were regarded as occupying an inferior position. They were frequently called 'mere technicians', and their jobs offered no chances of advancement.[3]

On both sides of the Atlantic it is frequently said that in America business values, incentives and methods were impressed on the university, but in one of England's fairest educational institutions anti-philistinism survived. The result, critics have said, is the failure of Cambridge, as well as Oxford, to play a vigorous role in building up the economy and facilitating technological change. The disdain of *homo oeconomicus* in Cambridge was altogether too complete. Recently the state has once again emerged as a third party to remind both the university and the business community of the service they must perform in promoting economic activity at home and abroad. To what extent or in what way Cambridge will respond to this pressure is not a question history can answer with any precision. No doubt part of the university response will be predictable, as part was predictable in the 1860's. But will there be no surprises, is another 'round about' impossible?

[1] Ibid., Tables V and VI, p. 68.   [2] Ibid., pp. 3, 17.
[3] Ibid., pp. 13–15, 27, 31.

APPENDICES

APPENDIX I

Fees of Grammar Schools or Similar Foundations in the Headmasters' Conference 1913[1]

	Day £	Tuition and Board £
1. Abingdon (refounded 1563, reorganized 1878)	14	60
2. Aldenham (1597, reorganized 1875)	none	71
3. Bedford School (1552, rebuilt 1891)	4–5	c. 30
4. Berkhampsted (16th cent., re-established 1841)	12	60
5. Birmingham (1552)	15 (⅓ pay nothing)	—
6. Blundell's, Tiverton (1604, reorganized 1876)	—	75–84
7. Bradford (1553, reorganized 1871)	16	—
8. Bristol Grammar (1532)	15	60
9. Bromsgrove (1553) (only a few day boys)	16	84
10. Perse (1615)	18	—
11. King's School, Canterbury (refounded 1541)	22	63
12. St. Edmund's, Canterbury (1749)	—	70
13. Carlisle Grammar (refounded 1541)	11	42
14. King's School, Chester (1541, reorganized 1873)	15	54
15. Chigwell (1629)	18	72
16. Christ's Hospital, West Horsham (1552)	?	?

[1] See the discussion *supra*, pp. 57–8. These schools entered the Conference at various times after 1889. Fees are taken from the *PSTB*.

277

	Day £	Tuition and Board £
17. Whitgift, Croydon (1596)	24	c. 60
18. Dulwich College (1619, reorganized 1857)	24	c. 80
19. Durham School (1541)	12–16	73
20. Exeter (refounded 1629, reorganized 1876)	12–20	50–70
21. Felsted (1564, reconstituted 1852)	20	70
22. Giggleswick (1512)	14	78
23. Hereford (1381, reconstituted 1894)	14	55–65
24. Elizabeth College, Guernsey (1563)	14	69
25. Highgate School (1562, reconstituted 1876)	24	84
26. Gresham's School, Holt (1555)	12	75
27. Ipswich School (1477)	16	c. 60 and up
28. Owen's School, Islington (1613, reconstituted 1878)	10	—
29. Lancaster (1469, reconstituted 1896)	6	—
30. Leeds Grammar (1552)	15	—
31. Wyggeston Grammar	9	—
32. Merchant Taylors' (1561)	15	special arrangement
33. Merchant Taylors', Crosby (1618)	15 (mainly a day school)	c. 60
34. Monmouth Grammar (1614)	10	40–50
35. Newcastle-under-Lyme (1602, reconstituted 1872)	16	60
36. Norwich (refounded 1547)	15	70
37. Nottingham High (1513, reconstituted 1882)	15	68–78
38. Oakham (1584)	10–15	c. 70
39. Oundle	32	95
40. Magdalen College School, Oxford (1480)	23	71
41. Portsmouth Grammar (1732, remodelled 1874)	12	by arrangement

APPENDIX I

	Day £	Tuition and Board £
42. Reading (refounded 1485)	18	68
43. Repton (1557)	40 (only a few)	115
44. King's School, Rochester (1542)	20	70
45. St. Alban's (1553)	10	50
46. St. Bees, Cumberland (1587)	15 (only c. 20)	60
47. St. Olave's and St. Saviour's Grammar (1571 and 1562, amalgamated 1899)	4–8 (or rated to means)	—
48. Sedbergh (1525, reorganized 1874)	24	79
49. Sherborne (1550, reorganized 1870)	30	c. 95
50. Tonbridge (1553)	20–30	c. 100
51. Uppingham (1584)	30	112
52. Wakefield Grammar (1591)	12	51–67
53. Warwick (1545, reorganized 1875)	—	60
54. Wolverhampton School (1515, reorganized 1874)	15	55–60
55. Woodbridge (1662)	8	58
56. King's School, Worcester (1541, reorganized 1884)	15	60
57. Worcester Royal Grammar (1370, reorganized 1893)	—	60
58. St. Peter's, York (eighth century, refounded in Tudor period and reorganized 1898)	9–18	60–70

SOCIAL BACKGROUNDS OF SIDNEY SUSSEX COLLEGE STUDENTS, 1843–1914

Occupation	1843–1849	1850–1859	1860–1869	1870–1879	1880–1889	1890–1899	1900–1914	Total
Anglican Clergy	22	25	49	34	42	53	80	305
Landed Gentlemen[2]	5	2	16	12	9	5	16	65
Civil Service, Local Gov't	0	1	3	2	7	6	18	37
Dissenting Clergy	1	0	0	3	3	4	8	19
Farmers	4	3	5	6	5	1	6	30
Legal	3	6	7	8	4	5	18	51
Medical	1	10	17	7	7	18	29	89
Services	3	4	4	2	2	11	12	38
Teachers and Academic[3]	1	5	9	5	13	8	23	64
Secretarial	1	0	0	2	4	2	8	17
Artisans and Tradesmen[4]	2	6	12	3	9	3	16	51
Businessmen[5]	9	12	15	19	23	12	63	153
Civil Engineers and Applied Scientists	0	0	3	3	1	2	10	19
Miscellaneous Professional[6]	1	1	4	1	6	6	10	29
Miscellaneous[7]	1	2	2	1	0	2	8	16
TOTAL	54	77	146	108	135	138	325	983
Unknown Backgrounds[8]	13	19	7	8	16	89	92	244
Total Matriculations	67	96	153	116	151	227	417	1227
Percentage Complete	81	80	95	93	89	61	78	80

[1] Compiled from the Sidney Sussex College Admissions Register, 1843–1933, and Venn, *Alumni Cantabrigiensis*.

[2] A negligible number of titular aristocrats matriculated at Sidney in the period 1843–1914. The greater majority of persons in this category are sons of 'gentlemen', to include rentiers.

[3] Some are in holy orders.   [4] See II : C for details.

[5] See II : D for details.   [6] See II : E for details.   [7] See II : F for details.

[8] Some of the unknowns may be sons of 'gentlemen'.

APPENDIX II: B

Awards Distribution in Sidney Sussex College, 1843–1914

Occupation	1843-9			1850-9			1860-9			1870-9			1880-9			1890-9			1900-14[1]			Total		
	Sizars	Scholars	Exh	Sizars	Scholars	Exh	Sizars	Scholars	Exh	Sizars	Scholars	Exh	Sizars	Scholars	Exh	Sizars	Scholars	Exh	Sizars	Scholars	Exh	Sizars	Scholars	Exh
Anglican Clergy	1	1	0	5	2	1	2	16	7	6	5	8	8	11	6	7	10	17	0	11	10	29	56	49
Landed Gentlemen	0	0	0	1	0	0	0	1	1	0	2	0	0	2	0	1	1	0	1	4	3	3	10	4
Civil Service, Local Gov't	0	0	0	1	0	0	0	0	0	0	1	0	0	4	0	0	3	3	0	5	3	1	13	6
Dissenting Clergy	1	0	0	0	0	0	0	0	0	1	0	0	0	3	0	0	1	3	0	1	1	2	5	4
Farmers	0	1	0	2	1	0	1	3	0	0	4	0	2	0	0	1	0	0	1	1	0	7	10	0
Legal	0	0	0	0	1	0	0	0	1	1	2	0	0	2	1	0	0	2	1	3	4	2	8	8
Medical	0	0	0	1	1	0	3	3	0	0	0	0	1	2	0	0	5	4	3	3	5	8	14	9
Services	0	1	1	1	1	0	1	1	0	0	0	0	0	0	0	3	3	1	2	1	2	7	7	4
Teachers and Academic	0	0	0	2	0	0	1	1	0	0	2	0	1	7	2	1	4	0	2	8	1	7	22	3
Secretarial	0	0	0	0	0	0	0	0	0	1	0	0	0	3	0	0	1	0	1	2	0	2	6	0
Artisans and Tradesmen	0	0	0	1	0	0	5	1	0	1	0	0	3	0	1	0	1	0	1	4	3	11	6	4
Businessmen	2	0	0	3	4	0	2	1	2	1	3	0	2	6	1	2	3	1	3	12	4	15	29	8
Civil Engineers and Applied Scientists	0	0	0	0	0	0	0	1	0	0	0	0	0	0	0	0	0	0	0	2	0	0	3	1
Miscellaneous Professional	0	0	0	0	0	0	0	2	0	0	1	0	1	3	0	0	4	1	0	5	0	0	15	1
Miscellaneous	0	0	0	0	0	0	0	0	0	0	0	0	0	0	0	0	0	0	0	3	0	0	3	0
TOTAL	4	3	1	17	10	1	15	30	11	11	20	8	18	44	12	16	36	31	14	64	36	95	207	100

[1] Entries for this period do not appear complete. A number of sizarships especially may be missing.

APPENDIX II

APPENDIX II: C

SONS OF ARTISANS AND TRADESMEN, SIDNEY SUSSEX COLLEGE, 1843–1914

Occupation	1843–1849	1850–1859	1860–1869	1870–1879	1880–1889	1890–1899	1900–1914	Total
Baker	0	0	2	0	0	0	1	3
Blacksmith	0	0	1	0	0	0	0	1
Bookseller	0	0	2	0	1	1	2	6
Butcher	0	1	0	0	0	0	1	2
Chemist	0	0	1	1	0	1	0	3
Cobbler	0	0	1	0	0	0	0	1
Draper	0	0	0	0	3	0	1	4
Dyer	1	0	0	0	0	0	0	1
'Engineer' (Mechanic)	1	0	0	0	1	0	2	4
Engraver	0	0	0	0	1	0	0	1
Grocer	0	0	0	0	2	0	1	3
Ironmonger	0	0	0	0	1	0	0	1
Jeweller	0	0	1	0	0	0	3	4
Metalworker	0	0	1	0	0	0	0	1
Miller	0	1	0	0	0	0	0	1
Nurseryman	0	0	0	0	0	0	1	1
Oak Carver	0	0	0	1	0	0	0	1
Printer	0	0	0	0	0	1	1	2
Robe Maker	0	0	0	1	0	0	0	1
Saddler	0	0	1	0	0	0	0	1
Tailor	0	0	1	0	0	0	2	3
Tanner	0	2	0	0	0	0	0	2
Tradesman unspecified	0	0	0	0	0	0	1	1
Turner	0	0	1	0	0	0	0	1
Silversmith	0	2	0	0	0	0	0	2
TOTAL	2	6	12	3	9	3	16	51

APPENDIX II: D

SONS OF BUSINESSMEN, SIDNEY SUSSEX COLLEGE, 1843–1914

Occupation	1843–1849	1850–1859	1860–1869	1870–1879	1880–1889	1890–1899	1900–1914	Total
Advertising	0	0	0	0	0	0	1	1
Auctioneer	0	0	0	1	0	0	0	1
Banker	1	0	1	0	1	2	6	11
Bleacher	0	0	0	1	0	0	0	1
Brewer	1	0	0	0	0	0	1	2
Builder	0	0	1	1	0	0	4	6
Business Agent	0	1	0	4	3	0	1	9
Contractor	0	0	0	0	1	0	1	2
Director	0	0	0	0	0	0	1	1
Estate Agent	0	1	0	1	2	0	1	5
Executive	0	0	0	0	0	0	1	1
Insurance Broker	0	0	0	0	0	1	2	3
Manufacturer	0	0	0	0	5	0	10	15
Merchant	6	10	13	9	10	7	22	77
Mine Owner	0	0	0	0	0	0	1	1
Money Broker	1	0	0	0	0	0	0	1
Publisher	0	0	0	2	0	0	1	3
Railway Director	0	0	0	0	0	0	1	1
Salesman	0	0	0	0	0	1	1	2
Stock Broker	0	0	0	0	0	1	7	8
Tug Owner	0	0	0	0	0	0	1	1
Wholesaler	0	0	0	0	1	0	0	1
TOTAL	9	12	15	19	23	12	63	153

APPENDIX II

APPENDIX II: E

SONS OF PROFESSIONAL MEN (MISCELLANEOUS), SIDNEY SUSSEX COLLEGE, 1843–1914

Occupation	1843–1849	1850–1859	1860–1869	1870–1879	1880–1889	1890–1899	1900–1914	Total
Accountant	0	0	0	0	3	2	2	7
Analyst	0	0	0	0	1	0	0	1
Architect	1	1	1	0	1	2	2	8
Archivist	0	0	1	0	1	0	0	2
Artist	0	0	0	1	0	0	2	3
Author	0	0	1	0	0	0	1	2
Geological Surveyor	0	0	0	0	0	1	1	2
Journalist	0	0	0	0	0	0	1	1
Law Writer	0	0	0	0	0	0	1	1
Musician	0	0	0	0	0	1	0	1
Naval Interpreter	0	0	1	0	0	0	0	1
TOTAL	1	1	4	1	6	6	10	29

APPENDIX II: F

SONS FROM MISCELLANEOUS BACKGROUNDS, SIDNEY SUSSEX COLLEGE, 1843–1914

Occupation	1843–1849	1850–1859	1860–1869	1870–1879	1880–1889	1890–1899	1900–1914	Total
Bailiff	0	0	2	0	0	0	0	2
Cashier	0	0	0	0	0	0	1	1
College Steward	1	0	0	0	0	0	0	1
Colonist	0	1	0	0	0	0	0	1
Dock Yard Officer	0	1	0	0	0	0	0	1
Foreign Rulers	0	0	0	0	0	2	0	2
Foreman	0	0	0	0	0	0	1	1
Herbalist	0	0	0	1	0	0	0	1
Railway Inspector	0	0	0	0	0	0	1	1
Sailor	0	0	0	0	0	0	2	2
Secretary of a Leper Mission	0	0	0	0	0	0	1	1
Secretary of a Public Company	0	0	0	0	0	0	2	2
TOTAL	1	2	2	1	0	2	8	16

APPENDIX III

The Employment of Cambridge Engineers[1]

Position	Number	Salary
Directors or Partners in Manufacturing Firms. (Some started their own businesses.)	10	not stated
Partners in Consulting Engineering Firms. (Some started their own businesses.)	14	not stated
Subordinate Positions in Manufacturing Firms (Draftsman or Works-Manager's Assistant to Works Manager)	49	£150–500, average about £200.
Assistants to Consulting Engineers	9	not stated
Teaching 1. Professors or Heads of Teaching Institutions 2. Assistant Teachers	6 17	£170–1,000, average about £400.
Government, Municipalities or Railways (U.K.)	12	not stated
Government Engineering Services Abroad	28	Perhaps £460 for a man of 29 serving in India.
Miscellaneous (seven barristers, three journalists, two soldiers, two architects, one artist, one clergyman and one missionary, three in research, the remainder in commercial pursuits)	31	not stated

[1] From a return of 1910 on the employment of one hundred and seventy-six Cambridge engineers, H. A. Roberts, *Careers for University Men* (Cambridge, 1914), pp. 20–1.

APPENDIX IV

A Select List of Sources for the History of the
University and Colleges

Table of Contents

APPENDIX IV

I. History of the University and Colleges of Cambridge—Manuscript Sources

A. University
  1. Library
    a. Letters: There is a voluminous and invaluable collection of letters, far too extensive to list, which may be used in studies of the history of Cambridge. Letters, as well as other manuscript sources, are listed in various publications of the University Library, the latest being a *Summary Guide to Accessions of Western Manuscripts (Other than Medieval) Since 1867* (Cambridge, 1966).
    b. Minute Book of the Cambridge Clerical Education Society, Add. 6984(E).
    c. Filby, P. W., 'Life with the Frazers' (1958). Cam. b. 958.3^1. 'Sir James George Frazer, 1854–1941, Anthropologist, Essayist, Classical Scholar' (1958). Cam.b.958.3^2.
    d. Memoranda and Notes of Evidence submitted to the Royal Commission on Oxford and Cambridge (1919). Cam.a.922.4–9.
    e. Petitions v. Pembroke and Queens' College Statutes, Cam.a.933.3.
    f. Whittaker, John William, accounts of expenditure, Add. 7457.
  2. Archives
    a. Matriculation Records
    b. Minutes of Meetings, Mathematical Studies Syndicate, 1877–8.

B. Colleges
  1. King's College Library
    a. Wedd Memoirs and Correspondence.
    b. Letters: Misc. 17.
    c. Roger Fry Papers and Correspondence.
    d. Walter Headlam Papers and Correspondence.
    e. Doncaster, Leonard, 'The Interpretation of Life' (1918), Misc. 17^{11}.
    f. Whitney, J. P., 'Sir George Prothero as a Historian', Q.32.33.

287

2. Trinity College
   a. Library
      (1) Thompson Papers, Add. c.72, 73.
      (2) Notices of William Edmund Currey, Add. c.27$^{87-119}$.
      (3) Broad, C. D., 'Autobiography' (1954).
      (4) Eddington, Arthur Stanley, Journal, Add. b.48.
      (5) Minutes of Meetings of the Sizarship Committee, June 17, 1899–July 29, 1926. Rec.24.1.
      (6) Minutes of the Education Committee, February 13, 1869–April 26, 1929. Rec.5.1–3.
      (7) Meetings of Tutors and Lecturers, May 22, 1868–79. Rec.16.1.
      (8) Collection of College Notices.
   b. Senior Bursar
      (1) Trinity College Council, Reports.
      (2) Minutes of the Meetings of the Council.
      (3) Envelope VI (L) – 'Tutorial System 1889'.
   c. Junior Bursar
      Minute Book of the Tutorial System Committee, January 1889–November 17, 1890.

3. Sidney Sussex College
   a. Admissions Register, 1843–1933.
   b. Scholarship Book (Examinations Book).
   c. Minutes of College Meetings, 1876–1919.
   d. Financial Book.
   e. Audit Books, 1800–1866.

4. Pembroke College Library
   a. Statutory Commission, 1923, 350.45.
   b. Leonard Whibley Papers.
   c. Attwater Papers, 350.1–

II. History of the University and Colleges of Cambridge – Printed Sources

   A. University Library
      1. Flysheets
         a. Greek Question, 1905. Cam.b.905.20.

b. Flysheets called forth by the Report of the Special
Board for Mathematics issued November 7, 1899.
Cam.b.899.6.

c. Flysheets, Theological Tripos, 1896. Cam.b.896.3.

d. Darwin, G. H., *To the Fellows of Trinity College*,
May 1900. Cam.c.900.4.

e. Selwyn College, flysheets. Cam.a.500.6, items
111–137.

f. Nixon, J. E., *On the Position of a Lecturer in King's
College, Cambridge* (November 19, 1891). Cam.c.
891.13.

g. Hammond, James Lemprière, *Sizarships* (December, 1866). Cam.c.866.19.

h. Gaye, R. K., *To the Master and Fellows of Trinity
College, Cambridge* (1904). Cam.c.904.40.

2. Cambridge Societies, Clubs, Associations
   a. Cradock, Percy, ed., *Recollections of the Cambridge
   Union, 1815–1939* (Cambridge, 1953).
   b. Reports of the Cambridge Clerical Education
   Society, 1838–1903. Cam.b.21.16.1.
   c. Clark, J. W., *Miscellaneous Papers*, I. Cam.c.291.
   6.1.
   d. Clark, J. W., *The Foundation and Early Years of the
   Cambridge Philosophical Society* (October 27, 1890).
   Cam.c.891.19.
   e. *Proceedings of the Cambridge Philosophical Society*
   (1866), CC 5 1.
   f. *Transactions of the Cambridge Philosophical Society*
   (1883–1928), CC 4 1.
   g. *Proceedings of the Society for Psychical Research.*
   h. *Journal of the Society for Psychical Research.*
   i. The Cambridge Appointments Association, Report of a Meeting held November 4, 1889, in the
   Senate House. Cam.b.899.11.
   j. Cambridge University Appointments Board, *University Education and Business* (Cambridge, 1946).

3. Periodicals and Bulletins
   a. *The Eagle.*
   b. *The Cambridge Review.*

c. *The Cambridge University Magazine.*
d. *The Cambridge University Reporter.*
e. *The Christ's College Magazine.*

4. University Handbooks and Guides
   a. Venn, J. A., *Entries of the Various Colleges in the University of Cambridge, 1544–1906* (Cambridge, 1908). Cam.c.908.48. Accompanying graphs, Cam.a. 908.2.$^{1-2}$, Cam.a.908.2^3.
   b. Tanner, Joseph Robson, *The Historical Register of the University of Cambridge* (Cambridge, 1917). Cam.d.1.4.1–
   c. *The Student's Guide.*
   d. *The Student's Handbook.*
   e. *The Cambridge University Calendar.*

5. Reports
   a. Cambridge University Reform (1909). Cam.b. 909.10.
   b. Report of a Conference on Secondary Education Convened of the Vice-Chancellor of the University of Cambridge and held in the Senate House, April 21–22, 1896. Cam.c.896.9.

6. Statutes
   a. Bradshaw, Henry, ed., *Statutes for the University of Cambridge and for the Colleges within it, Made, Published, and Approved (1878–1882) under the Universities of Oxford and Cambridge Act, 1877* (Cambridge, 1883).
   b. Statutes of the College of the Lady Frances Sidney Sussex. 1860, 1861–Cam.c.861.35. 1926–Cam.c. 926.27.
   c. *The Statutes of Trinity College, Cambridge* (Cambridge, 1926).

7. Biographical Registers
   a. Venn, J. and J. A., *Alumni Cantabrigienses.*
   b. *Christ's College Biographical Register.*
   c. Withers, John J., *A Register of Admissions to King's College, Cambridge, 1850–1900* (London, 1903).

d. Ball, W. W. Rouse, and Venn, J. A., eds., *Admissions to Trinity College, Cambridge* (London, 1911).

8. University and College Histories

a. University

Bristed, Charles Astor, *Five Years in an English University*, 2 vols. (New York, 1852). Also other editions.

Everett, William, *On the Cam* (London, 1869).

Gray, Arthur, *Cambridge University, an Episodical History* (Cambridge, 1926).

Jackson, Henry, 'Cambridge Fifty Years Ago', *The Cambridge Review*, XXXI (June 2, 1910), pp. 449–51.

Jesse, William, 'Cambridge in the 80's', *Cornhill Magazine*, CLV (March, 1937), pp. 340–56.

Mansbridge, Albert, *The Older Universities of England* (London, 1923).

Roach, John, 'The Victoria County History of Cambridge', *Proceedings of the Cambridge Antiquarian Society*, LIV (1960), pp. 112–26.

Roach, John, ed., *The Victoria History of the County of Cambridge and the Isle of Ely*, III (London, 1959).

Stephen, Leslie, *Sketches from Cambridge* (London and Cambridge, 1865).

Tennyson, Charles, *Cambridge from Within* (London, 1913).

The Twentieth Century (February, 1955).

Tillyard, Alfred Isaac, *A History of University Reform from 1800 to the Present Time* (Cambridge, 1913).

Winstanley, D. A., *Unreformed Cambridge* (Cambridge, 1935).

The University of Cambridge in the Eighteenth Century (Cambridge, 1922).

Early Victorian Cambridge (Cambridge, 1940).

Later Victorian Cambridge (Cambridge, 1947).

[Wright, John Martin Frederick], *Alma Mater; or Seven Years at the University of Cambridge*, 2 vols. (Cambridge, 1827).

b. College Histories

Attwater, Aubrey, *Pembroke College, Cambridge: A Short History* (Cambridge, 1936).

Brown, A. L., *Selwyn College, Cambridge* (London, 1906).

Bury, John Patrick Tuer, *History of Corpus Christi College, 1822–1952* (Cambridge, 1952).

Clare College, 1326–1926, 2 vols. (Cambridge, 1928).

Gray, Arthur, and Brittain, Frederick, *A History of Jesus College, Cambridge* (London, 1960).

Harrison, William John, *Notes on the Masters, Fellows, Scholars, and Exhibitioners of Clare College, Cambridge* (Cambridge, 1953).

Howard, Henry Fraser, *An Account of the Finances of the College of St. John the Evangelist, 1511–1926* (Cambridge, 1935).

Jones, W. H. S., *A History of St. Catharine's College* (Cambridge, 1936).

Miller, Edward, *Portrait of a College: A History of the College of St. John the Evangelist, Cambridge* (Cambridge, 1961).

Mullinger, James Bass, *St. John's College* (London, 1901).

Peile, John, *Christ's College, Cambridge* (London, 1900).

Rackham, H., *Christ's College in Former Days* (Cambridge, 1939).

Saltmarsh, John, *King's College: A Short History* (Cambridge, 1958).

Trevelyan, George Macaulay, *Trinity College, Cambridge; a History and Guide* (Cambridge, 1953).

9. History of the Colleges and University of Cambridge: Miscellaneous

Ashby, Eric, *Technology and the Academics* (London, 1958).

Ball, W. W. Rouse, *Cambridge Papers* (London, 1918).

The Origin and History of the Mathematical Tripos (Cambridge, 1880).

A History of the Study of Mathematics at Cambridge (Cambridge, 1889).

Cambridge Notes, 2nd ed. (Cambridge, 1921).

Brand, C. P., et al., *Italian Studies Presented to Eric Reginald Pearce Vincent* (Cambridge, 1962).

Breul, Karl, *Student's Life and Work in the University of Cambridge* (Cambridge, 1908).

Greek and Its Humanistic Alternatives in the 'Little-Go' (Cambridge, 1905).

Brookfield, Mrs. Charles, *The Cambridge Apostles* (New York, 1907).

Cambridge Essays, 1856 (Cambridge, 1856).

Cambridge Historical Essays (Cambridge, 1889).

Cambridge University Association, *Statement of the Needs of the University* (Cambridge, 1899).

Campbell, Lewis, *The Nationalization of the Old English Universities* (London, 1901).

Clark, George N., 'The Origins of the Cambridge Modern History', *Cambridge Historical Journal*, VIII (1945).

Clark, John Willis, *Endowments of the University of Cambridge* (Cambridge, 1904).

Cornford, F. M., *The Cambridge Classical Course: An Essay in Anticipation of Further Reform* (Cambridge, 1903).

Microcosmographia Academica (Cambridge, 1908).

Religion in the University (Cambridge, 1911).

Dimsdale, Marcus Southwell, *Happy Days and Other Essays* (Cambridge, 1921).

Drosier, W. H., *On the Duties of a Professor of Zoology and Comparative Anatomy* (1886). Cam.c. 866.[24].

Evennett, Outram, 'The Cambridge Prelude to 1895: the Story of the Removal of the Ban on Universities Told from the Cambridge Angle', *Dublin Review*, CCXVIII (April, May, June, 1946), pp. 107–26.

Foster, Sir Michael, *On Medical Education at Cambridge* (London, 1878).

Gill, Henry V., 'Brave Days at Cambridge', *Studies*, XXVI, pp. 267–79.

Green, W. C., *Greek at the Universities: A Dialogue* (December, 1904).

Hardy, Godfrey Harold, *Bertrand Russell and Trinity* (Cambridge, 1942).

Hopkins, William, *Remarks on the Mathematical Teaching of the University of Cambridge* (1854).

Kellett, E. E., ed., *A Book of Cambridge Verse* (Cambridge, 1911).

Langdon-Brown, Sir Walter, *Some Chapters in Cambridge Medical History* (Cambridge, 1946).

Lapsley, Gaillard Thomas, *Religious Difficulties and Doubts of the Present Generation* (1907). Cam.d. 907.20.

Larsen, Egon (pseud.), *The Cavendish Laboratory* (London, 1962).

Morgan, Henry Arthur, *The Tenure of Fellowships* (London, Oxford, and Cambridge, 1871).
The Mathematical Tripos, an Enquiry into Its Influence on a Liberal Education (London, Oxford, Cambridge, 1871).

Neale, C. M., *The Senior Wranglers of the University of Cambridge, 1748–1907* (Bury St. Edmunds, 1907).

Philpott, Henry, *Remarks on the Question of Adopting the Regulations Recommended by the Syndicate Appointed February 9, 1848* (1848).

Pollock, John Charles, *A Cambridge Movement* (London, 1953).

Pros and Cons of the Celibate System in the Universities by 'a Philogamous Fellow' (Cambridge, 1871).

Rice, F. A., *The Granta and Its Contributors, 1889–1914* (London, 1924).

Shipley, A. E., and Roberts, H. A., 'A Plea for Cambridge', *The Quarterly Review*, CCV (April, 1906), pp. 499–525.

Sidgwick, Henry, *On the Classical Tripos Examination* (1866). Cam.c.866.17.

Tillyard, Aelfrida, *Cambridge Poets, 1900–13* (Cambridge, 1913).

Trotter, Coutts, *University Finance and New Buildings* (1885). Cam.c.885.27.

Whibley, C., *In Cap and Gown. Three Centuries of Cambridge Wit* (1898).

White, James F., *The Cambridge Movement: the Ecclesiologists and the Gothic Revival* (Cambridge, 1962).

Williams, James, *The Law of the Universities* (London, 1910).

Wood, John Spicer, *The Position of Members of the Church of England in a College in the University of Cambridge* (Cambridge, 1882). Cam.c.882.29.

Wright, Harold, ed., *Cambridge University Studies 1933* (London, 1933).

B. Printed Sources – College Libraries
Pembroke College Cambridge Society, *Annual Gazette*.

III. Autobiographies, Biographies, Biographical Notices, Correspondence

Adami, John George, *A Great Teacher – Sir Michael Foster – and His Influence* (Kingston, Ontario, 1914).

Airy, Sir George Biddell, *Autobiography* (Cambridge, 1896).

Annan, Noel, *Leslie Stephen* (London, 1951).

Badley, John Haden, *Memories and Reflections* (London, 1955).

Barker, Sir Ernest, *Age and Youth* (London, 1953).

Baynes, Norman H., ed., *A Bibliography of the Works of J. B. Bury, compiled with a Memoir* (Cambridge, 1929).

Bell, Clive, *Old Friends* (London, 1956).

Benson, Arthur Christopher, *Memories and Friends* (London, 1924). *Rambles and Reflections* (London, 1926).

Benson, Edward Frederic, *As We Were* (London, 1930).

Black, John Sutherland, and Chrystal, George, *The Life of William Robertson Smith* (London, 1912).

Blennerhassett, W. L., 'Acton: 1834–1902', *Dublin Review*, CXCIV, pp. 169–88.

Bobbitt, Mary Reed, *Dearest Love to All: Life and Letters of Lady Jebb* (London, 1960).

Bonney, Thomas George, *Memories of a Long Life* (Cambridge, 1921).

Bowen, W. E., *Edward Bowen* (London, 1902).

Browning, Oscar, *Memories of Sixty Years* (London, 1910).

Bryce, James, *Studies in Contemporary Biography* (London, 1903).

Butler, James Ramsay Montagu, *Henry Montagu Butler: A Memoir* (London, 1925).

Campbell, Lewis, and Garnett, William, *The Life of James Clerk Maxwell* (London, 1882).

Campbell, Olwen Ward, Memoir of James Ward, prefixed to James Ward, *Essays in Philosophy* (Cambridge, 1927).

Campion, Sarah, *Father: A Portrait of G. G. Coulton at Home* (London, 1948).

Carlyle, Thomas, *Life of John Sterling* (London, 1851).

Chadwick, Owen, *Westcott and the University* (Cambridge, 1962).

Charteris, Evan Richard, *Life and Letters of Sir Edmund Gosse* (London, 1931).

Clark, George N., 'Sir John Harold Clapham, 1873–1946', *Proceedings of the British Academy*, XXXII (1946), pp. 339–52.

Clark, John Willis, *Old Friends at Cambridge and Elsewhere* (London, 1900).

Clark, William George, 'William Whewell, In Memoriam', *Macmillan's Magazine*, XIII (April, 1866), pp. 545–52.

Coleridge, Arthur, *Reminiscences* (London, 1921).

Cornford, Francis M., *The Unwritten Philosophy and Other Essays*, with a memoir by W. K. C. Guthrie (Cambridge, 1950).

Coulton, G. G., *Fourscore Years, An Autobiography* (Cambridge, 1943).

Coutts Trotter, In Memoriam (Cambridge, 1888). Cam.c. 291.6.5.[4].

Cowell, George, *Life and Letters of Edward Byles Cowell* (London, 1904).

Creighton, Mandell, *Life and Letters of Mandell Creighton*, ed. Louise Creighton, 2 vols. (London, 1904).

Crone, John S., *Henry Bradshaw, His Life and Work* (Dublin, 1931).

Cunningham, Audrey, *William Cunningham, Teacher and Priest* (London, 1950).

Dampier, Sir William Cecil, *Cambridge and Elsewhere* (London, 1950).

Dickinson, Goldsworthy Lowes, *John McTaggart Ellis McTaggart* (Cambridge, 1931).

Douglas, Mrs. Stair, *Life of William Whewell* (London, 1881).

Douglas, Allie Vibert, *Life of Arthur Stanley Eddington* (London, 1956).

Downie, R. Angus, *J. G. Frazer, Portrait of a Scholar* (London, 1940).

Eden, George R., *Lightfoot of Durham* (Cambridge, 1932).

Eve, Arthur Stewart, *Rutherford* (Cambridge, 1939).

Fifoot, C. H. S., ed., *The Letters of Frederic William Maitland* (Cambridge, 1965).

Firth, John D'Ewes Evelyn, *Rendall of Winchester* (London, 1954).

Fisher, Herbert Albert Laurens, *Frederic William Maitland, A Biographical Sketch* (Cambridge, 1910).

Forster, E. M., *Goldsworthy Lowes Dickinson* (London, 1962).

Forsyth, A. R., 'Edward John Routh', *Proceedings of the London Mathematical Society*, 2nd ser., V, Part 7 (July 5, 1907), pp. xiv–xx.

Gaskell, Walter Holbrook, *Sir Michael Foster, 1836–1907* (London, 1908).

Glover, Terrot Reaveley, *Cambridge Retrospect* (Cambridge, 1943).

Gooch, G. P., 'Victorian Memories', *Contemporary Review*, CLXXXVIII (Oct., Nov., Dec., 1955), pp. 235–41; 307–11; 382–86; CLXXXIX (Jan., Feb., April, 1956), pp. 24–8, 101–6, 204–9.

Graham, Edward, *The Harrow Life of Henry Montagu Butler* (London, 1920).

Hardy, Godfrey Harold, *A Mathematician's Apology* (Cambridge, 1940).

Harrison, Jane Ellen, *Reminiscences of a Student's Life* (London, 1925).

Harrod, Roy F., *The Life of John Maynard Keynes* (London, 1951).

Headlam, Walter George, *Letters and Poems*, with a memoir by Cecil Headlam (London, 1910).

Heilbrun, Carolyn G., *The Garnett Family* (London, 1961).

Heitland, William Emerton, *After Many Years* (Cambridge, 1926).

Holland, Henry Arthur, *Frederic William Maitland* (London, 1953).

Hort, Arthur Fenton, *Life and Letters of Fenton John Anthony Hort*, 2 vols. (London, 1896).

James, Montagu Rhodes, *Eton and King's* (London, 1926).

Jebb, Carolyn, *Life and Letters of Sir Richard Claverhouse Jebb* (Cambridge, 1907).

Johnstone, J. K., *The Bloomsbury Group* (London, 1954).

Keynes, John Maynard, *Two Memoirs* (London, 1949). *Essays in Biography* (London, 1951).

Kingsley, Charles, *His Letters and Memories of His Life*, ed. by his wife, 2 vols. (London, 1877).

Leaf, Walter, *Some Chapters of Autobiography* (London, 1932).

Leigh, William Austen, *Augustus Austen Leigh* (London, 1906).

Leslie, Shane, *The Film of Memory* (London, 1938).

Marshall, Mary Paley, *What I Remember* (Cambridge, 1947).

Maurice, Frederick Denison, *The Life of F. D. Maurice*, ed. Frederick Maurice, 2 vols. (London, 1885).

Mayor, J. E. B., *Twelve Cambridge Sermons*, with a memoir by H. F. Stewart (Cambridge, 1911).

Milne, E. A., *Sir James Hopwood Jeans* (Cambridge, 1952).

Morgan, Iris L. Osborne, *Memoirs of Henry Arthur Morgan* (London, 1927).

Moule, Handley Carr Glyn, *My Cambridge Classical Teachers* (Durham, 1913).

Murray, Gilbert, *Jane Ellen Harrison, An Address* (Cambridge, 1928).

Parry, Reginald St. John, *Henry Jackson, O.M.* (Cambridge, 1926).

Pearson, Karl, *The Life, Letters, and Labours of Francis Galton*, 4 vols. (Cambridge, 1914–1930).

Pell, Albert, *Reminiscences* (London, 1908).

Pethick-Lawrence, Frederick William, *Fate Has Been Kind* (London, 1942).

APPENDIX IV

Pigou, A. C., 'John Maynard Keynes', *Proceedings of the British Academy*, XXXII (1946), pp. 395–414.

Plucknett, T. F. T., 'Maitland's View of Law and History', *Law Quarterly Review*, LXVII (April, 1951), pp. 179–94.

Pollock, Frederick, 'For my Grandson: Cambridge and the "Apostles": Oxford Scholars and Historians: University Memories', *Cornhill Magazine*, LXXIV (January, 1933), pp. 1–15. *For My Grandson: Remembrances of an Ancient Victorian* (London, 1933).

Powicke, Maurice, 'Three Cambridge Scholars: C. W. Previté-Orton, Z. N. Brooke, and G. G. Coulton', *The Cambridge Historical Journal*, IX (1947), pp. 106–25.

Powys, John Cowper, *Autobiography* (London, 1934).

Prothero, George W., *A Memoir of Henry Bradshaw* (London, 1888).

Pryme, George, *Autobiographic Recollections*, ed. by his daughter (Cambridge, 1870).

Raverat, Gwen, *Period Piece, A Cambridge Childhood* (London, 1952).

Rayleigh (Robert John Strutt), Fourth Baron, *Life of J. J. Thomson* (Cambridge, 1942). *John William Strutt, Third Baron Rayleigh* (London, 1924).

Reddaway, W. F., *Cambridge in 1891* (privately printed, 1943).

Roberts, Mrs. Ernest Stewart, *Sherborne, Oxford, and Cambridge* (London, 1934).

Rolleston, Humphrey Davy, *Life of Sir Clifford Allbutt* (London, 1929).

Russell, Bertrand, *Portraits from Memory and Other Essays* (London, 1956).

Shipley, Arthur E., '*J.*' *A Memoir of John Willis Clark* (London, 1913).

Shove, Fredegond, *Fredegond and Gerald Shove* (Cambridge, 1952).

Sidgwick, Arthur, and Sidgwick, E. M., *Henry Sidgwick, A Memoir* (London, 1906).

Sidgwick, Ethyl, *Mrs. Henry Sidgwick* (London, 1938).

Skeat, Walter W., 'John Peile, Litt.D., 1838–1910', *Proceedings of the British Academy*, IV (1909–10), pp. 1–4.

Smith, A. L., *Maitland* (Oxford, 1908).

Stephen, Leslie, *Life of Henry Fawcett* (London, 1885).

Stewart, H. F., *Francis Jenkinson* (Cambridge, 1926).

Stewart, Jessie, *Jane Ellen Harrison: A Portrait from Letters* (London, 1959).

Stokes, Sir George Gabriel, *Memoir and Scientific Correspondence*, 2 vols. (Cambridge, 1907).

Stuart, James Montgomery, *Reminiscences and Essays* (London, 1884). *Reminiscences* (London, 1912).

Thomson, J. J., *Recollections and Reflections* (London, 1936).

Thornely, Thomas, *Cambridge Memories* (London, 1936).

Thirlwall, John Connop, Jr., *Connop Thirlwall* (London, 1936).

Todhunter, Isaac, *William Whewell, D.D.*, 2 vols. (London, 1876).

Trevelyan, George Macaulay, *An Autobiography and Other Essays* (London, 1949).

Trevelyan, George Otto, *The Life and Letters of Thomas Babington Macaulay*, 2 vols. (London, 1932).

Verall, Arthur Woollgar, *Collected Literary Essays with a memoir*, eds. M. A. Bayfield and J. D. Duff (Cambridge, 1913).

Wedd, Nathaniel, 'Goldie Dickinson: The Latest Cambridge Platonist', *The Criterion*, XII (January, 1933), pp. 175–83.

Wedgwood, Julia, *Nineteenth-Century Teachers* (London, 1909).

Westcott, Arthur, *Life and Letters of Brooke Foss Westcott*, 2 vols. (London, 1903).

White, John F. and Geddes, William D., *Two Professors of Oriental Languages* (Aberdeen, 1899).

White, R. J., 'F. W. Maitland: 1850–1950', *The Cambridge Journal*, IV (December, 1950), pp. 131–43.

Wollaston, A. F. R., *Letters and Diaries*, ed. Mary Wollaston (Cambridge, 1933).

Wood, Herbert George, *Terrot Reaveley Glover* (Cambridge, 1953).

Woolf, Leonard, *Sowing, An Autobiography of the Years, 1880–1904* (London, 1960). *Beginning Again* (London, 1964).

Woolf, Virginia, *Roger Fry* (New York, 1940).

APPENDIX IV

Wortham, Hugo, *Victorian Eton and Cambridge: Being the Life and Times of Oscar Browning* (London, 1956).

Young, Kenneth, *Arthur James Balfour* (London, 1963).

IV. Parliamentary Papers and Government Reports

Report of the Commissioners appointed to inquire into the state, discipline, studies and revenues of the University and colleges of Cambridge; together with the evidence, and an appendix and index (Graham Commission). 1852–3 (1559) xliv.

Report of the Cambridge University Commissioners. 1861, xx.

Special Report from the Select Committee on the Oxford and Cambridge Universities Bill, together with the proceedings of the Committee, Minutes of Evidence, and Appendix (Ewart Committee). 1867. xiii.

Report from the Select Committee of the House of Lords on university tests, together with the proceedings of the Committee, minutes of evidence, and appendix (1870). 1871, ix.

Report of the Commissioners appointed to inquire into the property and income of the Universities of Oxford and Cambridge and of the colleges and halls therein, together with returns and appendix (Cleveland Commission). 1873 (c. 856), xxxvii.

Return from the Universities of Oxford and Cambridge separately, stating, so far as possible for each year, from 1870–1875, inclusive–number, names, and description of professors and mode of appointment of each professor, emoluments of each professor, distinguishing the amounts accruing from fees, salary, and other sources, number of lectures delivered, number of audits at each lecture, the amount transferred from the press fund to the general account of the university. . . . 1876 (327) lix.

Copy of the report, dated March 27, 1876, of the syndicate appointed May 27, 1875 by the University of Cambridge, to consider the requirements of the university in different departments of study, with appendices. 1876. lix.

Royal Commission on Technical Education. 1884 (c. 3981), xxxi, Vol. I, Part III.

Return relating to the Universities of Oxford and Cambridge. 1886, li.

Royal Commission on Secondary Education (Bryce Commission). 9 vols. 1895 (c. 7862), xliii.

Return showing the occupation of the parents of the winners of county council scholarships during the past three years; the amount of each scholarship, and the period for which it was tenable. The name of the school in which the scholarship was won, and whether the school was a voluntary or board school; whether the scholar availed himself of the scholarship and whether he won other scholarships. 1900, lxxiii.

General Reports on higher education, with appendices for the year 1902. 1903 (Cmd. 1738), xxi.

Tables showing the number of pupils exempt from fees in grant-earning secondary schools in England and Wales on January 31, 1911, and the number of pupils who proceeded with scholarships for grant-earning secondary schools to universities during the year 1909–10. 1914 (Cd. 7339), xvi.

Interim Report of the Consultative Committee on Scholarships for Higher Education (Acland Committee of the Board of Education). 1916 (Cmd. 8291), viii.

Royal Commission on Oxford and Cambridge Universities, report and appendices. 1922 (Cmd. 1588), x.

Board of Education, The Public Schools and the General Educational System, Report of the Committee on Public Schools appointed by the President of the Board of Education in July 1942 (Fleming Report), 1944.

Committee on Higher Education appointed by the Prime Minister under the Chairmanship of Lord Robbins, report and appendices. 1963 (Cmnd. 2154).

University Grants Committee, Report of the Committee on University Teaching Methods (Hale Committee), 1964.

APPENDIX IV

V. Miscellaneous

Altick, Richard D., 'The Sociology of Authorship: The Social Origins, Education, and Occupations of 1100 British Writers, 1800–1935', *Bulletin of the New York Public Library*, LXVI (June, 1962), pp. 389–404.

Ben-David, Joseph, and Zloczower, Awraham, 'Universities and Academic Systems in Modern Societies', *European Journal of Sociology*, III (1962), pp. 45–84.

Butterfield, Herbert, *The University and Education Today* (London, 1962).

Davie, George Elder, *The Democratic Intellect: Scotland and Her Universities in the Nineteenth Century* (Edinburgh, 1961).

Forbes, Duncan, *The Liberal Anglican Idea of History* (Cambridge, 1952).

Grosskurth, Phyllis, *The Woeful Victorian* (New York, 1965).

Halsey, A. H., 'British Universities and Intellectual Life', in A. H. Halsey, Jean Floud, and C. Arnold Anderson, eds., *Education, Economy* and *Society* (New York, 1961), pp. 502–12.
'British Universities', *European Journal of Sociology*, III (1962), pp. 85–101.

Hans, Nicholas, *New Trends in Education in the Eighteenth Century* (London, 1951).

McDonald, Ellen, 'English Education and Social Reform in Late Nineteenth Century Bombay: A Case Study in the Transmission of a Cultural Ideal', *The Journal of Asian Studies*, XXV (May, 1966), pp. 453–70.

Marris, Peter, *The Experience of Higher Education* (London, 1964).

Newsome, David, *Godliness and Good Learning* (London, 1961).

Oxford University, Report of Commission of Inquiry – Franks Report, 2 vols. (Oxford, 1966).

'The Popularity of Oxford and Cambridge', *Universities Quarterly*, XV (1960–61), pp. 327–60.

Richter, Melvin, *The Politics of Conscience* (London, 1964).
'Intellectual and Class Alienation: Oxford Idealist Diagnoses and Prescriptions', *European Journal of Sociology*, VII (1966).

Roach, John, 'Victorian Universities and the National Intelligentsia', *Victorian Studies*, III (December, 1959), pp. 131–50.

'Liberalism and the Victorian Intelligentsia', *Cambridge Historical Journal*, XIII (1957), pp. 58–81.

Lord Robbins, *The University in the Modern World* (London, 1966).

Rose, Jasper, and Ziman, John, *Camford Observed* (London, 1964).

Simon, Brian, *Studies in the History of Education, 1780–1870* (London, 1960).

Ward, W. R., *Victorian Oxford* (London, 1965).

Williams, Raymond, *Culture and Society* (New York, 1960).

INDEX

agrarian depression: and Cambridge income, 71, 254–6; and Trinity College supervisorial system, 232

agrarian labourers, 29, 30 n.; *see also* working classes

Airy, William, 66, 66 n.

alienation: professionalization, career and teaching as solution to, 91–2, 135–6, 152–3, 180, 240–7, 250, 258; and Victorian intellectual aristocracy, 93; and J. S. Mill, 97–115; and M. Arnold, 117–18, 126–130; J. H. Newman's description of, 128–9; resisted by F. D. Maurice, 148–9, 151; J. R. Seeley's solution to, 157, 167–8, 178–80; dons do not wish to be solely *gelehrten*, 201, 258; related to problems of employment of graduates, 259–73; *see also* Victorian problem of duty, dons, character formation, professional men and professions

Allbutt, T. Clifford, 185, 225

Apostles, Society of, 211, 220–1; revived by F. D. Maurice, 143

Appointments Association, Cambridge University, 258–73

aristocracy: and ancient universities, 18–19, at public schools, 49, 54–5; special position in Cambridge, 72, 181; expect toadying from dons, 209; extravagant behaviour of, 72–5, 187–9; percentage at Cambridge, 86–7; declining impor-

tance of, 18, 72–3, 87, 89, 90, 238; Bentham on, 99; J. S. Mill's sentimentalism about, 108; in M. Arnold's writings, 118, 126–7; redefined by J. R. Seeley, 157, 179; social responsibility of, 90; 'manly' tradition of, 228, 241, 245; *see also* dons, undergraduates

Arnold, Matthew: influence of Dr. Arnold on, 116; and cultural relativism (or pluralism), 116–18, 130; evidence for alienation of, 117–18, 126–9, 128–30, 148, 168; England in anarchy, 118–19, 126; need for authority, 119; culture as authority, 124–6, 146; importance of a national church, 119–20 (*see also* F. D. Maurice, 149, and J. R. Seeley, 161); Hebraism, 121–4; Hellenism, 123–4, 130; 'dandy' phase, 126, 142; dismisses aristocracy, 126–7; J. H. Newman's influence on, 128–9; and democracy, 130; agrees with J. S. Mill, 93, 116, 131–2; disagrees with J. S. Mill, 93, 130–1; new humanism of, 123–4, 130–1 (*see also* R. C. Jebb, 220–1); environmentalism of, 131; belief in social regeneration, 131 (*see also* alienation); as guide to thinking of Victorian dons, 93, Chapter 3 (*see also* dons); criticized by H. Sidgwick, 121, 142–3; and F. D. Maurice, 144,

INDEX

INDEX

sity should not prepare for business careers, 88–93; and professional education, 248–59; and liberal education, 248–54, 265; Appointments Board, 262–6, 269; and employment of graduates, 258–73; and compulsory Greek, 252–4, 257; and outside pressures in Edwardian period, 253–8; and Cambridge University Association, 255–6, 257, 257 n.; increase in matriculations, 48, 78, 87, 232, 254; changes in student behaviour, 72–4, 187–9, 238, 244, 244 n.; advancing age of students, 166, 183, 193, 236; 'old college system', 72, 188, 192–4; teaching revolution at, 90, 180, 189, 192, 216, 231–5; private tuition, 198–208, 210, 216–17, 231–5; idea of a college, 175–6, 194–6, 205, 209, 223, 231–49, 251, 258, 270–1; idea of a university, 175–6, 237, 248–50; tutorial system, 196–8; supervisorial system, 231–5, 243, new dons, 188–90, 194–6, 210–47; 'new school' of professors, 152, 154, 170–2, 176, 180, 199 (see also H. Sidgwick and J. R. Seeley); fellowships, 135, 181–182, 193, 198, 200, 203, 206, 217–218, 231, 242–3, 249, 259; discipline in, 182–4, 188, 223, 228; relations between university and colleges, 184; small colleges, 196, 205–7, 235–6; intercollegiate lectures, 205–7, 230–1; non-collegiate forms of residence, 70–1, 237–8; foundation of Selwyn College, 240–1, 241–2 n.; examination system, 179, 181–6; moral sciences in, 135, 166–7; classical teaching compared to Oxford, 166; new importance of history and historical method in, 153, 167–72; Comte in, 169, 177; 'manly' tradition of, 228 (see also aristocracy); town and gown, 183–4; intuitional philosophy in, 101–5, 136, 138–

141; Grote Club, 138; Society of Apostles, 143, 211, 220–1; F. D. Maurice's solution to the crisis between university and society, 148, 151; Maurice's influence on younger dons, 151; problem of university and social change, 138; see also class conflict or class interest theory of university history, Church of England, clergy, dons, private tuition, Christ's College, Jesus College, St. Catharine's College, King's College, Trinity College, Corpus Christi College, Selwyn College, professional men and professions, businessmen (and business), character formation

Carlisle, Nicholas, 35, 41 n., 57
Cavendish College, Cambridge, 71
Chamisso, *Peter Schlemiehl*, 149
character formation: J. S. Mill's ethology, 111–12; J. S. Mill, M. Arnold and regeneration of the self as solution to alienation, 131, 247; debated by intuitionists and utilitarians, 139–41, 180; C. Kingsley's muscular christian theory of, 170, 172; J. R. Seeley's use of Christianity in, 174; as part of Cambridge teaching revolution, 180, 227, 236–7, 239, 246–7; and Arnoldians, 180; missing from private tuition, 209; R. C. Jebb, 221; and idea of a college, 235–247; and use by businessmen, 269–273; as part of liberal education, 132, 248–50; see also dons, alienation

Christianity: M. Arnold's analysis of, 119–21; F. D. Maurice reconstructs social teaching of, 144, 158; H. Sidgwick's loss of faith in, 135, 144, 207, 218–19; discussed by J. R. Seeley, 158–60, 162–3, 174; contains principle of unity, 119–21, 160; importance for character formation, 139, 174,

INDEX

examinations: *cont.*
184–6; tripos or honours examination, 179, 181–5; competitive nature of, 181, 183, 186; pressures for success in, 193; situation in King's, 221; *see also* Cambridge University
exhibitions: *see* scholarships, sizars
experientialism: *see* utilitarianism

family: F. D. Maurice on, 145–7, 158; Henry Maine on, 157–8; importance for J. R. Seeley, 159–60, 175 n.; underlies idea of a college, 175, 210, 227, 237–41; see also *in loco parentis*
Fawcett, Henry, 137
fellowships: holy orders as precondition for, 135, 218; linked to honours examination, 181–2, 193, 198; aid to professional career, 198, 249, 259; monetary value of, 200, 206; celibacy requirement for, 198, 203, 206, 217, 242; compared to Trinity College praelectorship, 231; *see also* dons
Fitzwilliam House, Cambridge: attempt to reduce necessary costs of a Cambridge education, 69; success of, 69–70, 69 n.; social composition of, 70; Oxford non-collegiate house, 70 n.; as part of anti-college movement, 238
Foster, Michael: and Cambridge Medical School, 185; Trinity College praelector, 231
franchise reform: and Victorian intellectual aristocracy, 24; *see also* J. S. Mill, M. Arnold, J. R. Seeley, H. Sidgwick, dons

Galton, Francis, 182; description of W. Hopkins, 191–2 n.
gentility, 90, 90 n.; John Henry Newman's description of the alienated gentleman, 128
gentry: at public schools, 49, 54; *see* aristocracy

Germany, England's rivalry with, 257
Gibb, George Stegmann, 262, 268 *passim*
Gladstone, William Ewart: interest in J. R. Seeley and *Ecce Homo*, 177–8; offers Regius Professorship to Seeley, 178
Glover, T. R., 250
Gonville and Caius College, Cambridge, 242
Graham Commission, 72, 189; prepares teaching reforms, 204–5; recognizes changing nature of adolescence, 210–11; suggests non-collegiate forms of residence, 238
grammar schools, 21–2; social structure of, 34–6; decline, 37 *et seq.*; costs at, 37–43, 57, Appendix I; curriculum of, Chapter 1, 37–8, 60; *see also* scholarships, social mobility
Greek, compulsory: *see* classical education
Green, T. H., 219
Grote Club, 138–41, 143, 211; *see also* H. Sidgwick
Grote, George, 138–41
Grote, John: personality of, 138–9; intuitionism of, 138–41; connection with younger dons, 138–41, 143; and practical education, 258
Gunson, William Mandell, 197, 230 n.

Hamilton, Sir William: and intuitionism, 101, 105; quoted by R. C. Jebb, 220
Hammond, James Lemprière: and Trinity sizarships, 75; noted tutor, 197, 197 n.
Hare, Julius, 212
Headmasters' Conference, 21, 52, 57, 58, 60; *see also* public schools
Hebraism: *see* M. Arnold
Heitland, William, 204, 224
Hellenism: *see* M. Arnold
history and historical method: new

310

INDEX

importance of, 153; and H. Sidgwick, 153–4; and J. R. Seeley, 167–72; and C. Kingsley, 169–70; and theological tripos, 251; *see also* Regius Professor of History

homosexuality, 135

Hopkins, William: described by Francis Galton, 191–2 n.; and private tuition, 68 n., 198, 201–3, 210; proposes system of university lecturers, 205–6

Hort, Fenton John Anthony, 143, 251

hostel system, revival of, 70–1, 237–238

idea of a college: *see* Cambridge University

immiseration thesis: as applied to university history, *see* class conflict or class interest theory of university history; as applied to grammar schools, *see* Chapter 1; as applied to public schools, *see* Chapter 2

independent schools, 21 n.; *see also* public schools

industrialism: *see* class conflict or class interest theory of university history, J. S. Mill, M. Arnold, J. R. Seeley, businessmen (and business)

in loco parentis, 197, 227, 233–4; *see also* family

innate capacities, theory of: *see* intuitionism

intellectual aristocracy: and franchise reform, 24–5; professional ideal of, 93; M. Arnold and J. S. Mill as members of, 132; *clerisy* idea, 114, 148 n., 161

intuitionism: and J. S. Mill, 101–5; as advanced by Cambridge professoriate, 101–5, 136, 138–41; criticized by F. D. Maurice, 145; and practical education, 258; and character formation, 139–41, 180; *see also* utilitarianism

Jackson, Henry, 176, 197; on R. Shilleto, 204 n.; admires friendliness of King's College, 211, 222; and W. H. Thompson, 212–13, 215; as a socratic figure, 214–15; as a new don, 215–17, 219, 222; learns from private tuition, 215–217; appointed assistant tutor, 216; challenges private tuition, 216–17, 222; confused about career, 217; and intercollegiate lectures, 230; as praelector, 231; and introduction of supervisorial system, 233; and character formation, 247 n.; and Cambridge University Association, 257, 257 n.

Jebb, Richard Claverhouse: personality of, 219–20; disliked by F. W. Maitland, 219–20; best of Cambridge pure classical scholars, 219–20; appears donnish, 220; new humanism of, 220–1; (*see also* M. Arnold, 123–4, 130–1); interest in character formation, 221; likes *Ecce Homo*, 221 n.; and introduction of supervisorial system, 233; attitude towards business, 245, 245 n.

Jesus: as model for Victorian intellectual and teacher, 147, 151; as described by J. R. Seeley, 163–164, 172–4, 177–8; and H. Sidgwick, 245–6

Jesus College, Cambridge: preference for clergymen's sons in, 64–5; expenses of Thomas Malthus at, 66; intercollegiate lectures, 230; marriages in, 242

Jowett, Benjamin: on costs of Oxford education, 67 n.; on social origins of Oxford clergy, 84 n.; compared to J. R. Seeley, 155

Kant, Emmanuel, influence on Cambridge professoriate, 102, 104–5

Keynes, John Maynard, 63

INDEX

Keynes, John Neville, 63, 249

King's College, Cambridge: Etonian connection, 50, 56 n., 221–3; Etonian scholarships at, 63; Supplementary Exhibition Fund, 80 n.; examinations in, 181–2; joins attack on coaching, 211, 221–7; dons and students in, 222, 240; office of tutor revived, 223; non-Etonians in, 223, 223 n.; Augustus Austen Leigh, 223–4, 226; Henry Bradshaw, 224–7; Eton collegers at, 223–7; quarrel between collegers and oppidans, 226; Oscar Browning, 222, 227 n., 229–30, 240; Political Society in, 229; history teaching in, 236

Kingsley, Charles: and F. D. Maurice, 150, 152–3, 228; as Regius Professor of History, 169–172; compared to 'new school' professors, 170–1; goes out of residence, 152–3, 171; views on historical science, 169–71; and J. R. Seeley, 169–72, 177; influence on undergraduates, 170–1; eccentric behaviour of, 171, muscular christian theory of character, 170, 172

Latham, Henry: criticizes changes in student behaviour, 73; as tutor, 189 n.

Leaf, Walter, 72

Leigh, Augustus Austen: background, 223; gives up priesthood, 223; as a new don, 223–4, 226, 240

Lewis, William James, 262

liberal education, 90, 248–50; J. S. Mill, M. Arnold and, 131–2

Lightfoot, Joseph Barber, 251; as a new don, 227 n.

Local Taxation Act, 1890, 78–9

Macaulay, Thomas Babington: and dons, 190, 192–3, 239, 245; ideal of independent scholar, 204, 239–240

Maine, Henry: and utilitarianism,

136–7; interest in family, 157–8; influences J. R. Seeley, 157–8

maintained schools, 21 n., see also grammar schools

Maitland, Frederic William: attitude toward Regius Professorship, 176, 178; dislikes R. C. Jebb, 219–20; praises H. Sidgwick, 219 n.; and Cambridge University Association, 257, 257 n.

Malthus, Thomas, expenses at Jesus College, 66

Manchester Grammar School, 40–1, 61, 81

Mansbridge, Albert, 30–3

Marshall, Alfred, 219, 256

mathematical education, 31, 229; tripos, 181–2, 252; private tuition, 199–200; wranglers, 202–3; order of merit, 203–4, 234–5, 252; King's and, 221; at St. John's, 230–2

Maurice, Frederick Denison: criticism of J. S. Mill, 105; career, 143–4, continues Grote Club, 143; revives Society of Apostles, 143, 152; problems similar to Sidgwick's, 143–4; as a Coleridgean, 143; fear of class war and social disintegration, 144, 147, 151; uses word *clerisy*, 148 n.; meets utilitarians, 143; attacks utility doctrine, 145, 147; reconstructs Christian social teaching, 144, 158; intellectual characteristics of, 144–145, 150–1; doctrine of sacrifice or limitations, 146, 151; struggles against alienation, 148–9, 151; belief that universities should provide leadership, 148; professional man as a social leader, 148; public worship as a means to unity, 149, 162, 172; and Charles Kingsley, 150, 228; solves Victorian problem of duty, 145–6, 148–51, 165; elected Knightbridge Professor, 152–3; as a 'new school' professor, 152–3; important influence on J. R. Seeley, 157, 164–5; criticism

INDEX

of Whewell, 145, 146, 212; welcomed by W. H. Thompson, 213; comments on friendliness of Cambridge, 228

Mayor, Joseph Bickersteth: member of Grote Club, 138; moral sciences lecturer, 218; as a new don, 138, 229

Mill, James, psychology of, 100–1

Mill, John Stuart: difficulties with utility doctrine, 97–109, 115–17; as guide to thinking of Victorian dons, 93, Chapter 3; and problem of culture, 98–9, 108, 112, 114–15, 132; and problem of leadership, 99, 108, 112, 114–15, 132; debates intuitionists, 101–6, and Sir William Hamilton, 105; and problem of authority, 101, 106–7, 109, 112; and social and political changes in England, 108; environmentalism of, 109–12; and relativism, 100, 109, 112; and neurophysiology, 110–11; ethology and character formation, 111–12; interest in historical theory, 112–14; influence of St.-Simonians on, 113; influence of Comte on, 113; influence of Coleridge on, 113–14, 245; agrees with M. Arnold, 93, 116, 131–3; disagrees with M. Arnold, 130–1; favours pluralism, 115; belief in social regeneration, 131 (*see also* alienation); waning influence of in Cambridge, 136–141; and F. D. Maurice, 105, 143, 150; defines liberal education, 132, 248

Namier, Sir Lewis, 19, 25
national education: *see* University
nativism: *see* intuitionism
Newman, John Henry: influence of Coleridge on, 114; 'sweetness and light', 124; description of alienated gentleman, 128–9
Newnham College, Cambridge, 211
Noble, Sir Andrew, 262–3

non-collegiate education: *see* Oxford and Fitzwilliam House, Cambridge

Nonconformists: and business, 49, 120, 122; and behaviour, 122; at King's, 225; and problem of authority in Cambridge, 237, 241, 241–2 n.

oppidans, 50, 56, 223

Oxford University, 17 *passim*, 62, 153, 273; social mobility and, 30–33; educational costs at, 67 n.; employment opportunities for non-collegiate students in, 70 n.; scholarships and eleemosynary funds, 80 n., 85–6; John Henry Newman's idealization of, 127; classical teaching compared to Cambridge, 166–7; private tuition not as strong in, 198; financial problems of, 256 n.

paradox: Victorian use of, 150–1; Seeley's use of, 177; F. D. Maurice's use of, 144, 150, 165; and utilitarians, 109

Pattison, Mark, 155; idea of a college, 194–5, 247

Peacock, George, 188, 197; influences W. H. Thompson, 212

Peile, John: attended Christ's College, 156; among reformers, 211; participates in intercollegiate lectures, 230 n.

philistines, 142, 162–3, 175, 245, 255, 271, 273; *see also* businessmen (and business) and Matthew Arnold

philosophic radicalism: *see* utilitarianism

philosophy (moral sciences): new undergraduate subject, 135, 207; Knightbridge Professorship, 135; John Grote, 138–41; William Whewell, 101, 103–5, 136, 138; F. D. Maurice, 143–53; J. R. Seeley's interest in philosophy and moral sciences tripos, 165–6, 218

313